LONDON NIGHTS

FRONT COVER
The West End at night, 1960 *(detail)*

PAGES 14/15
Piccadilly, 1960

BOB COLLINS (1924–2002)

LONDON NIGHTS

HOXTON MINI PRESS

CONTENTS

This publication presents London at night through photographs, film stills and words. A poem by Inua Ellams introduces each of three sections, followed by interpretative text from Anna Sparham exploring the subsequent imagery.

BIOGRAPHIES

Born in Nigeria, INUA ELLAMS is a cross art form practitioner, a poet, playwright & performer, graphic artist & designer and founder of the Midnight Run – an international, arts-filled, night-time, playful, urban, walking experience. He is a Complete Works poet alumni and a designer at White Space Creative Agency. Across his work, Identity, Displacement & Destiny are reoccurring themes in which he also tries to mix the old with the new: traditional African storytelling with contemporary poetry, pencil with pixel, texture with vector images. His poetry is published by Flipped Eye, Akashic, Nine Arches and several plays by Oberon.

ANNA SPARHAM is Curator of Photographs at the Museum of London. Originally from Birmingham, Sparham graduated with a photography degree from Nottingham Trent University in 2001. After working with the British Empire & Commonwealth Museum's photographs collection, she joined the Museum of London in 2004, becoming a curator there in 2006. Working closely with photographers and historic and contemporary photographs, Sparham develops the museum's collections and realises temporary exhibitions, which have recently included *London Street Photography* (co-curated 2011) and publication, *Observing the Crowd: Photographs by Bob Collins* (2014), *Soldiers and Suffragettes: The Photography of Christina Broom* (2015) and publication, *Stomping Grounds: Photographs by Dick Scott-Stewart* (2016) and *London Nights* (2018).

THE MUSEUM OF LONDON tells the ever-changing story of this great world city and its people, from 450,000 BC to the present day. Our galleries, exhibitions, displays and activities seek to inspire a passion for London and provide a sense of the vibrancy that makes the city such a unique place. The museum's collection of photographs, from which many works in this book have been drawn, encompasses an estimated 150,000 items, comprising a visual encyclopaedia of London's physical and social fabric.

HOXTON MINI PRESS are a small independent publisher making collectable photobooks out of East London. Our goal is to make artistic books that are both beautiful and accessible. We hope that both collectors and everyday folk will keep them in neat piles on wooden shelves. We are Ann and Martin and have two dogs, Moose and Bug, both of whom hate art. East London is where we nurture our ideas, walk the dogs and meet people more talented than ourselves. Thank you for supporting us. You can find more of our books at:

www.hoxtonminipress.com

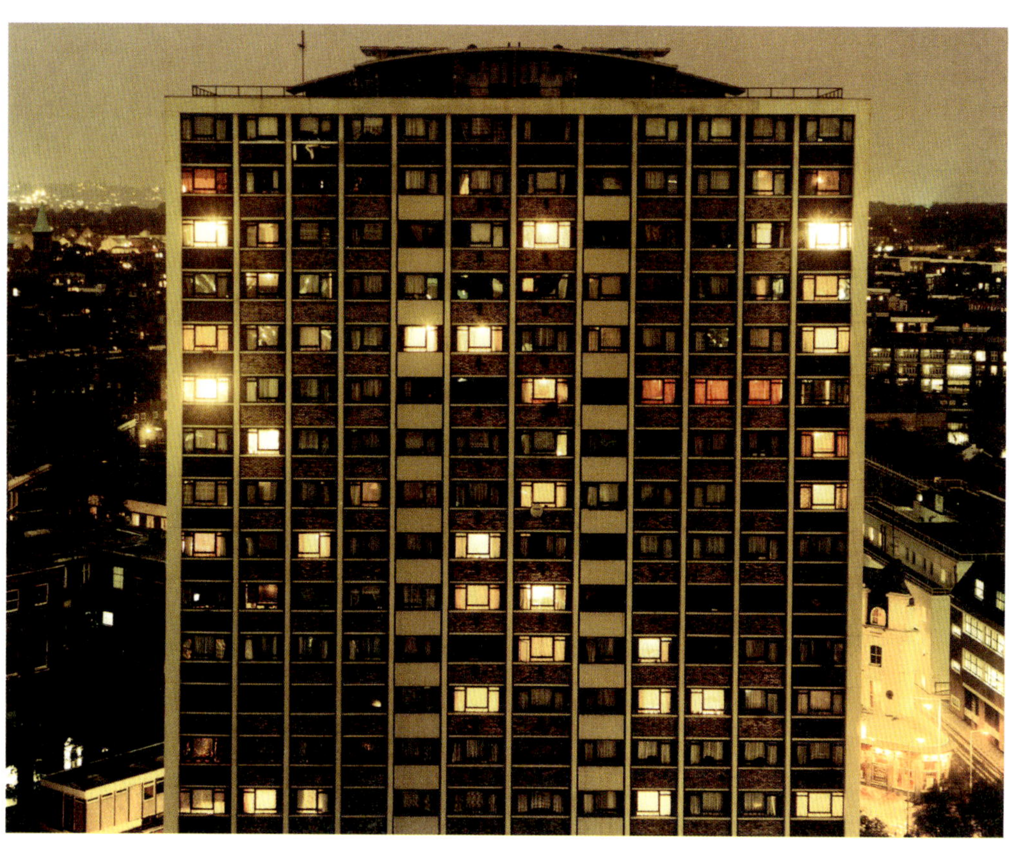

London: A Modern Project,
from the series *London: A Modern Project*, 1995

RUT BLEES LUXEMBURG (b 1967)

INTRODUCTION

As daylight fades and darkness falls, London visually transforms. From the West End's glittering bright lights to dimly-lit corners of suburbia, the city morphs to reveal its nightly persona. After dark, London's unique urban character – positive and negative – appears amplified in the night light, captivating the eye and heightening the senses.

Artificial exterior and interior illumination at night enables the metropolis to stay awake. The eye adjusts, alongside the mindset, to read and engage with London in this alternative nocturnal light. In so doing, infinite opportunities arise. There is so much to do, so much to see. The darkened city embraces the excited through to the exhausted, the daring to the fearful, the gregarious to the lonesome. London bears it all.

The eclectic cultural and aesthetic complexion of the capital at night presents rich ground for image-makers. Since the late 19th century, photographers have been enticed by the subject of London at night and the challenge of recording it. As a subject, night-time traverses the many genres of the photographic medium from social documentary to the conceptual. Whichever the output, there is an innate fascination with the visual potential offered by the urban night, and the immeasurable twists and turns photographic exploration may take. The notion of *night* is, after all, where the imagination has always run wild. Nightmares are conceived in the small hours by young and old. Secrets are born and hidden behind drawn curtains or down an unlit alleyway; we are kept, metaphorically, 'in the dark'.

The concept of night photography is best explored through imagery that stands distinct in appearance to daylight, despite the lighter late evenings of the UK summertime. Therefore, the photographs presented in *London Nights* capture, emulate or suggest a darkened night-time aesthetic. When the illuminated night itself is not obvious or visible at all, the images respond and relate to themes that London 'after hours' conjures up.

Photography depends of course upon light. Before photographic technology was sophisticated enough to allow the rendering of any recognisable results from the blackness of the night, photographers could only allude to it through reference, association or context. *Street Life in London* for example, published in 1877, includes the occasional glimpse of the night, not through John Thomson's renowned photographs of people on the street, but in the individual texts that accompanied them by journalist Adolphe Smith. In one example, *The Seller of Shell Fish*, a quote reads, 'When it's possible to work off some doubtful goods is at night, at the bar of a public house when the men drinking are too far gone to be nice about smell or taste, so long as they gets something strong.'[1] The viewer is encouraged to imaginatively place those photographed by day into the night scene.

Although there were earlier attempts at capturing the nocturnal city,[2] it was the pioneering work of Paul Martin in 1896, then a keen amateur photographer, that first succeeded in portraying London at night to a wide, receptive audience and paved the way forward.[3]

Anyone living in London and venturing beyond their own doorstep will recognise that this vast city diversifies at every corner. And yet, despite the distinct characteristics of each borough, if one is asked to imagine a nocturnal London scene, it is a generic picture of central London that will most likely enter the mind – Piccadilly, perhaps Theatreland, neon-lit Soho streets or floodlit iconic landmarks. Despite the myriad experiences encountered and offered in London at night, it is unlikely to be the sleepier suburbs or fringes of the capital that one thinks of. The best known depictions of the city at night are devised by advertising, feature films and other forms of popular culture, many of which have over time focused on the West End and renowned sights, informing both visitor and Londoner alike.

In 1915, walking home late at night among the 'monotonous-faced houses' of London's suburbia, author Thomas Burke asked his readers whether they too had considered that 'that street is but one of thousands and thousands which radiate to every point, and that all the night air of one city is holding the passions of those millions of creatures?'[4] This boundlessness of the nocturnal metropolis has sometimes been conveyed through photographs made from elevated vantage points. Looking across the city, they capture the ubiquitous dots of light meeting the infinite black of the night sky.

In more recent years, photographers have delved into the less frequently depicted areas, well away from the centre of the city. In the expansive suburbs a thriving nightlife can often be found, distinct from the familiar tourist spots of central London. In contrast, the edgelands – the industrial estates and waste ground – lie uninhabited after dark.

The multitudinous ways to photograph both obscure or iconic London localities at night remain powerfully inexhaustible. With current technological advances, the city is broadly accessible to anyone with a camera, professional and amateur alike. Achieving good results no longer demands cold hours spent huddled around a large format camera and tripod, enduring slow shutter speeds. Although contemporary photographers who continue to exploit the possibilities of this approach often produce remarkable images. A host of digital and analogue masterclasses, books and online guides exist to seduce the photographer with the possibilities of night-time photography.

Many photographers will contentedly find their own way, perhaps wandering alone on a journey of discovery. Becoming 'voyeuristic strollers',[5] they absorb and observe London's nightly moods while walking the darkened streets. In so doing, they follow in the footsteps of many creative minds and insomniacs before them, including the great visionary author Charles Dickens. His 1860 essay 'Night Walks' captured the eclectic and restless London night that is equally alluring to night photographers. 'Nightwalking was for Dickens a narcotic.'[6]

The photographs that follow offer a taste of the nocturnal London created by diverse practitioners over the decades and today. Collectively they represent the work of photographers included in the 2018 *London Nights* exhibition at the Museum of London. Many are drawn from the museum's own significant collection. A broad visual interpretation of the city is presented within three thematic sections: 'London Illuminated', which focuses on the aesthetic of the city in the limited light of the night; 'Dark Matters', addressing the more unsettling aspects of the urban night, and lastly 'Switch On Switch Off', which looks at people's interaction with London at night through work, rest and play. Each section is introduced by the words of poet, playwright and performer Inua Ellams, inspired by the photography and his own personal exploration of the London night.

Contemporary and historic images, colour and monochrome, criss-cross time and place. The ambiance, activities and individuals that co-exist in our night-time city are revealed and the imagination is unleashed. Low-light subtlety and dazzling high contrast collide and complement each other. These memorable images delve into the familiar and unknown, the charm and the alarm, emerging out of the darkness and into the light.

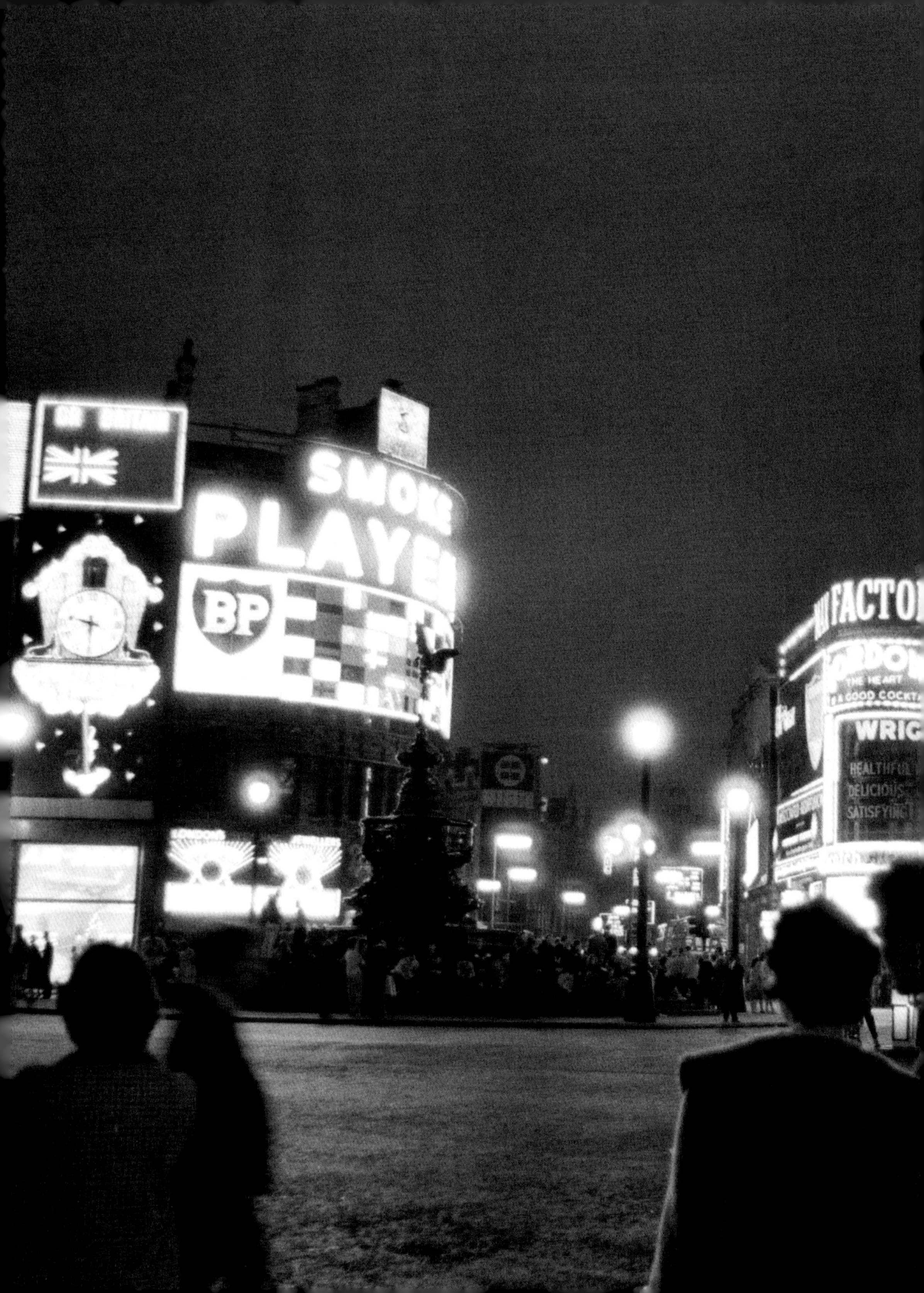
SMOKE
BP
FACTOR
THE HEART
HEALTHFUL
DELICIOUS
SATISFYING

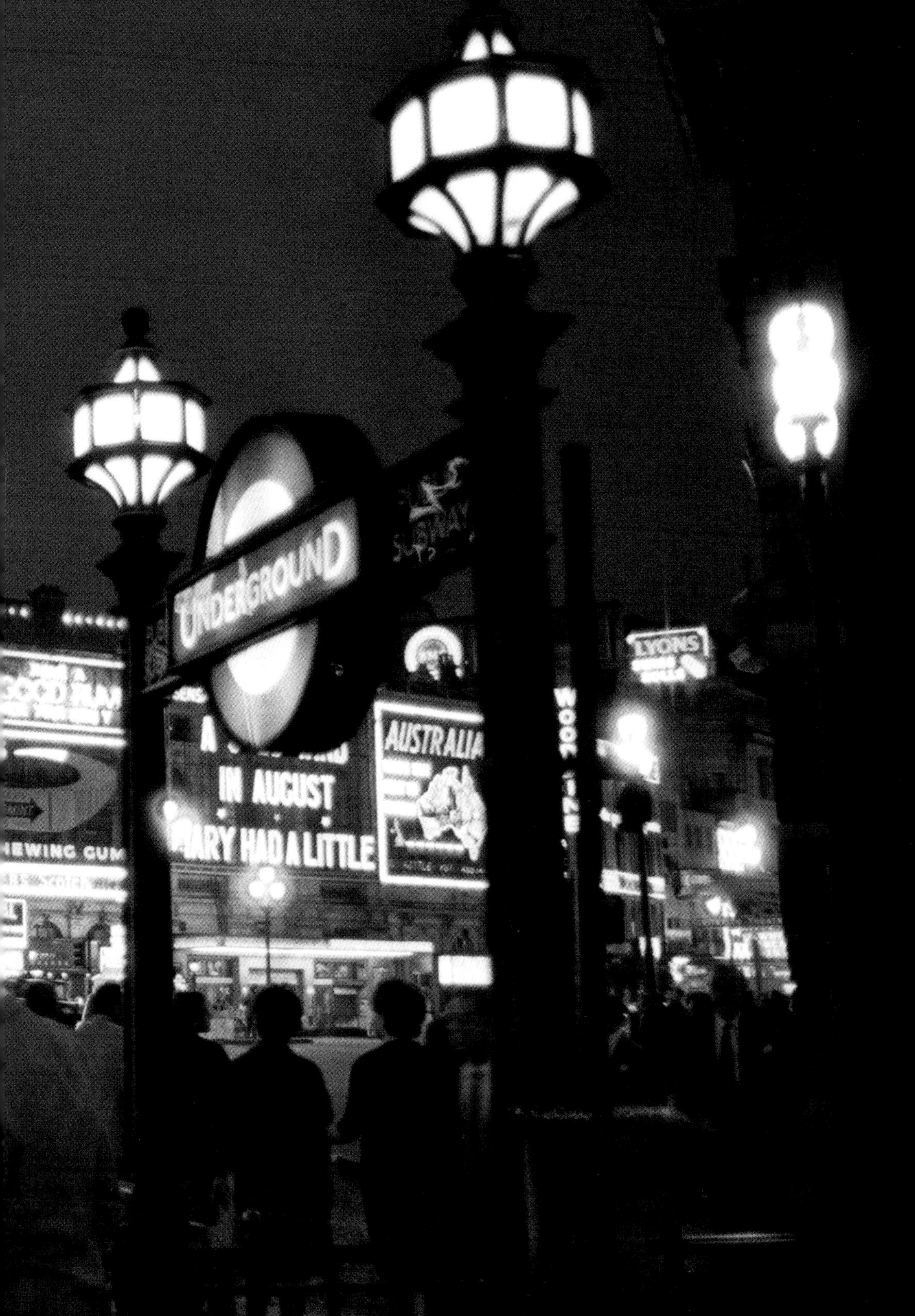
UNDERGROUND
IN AUGUST
MARY HAD A LITTLE
AUSTRALIA
LYONS
CHEWING GUM

Moth /

The mouth of a cobwebbed alley / and a woman with eyes narrow as blades / squinting as dusk falls on London / wants for a saviour / She huffs into the coming cold / stamps / BAM / on the pavement and the sound of her heel on stone gathers her loneliness in its sonic glove / and echoes out / clattering upwards / stirring a sleeping moth / Two wings beat / two twin swirls / and like a prayer the moth is gone / fluttering over flowing dustbins / jagged stairs / chimneys / flood-lit streets / neon signage / billboards / skeletal trees / spiked railings / across air vents / and warm air / that thrusts up through smog / The prayer floats up to clouds / which drift like ships / like rafts of spirits / the star-essence of unborn children / urban braves / incoming saviours / our future unformed selves.

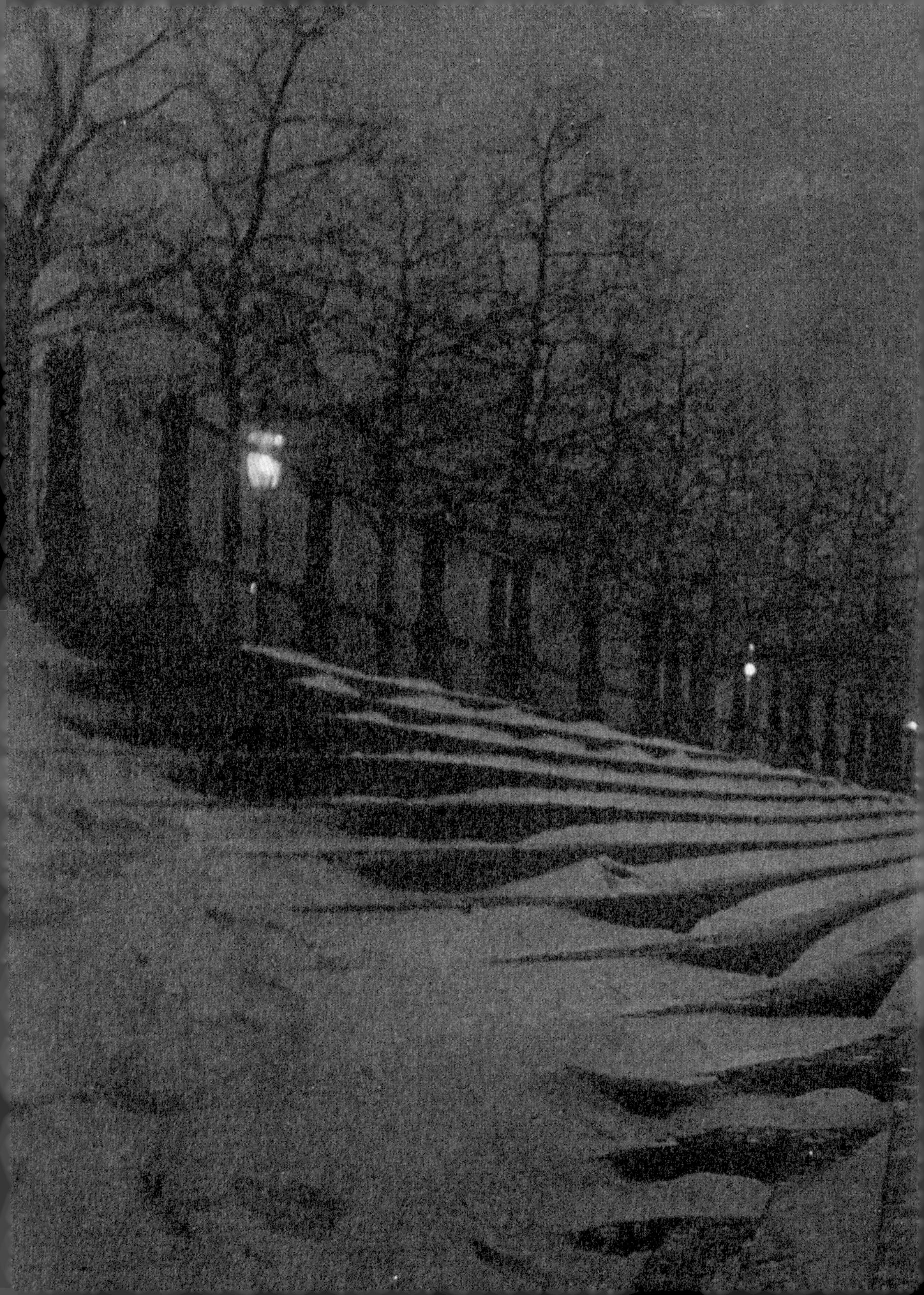

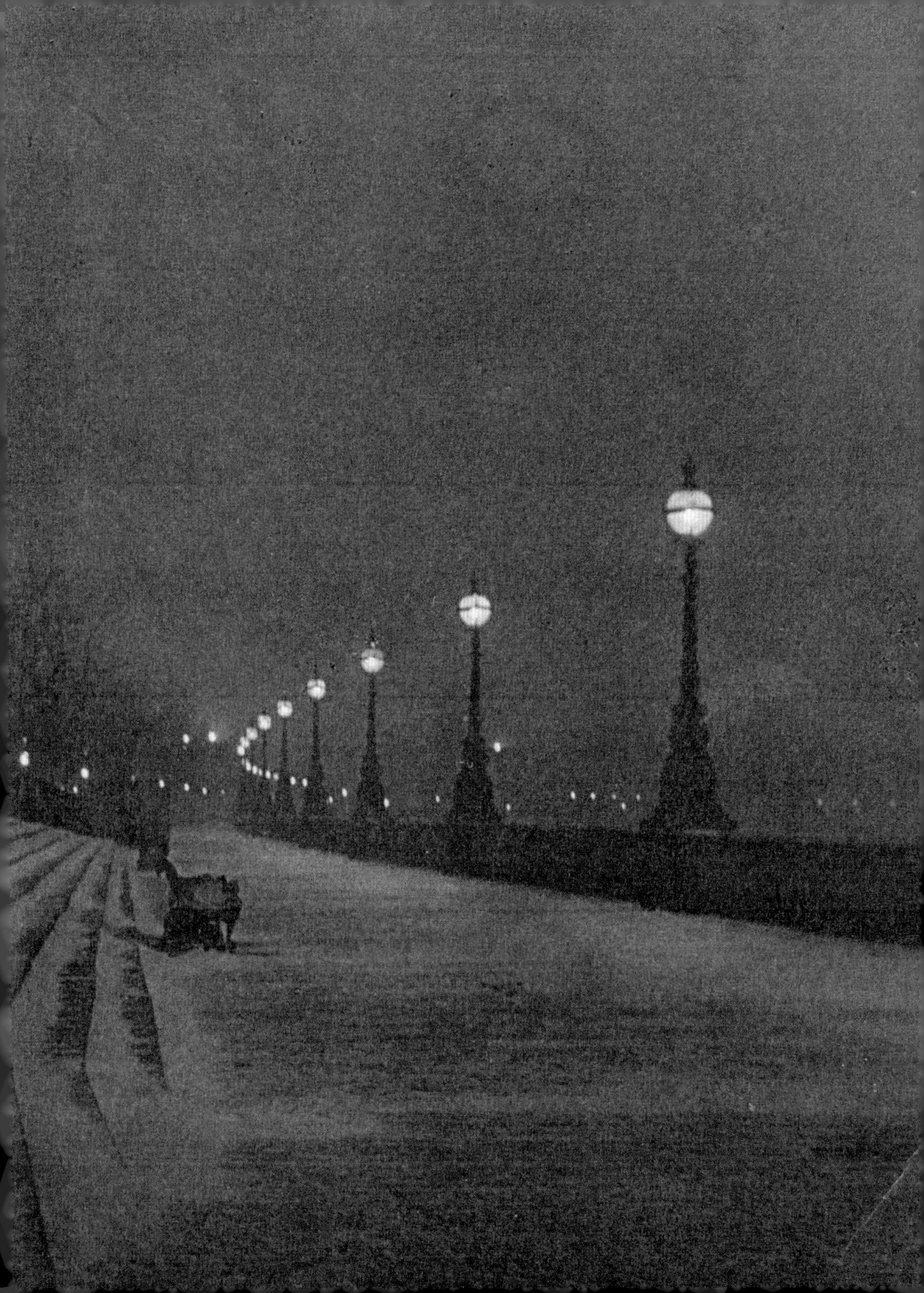

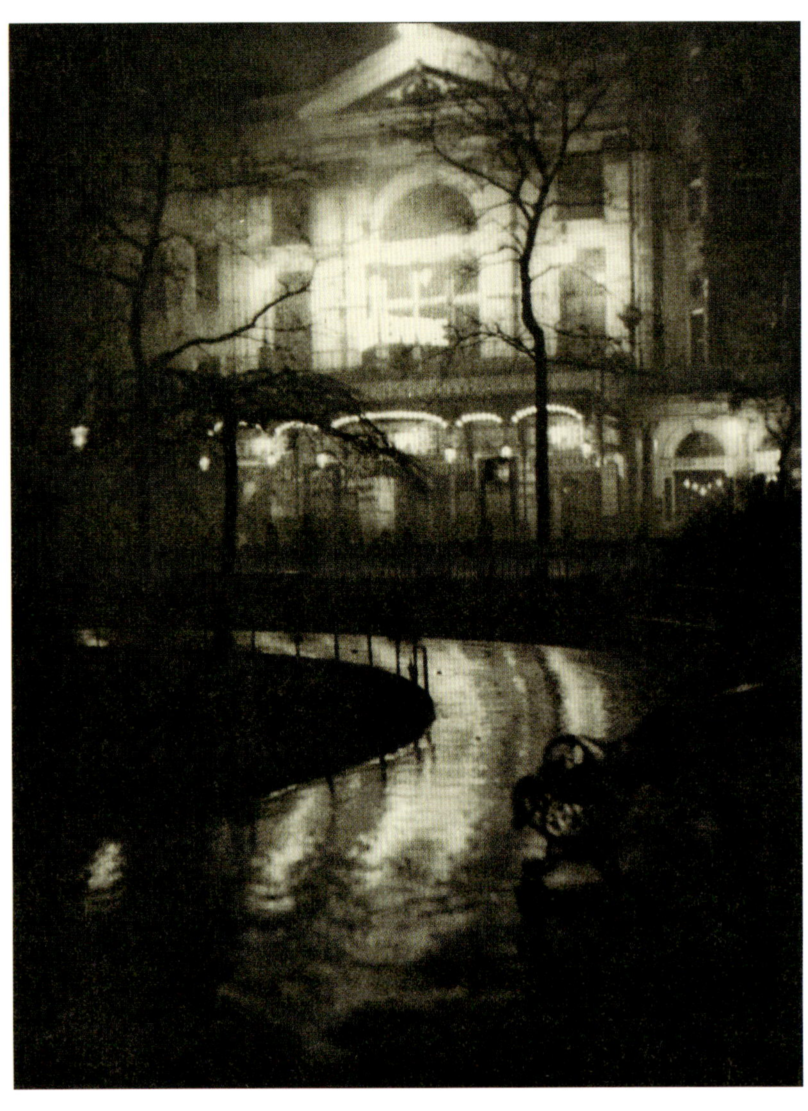

ABOVE
Leicester Square
from the series *London*, 1909

ALVIN LANGDON COBURN (1882–1966)

PREVIOUS PAGES
Embankment at Night,
from the series *London by Gaslight*, 1896

PAUL MARTIN (1864–1944)

LONDON ILLUMINATED

The glow of London after dark can be awe-inspiring. Floodlit landmarks, sodium-lit sprawling streets or a vista complete with twinkling skyline all add to the visual experience and aesthetic of the city at night. As a Londoner, or visitor to London, who hasn't found themselves crossing one of the River Thames' bridges at night and soaked up the view? Perhaps even stopping to take a photograph, so that the hypnotising moment might be recorded. After all, as Susan Sontag wrote, 'It is common for those who have glimpsed something beautiful to express regret at not having been able to photograph it.'[7]

Manoeuvring through the daily grind, many might take these grand views for granted, or just not look so acutely. 'London Illuminated' throws light on the work of photographers who, on the contrary, do make such observations. Specifically, they gravitate towards the effects and impact of limited natural and artificial night light. They are collectively intrigued by and drawn to the way such light plays upon the nightscape and how that can translate through the lens.

In the earliest days of night photography, it was the artistic and technical challenge of capturing London's iconic locations after dark that inspired practitioners to represent the night in photographic form. Photographer Paul Martin pioneered the possibilities through the notable *London by Gaslight* series he made in 1896 (pp 18–19). Using his wooden Facile magazine plate camera and tripod, the then amateur photographer persevered with experiments in central London until he achieved successful results. Exposure times were between ten and forty-five minutes, with Martin going to such lengths as to cover the camera lens when the lights of a cab passed by.[8] Martin aimed to emulate the tone of the gaslighting by presenting his work as glass lantern slides with blue tinting and yellow-coloured binding or projector filters. Brighter illumination later provided by electric lighting 'made the softly flickering gaslight it replaced seem almost as inconstant and intimate as candlelight.'[9] Martin's revolutionary efforts 'aroused great interest' in the photographic field. Night photography in London was truly inaugurated.[10]

In the early 20th century, pictorialist Alvin Langdon Coburn embraced the city's nocturnal ambience in his work *London,* published in 1909. Soft and painterly impressions, 'translating a personal vision'[11] of the city were printed in delicate photogravure to reveal London in both the day and night. In *Leicester Square* (p 20), the Empire Theatre radiant in electric light, Coburn incorporates a recurring motif in night photography of wet surfaces and reflections.

Dramatic floodlighting of London's architecture has attracted many photographers. In the late 1920s and early 1930s, able amateurs George Davison Reid (pp 32–3) and Mercie Lack (pp 28–31) both played with the directional light exuding from floodlit surrounds. Each photographer required a tripod and great patience, waiting for people to either incidentally enhance their compositions or be out of shot altogether.

London at night became an apt subject for the commercial photographic trade too. The humble picture postcard went a long way in disseminating visions of night-time London. Valentine & Sons Ltd., a successful picture postcard publisher, whose motto printed on their postcards' backs proclaimed them to be 'famous throughout the world', were official postcard publishers for the 1908 Franco-British exhibition at White City. Countless copies of their photographic postcards of the exhibition's centrepiece, the Court of Honour, shimmering in thousands of lights, were sold (p 38). Decades later, John Hinde Studios embedded boldly saturated depictions of 1960s Piccadilly and other iconic locations within the tourist trade (p 43).

Much night photography, particularly the more historic, focuses upon central London, but some photographers have eagerly looked to the outer boroughs and the city's fringes to explore the lesser known. How does the night light, and darkness, compare as the camera ventures further afield from London's nucleus? 'The darkness of Pall Mall is different from the darkness of Bishopsgate; the lights of Piccadilly are different from the lights of the Edgware Road,' wrote H.V. Morton in 1926.[12]

Devoid of people, William Eckersley's captivating *Dark City*, 2011, uncovers the intensely quiet inactivity across the broader night city (pp 46–9). An eeriness emerges from the dark streets as traces of everyday London life, from shopping trolleys to CCTV cameras, are thrown under colourful illumination. The alluring light reveals the beautiful as well as the inelegant in familiar and unassuming locations. Charting their way around street corners and vacant spaces, Eckersley's photographs echo something of the mood seen in earlier work of the genre; the blue-toned photogravures by Harold Burdekin, for example (pp 26–7), published in *London Night* in 1934. The accompanying author, John Morrison, wrote, 'Night reveals another, different world, real in its unreality. She heightens, detracts, hides and exposes, covers and distorts the world of day. But who shall say which world is the true, which the unreal?'[13]

Night photography can be incredibly immersive, both for the viewer and the creator. Extensive knowledge and familiarity with an area lead to considered locations and perspectives, as seen in the series *Hackney by Night* by David George (pp 55–7). A potentially romanticised view of Hackney, it depicts seemingly natural, unpopulated spaces, warmly illuminated in the available light. Yet details of local industry and man-made intervention arise from the darkness, reminding the viewer of the urban setting. George invites a closer look at and response to both the beauty and inherent mystery contained within.[14] Similarly, Niall McDiarmid's *Southwestern* transports the viewer to the domain of south-west London and the neighbourhoods of Wandsworth, Merton, Southfields and Earlsfield (pp 52–3). His familiarity with the glow of suburbia at night shines through, culminating in backlit drawn curtains, beaming signage, streetlighting and scatterings of occasional figures.

Some photographers have approached the night through more abstract image-making, embracing the textural qualities that surface. In his series *LDN*, Antony Cairns sought out the light within structures, from the Olympic Park to construction sites, transport hubs and subterranean passages (pp 62–3). Using analogue techniques including solarisation, which involves interrupting the development process of a negative or print by exposing it to light and altering the resulting lights and darks, Cairns finds patterns and shapes among light sources to create his unique visions of nocturnal London.[15]

Chloe Dewe Mathews' film piece *London River Burning* abstracts the River Thames, as, in her words, it 'tugs, ripples and whirlpools'. The fluctuating fluid surface reflects the available transmuting lights of the city (pp 67–9). Dewe Mathews' spellbinding film, while glorious in texture and colour, reminds the viewer of the river's natural force, potential danger and powerful history. As H.V. Morton wrote in *The Nights of London*, 'The Thames at night is the most mysterious thing in London. So much part of London, yet so remote from London, so cold, so indifferent, so wise; for there is nothing about London that the Thames does not know.'[16]

Other forces of nature are examined through Thierry Cohen's London skyline (pp 64–5). A densely starlit sky sits wondrously above the City. Yet who has witnessed such a sky in London? The photograph is in fact a digital composite. The buildings were photographed in daylight, free of any interior illumination. Traversing the globe along the exact same latitude, Cohen photographed the magnificent sky over Kazakhstan; the same sky that would be visible in London if not for light and atmospheric pollution.[17] This ultimate play with light, artifice and reality begs the viewer to look more imaginatively at the various interacting elements of the night environment.

Collectively, the photographs within 'London Illuminated' push both geographic and photographic boundaries. Their focus on the presence and impact of light within the dark encourages us to discover and tune in to the miscellany of moods running through London from dusk to dawn.

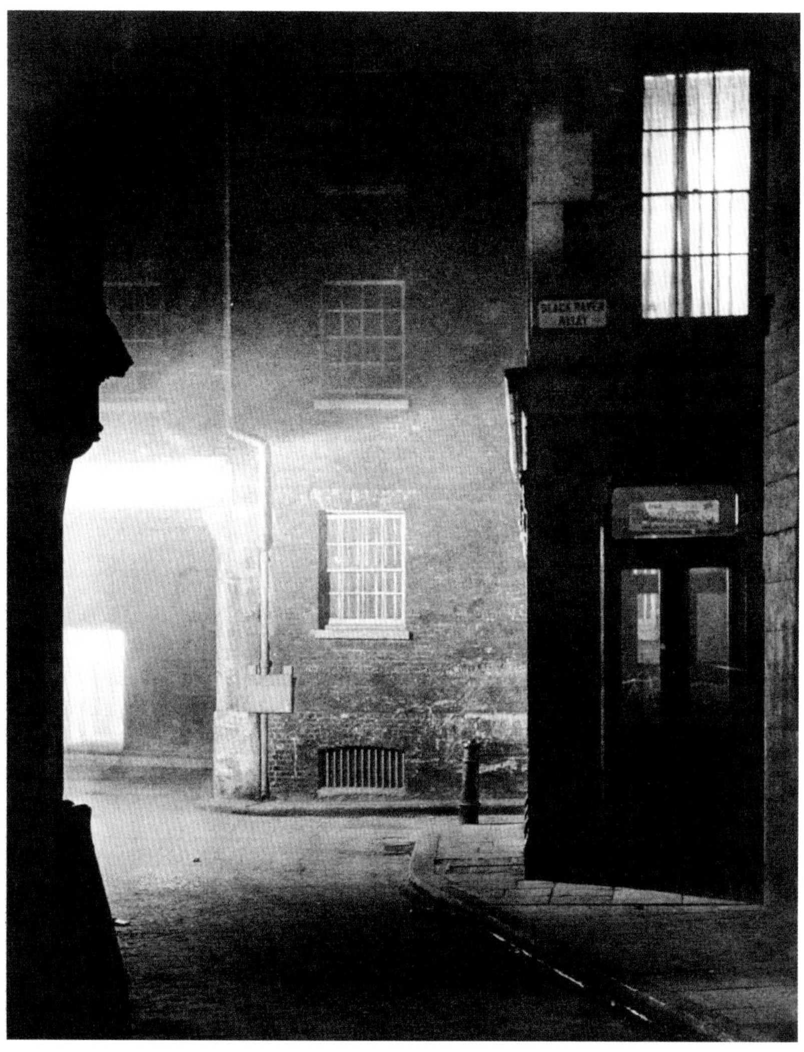

Sinister Street from *London Night*, 1934
Beyond the Pavement from *London Night*, 1934

HAROLD BURDEKIN (1899–1944)

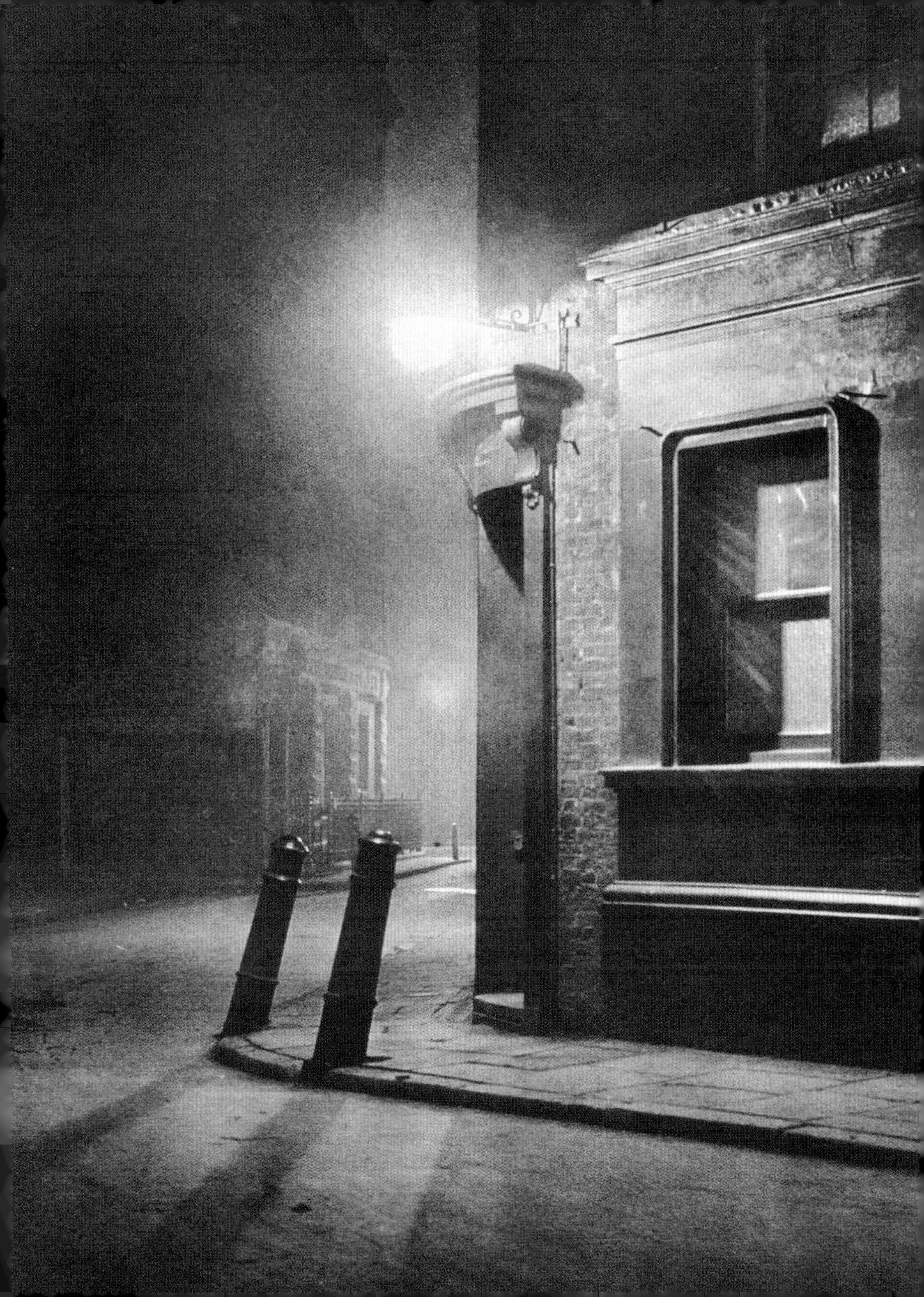

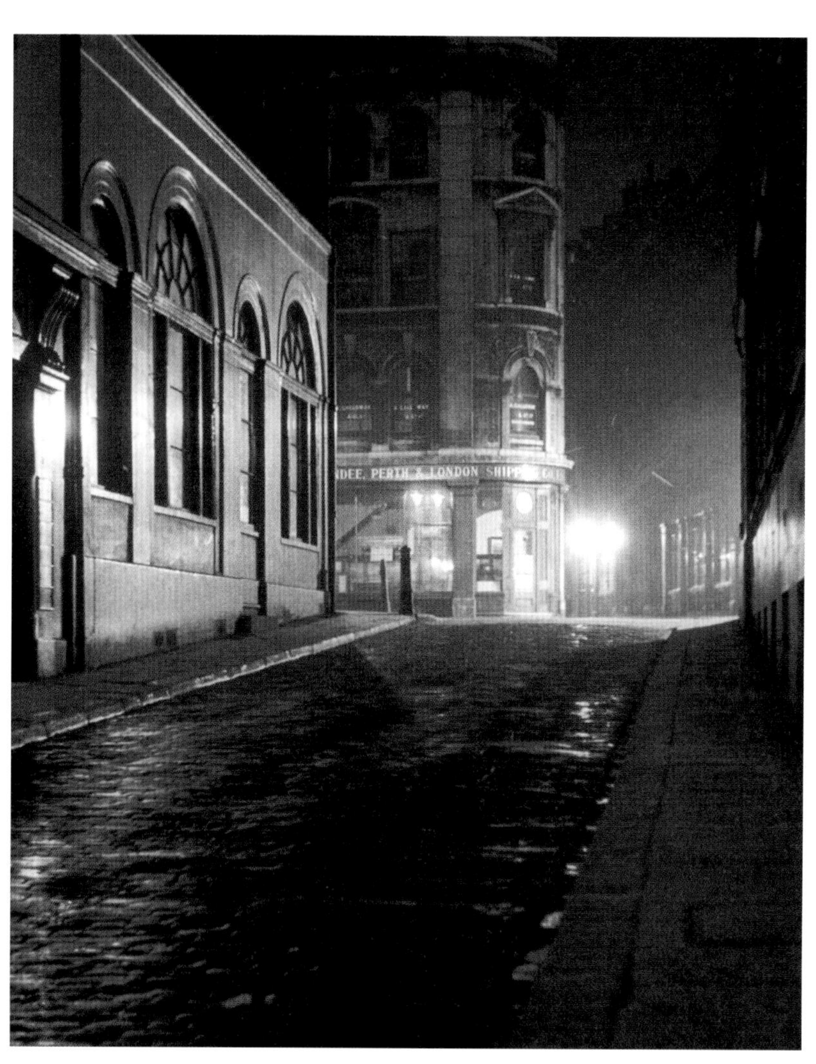
NDEE, PERTH & LONDON SHIPP

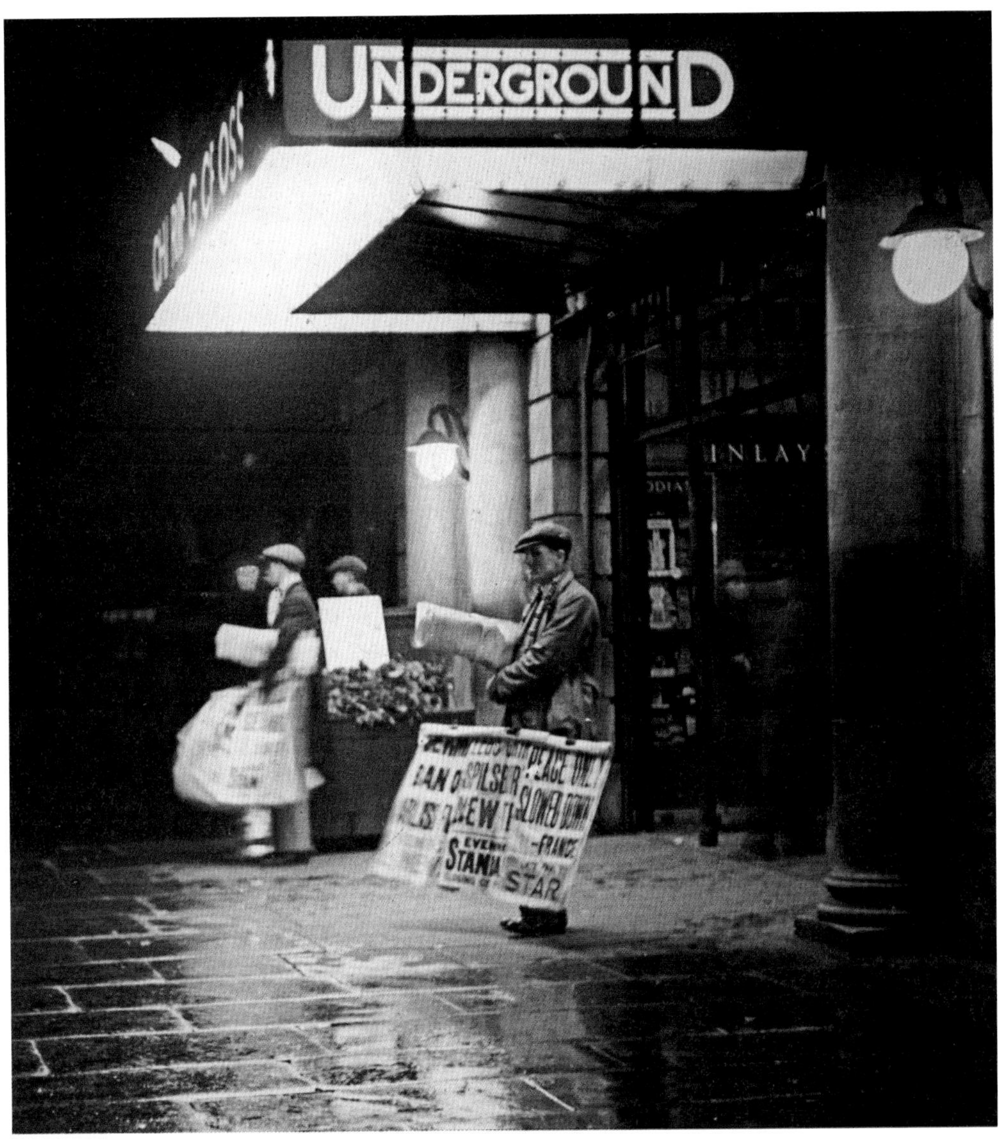

St. Dunstan's Hill, c 1930
Late Extra, c 1930

MERCIE LACK (1894–1985)

Embankment at Chelsea, c 1930

MERCIE LACK (1894–1985)

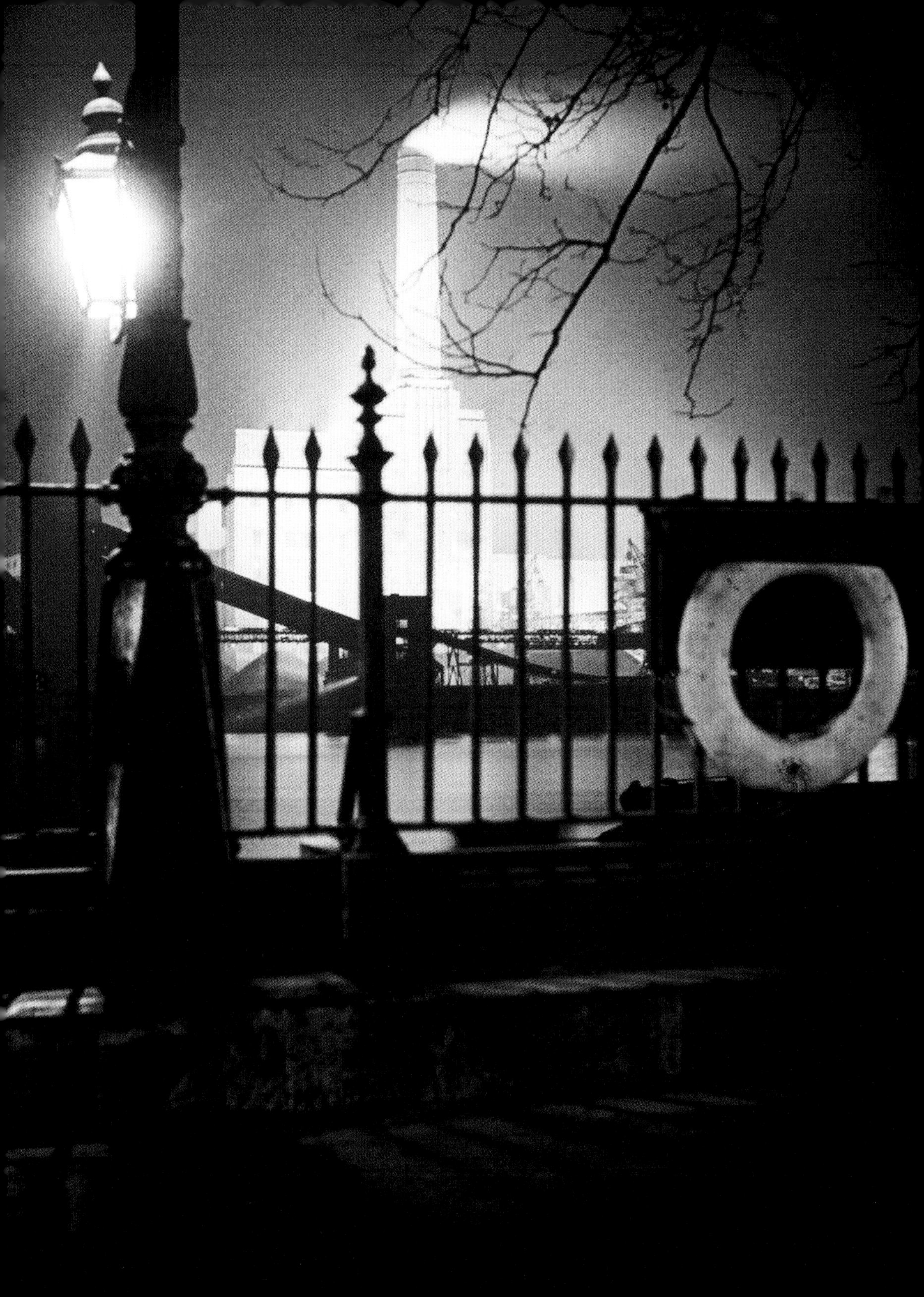

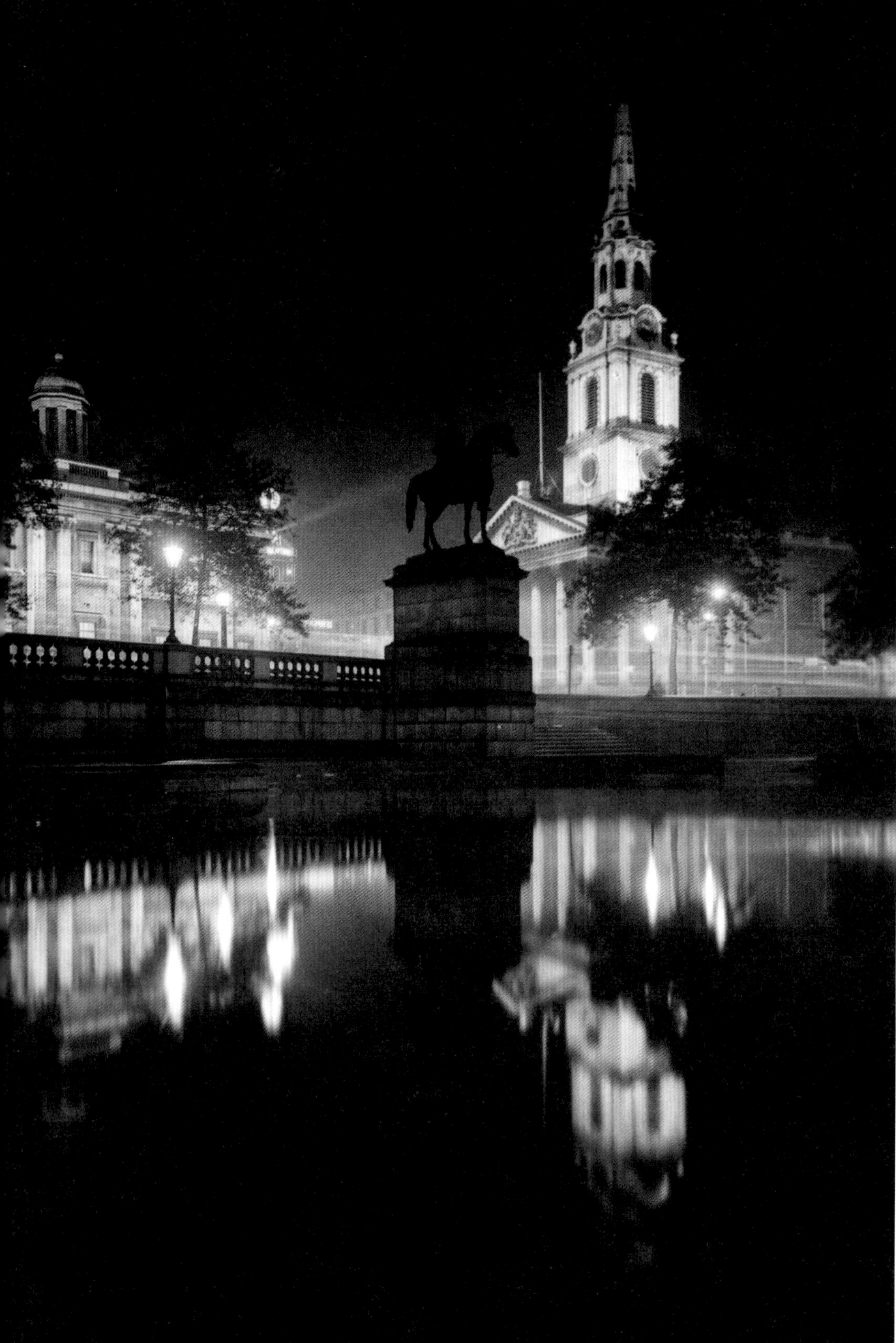

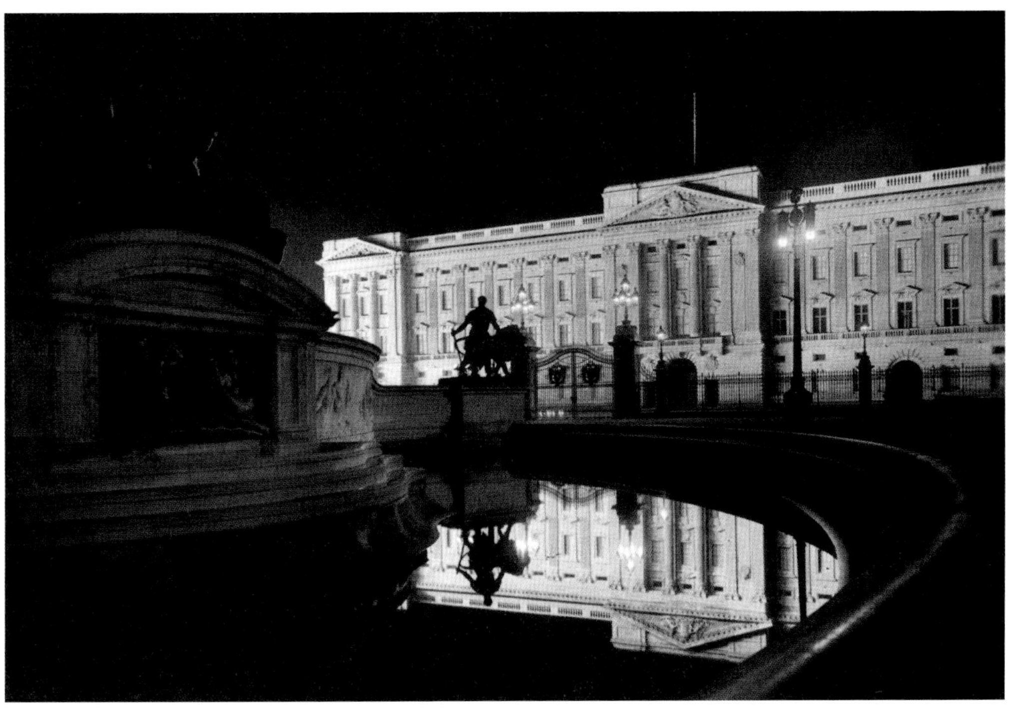

Trafalgar Square at Night, c 1930
Buckingham Palace, Floodlit, c 1930

GEORGE DAVISON REID (1871–1933)

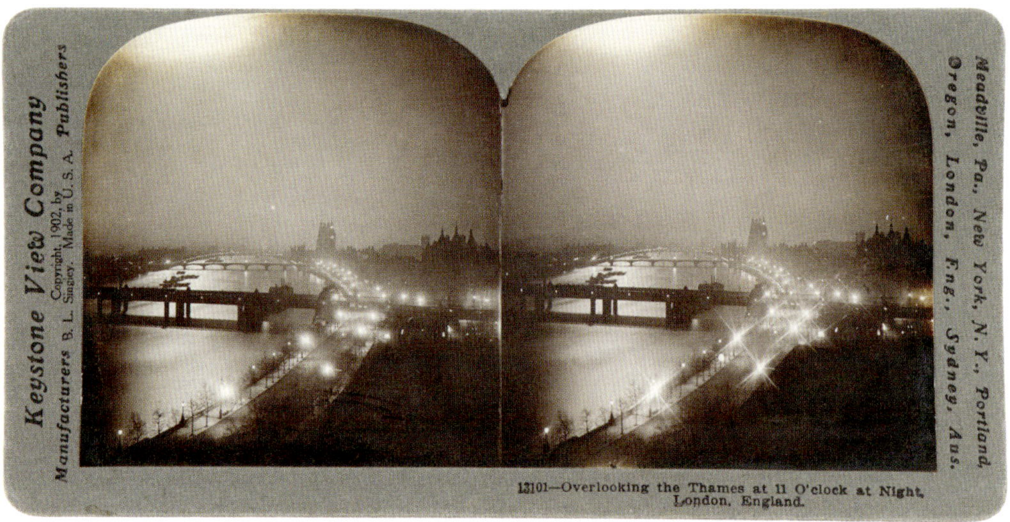

Overlooking the Thames at 11 O'clock at Night, c 1903

ANONYMOUS (Keystone View Company)

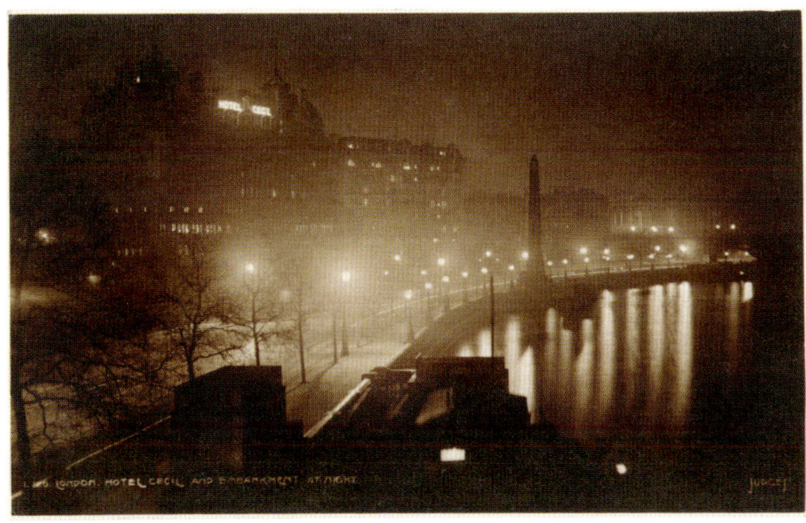

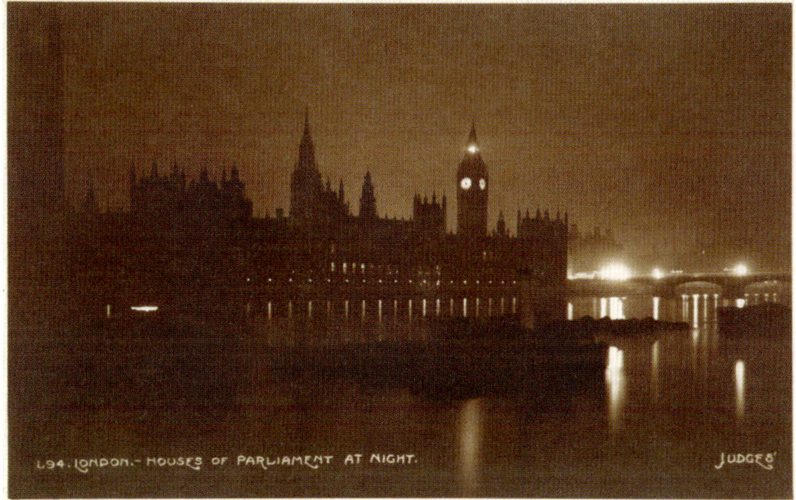

Postcard of Hotel Cecil and Embankment at night, c 1909
Postcard of the Houses of Parliament at night, c 1909

FRED JUDGE (1872–1950)

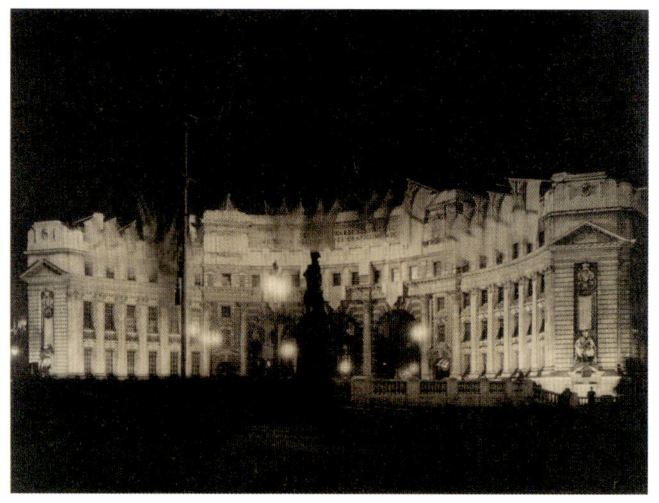

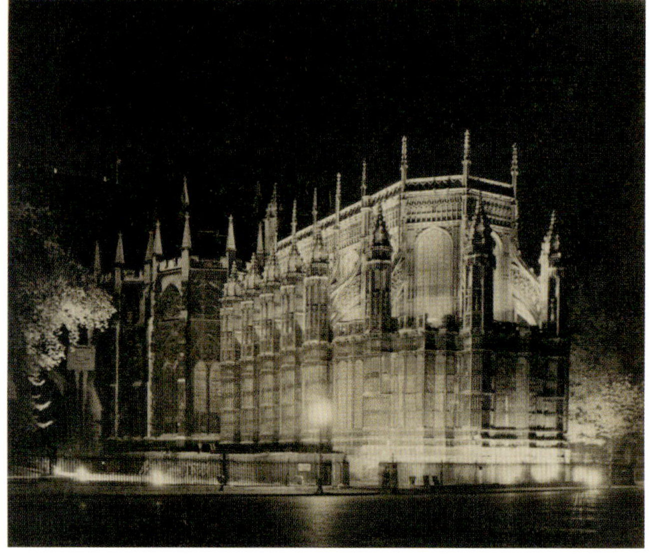

Victory Celebrations, Floodlighting, June 1946

ANONYMOUS (Ministry of Works)

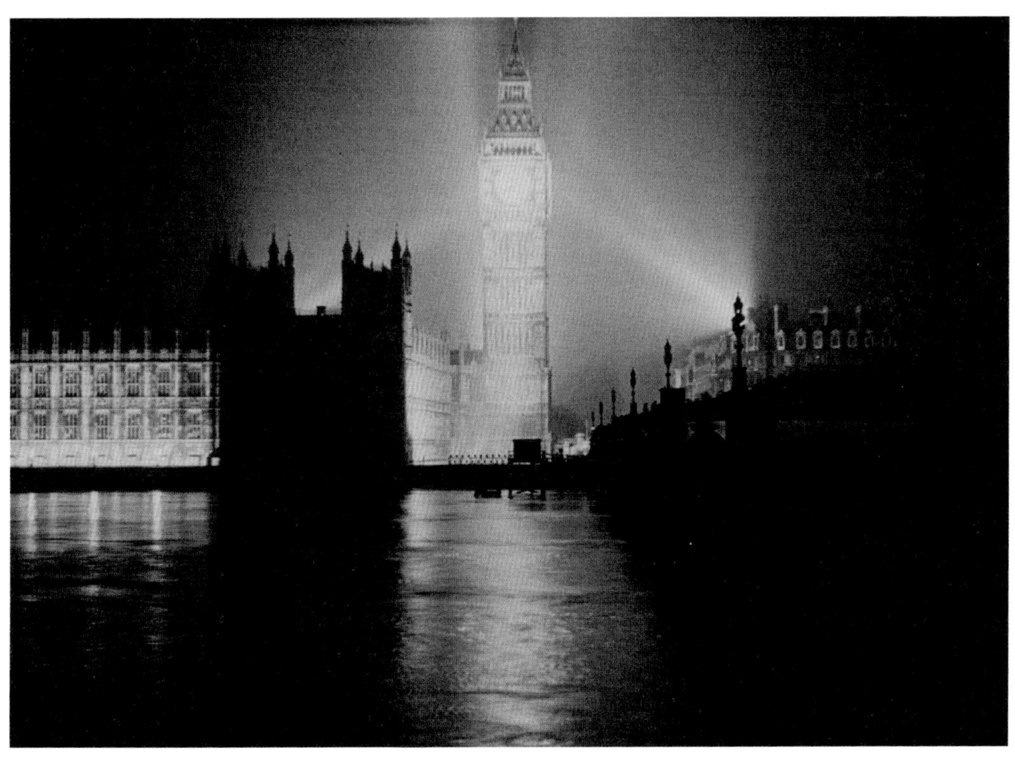

The lights go up in London, 1945

FELIX H. MAN (1893–1985)

The floodlit Houses of Parliament shone bold and bright to celebrate the end of the Second World War in Europe and the long years of blackout.

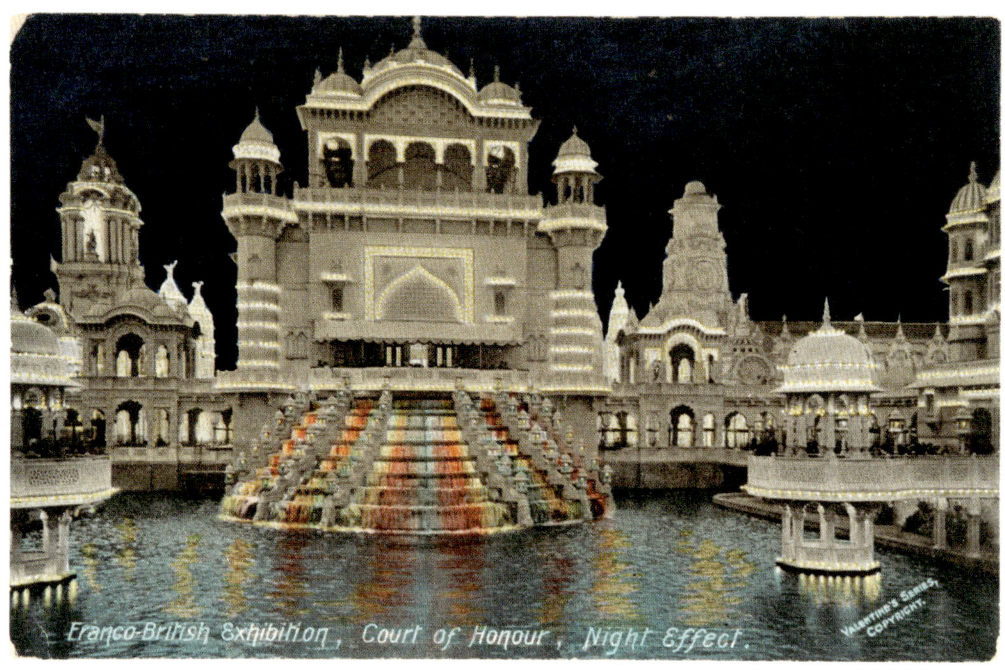

Postcard of Congress Hall, at night, 1910

VALENTINE & SONS LTD

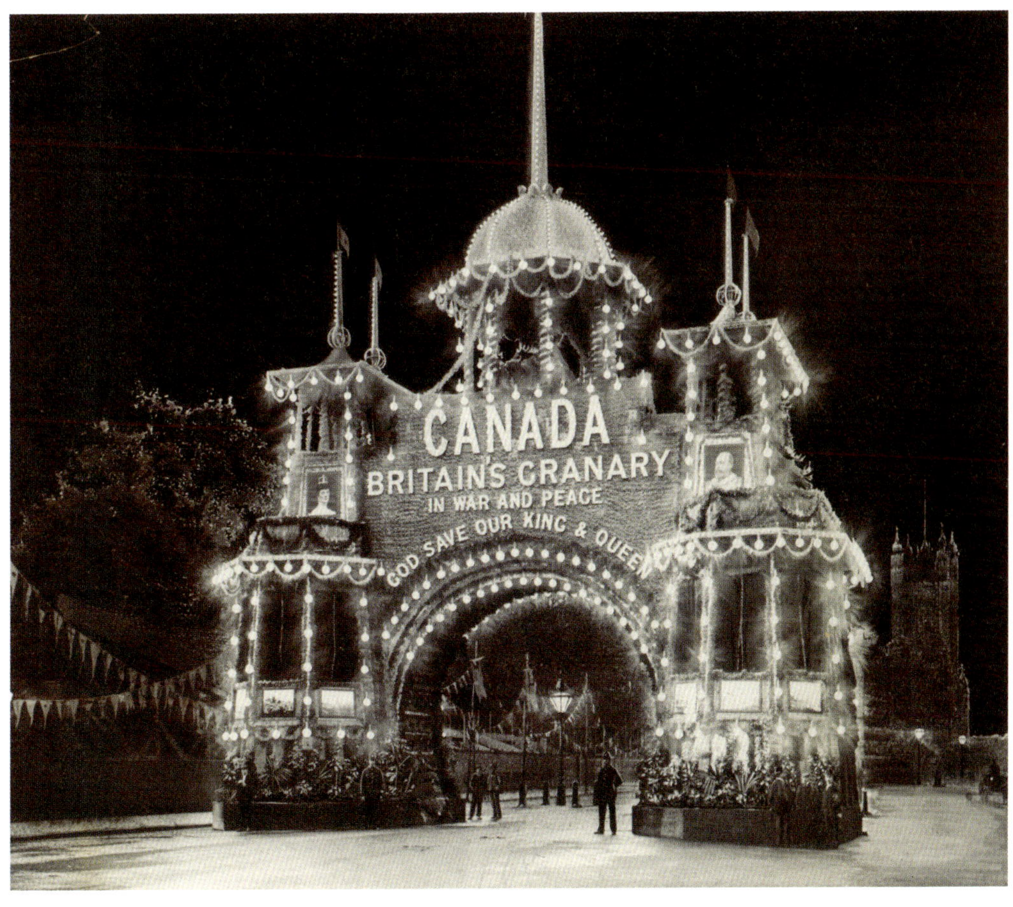

Canadian Arch on Victoria Embankment, 1902

EDWIN TAYLOR (1874–1947)

Working for an unknown photographic company, Taylor captured the prominent decorations illuminating the ceremonial route for the coronation of King Edward VII in 1902.

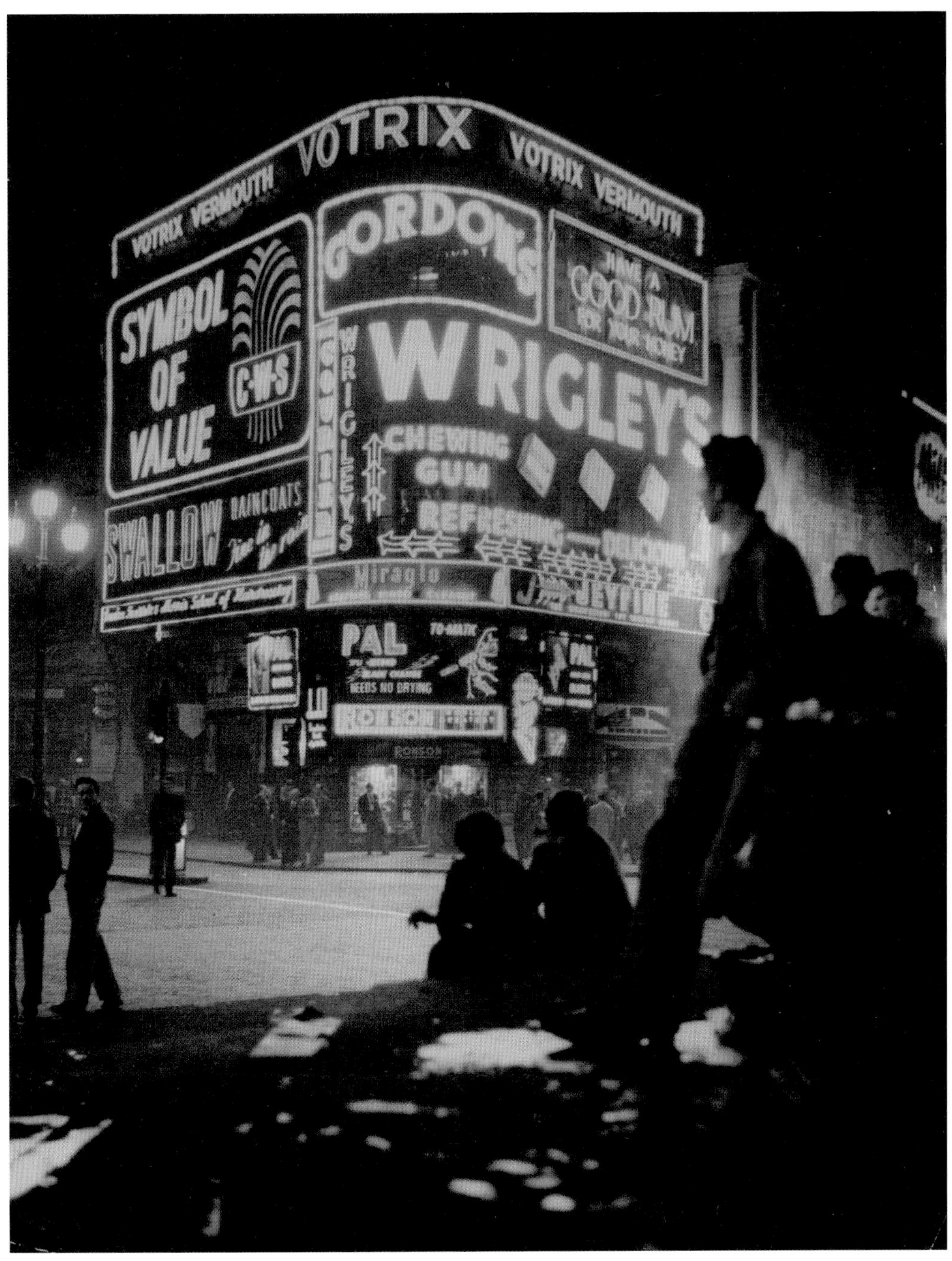

Piccadilly, 1955

HANNES KILIAN (1909–99)

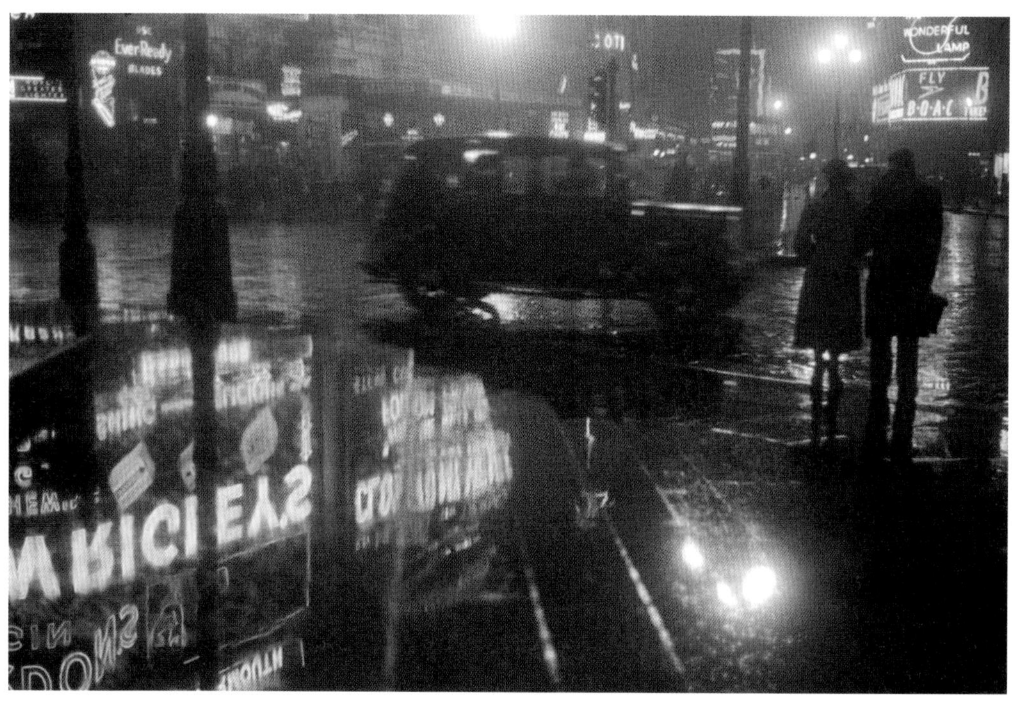

Piccadilly, 1958

HENRY GRANT (1907–2004)

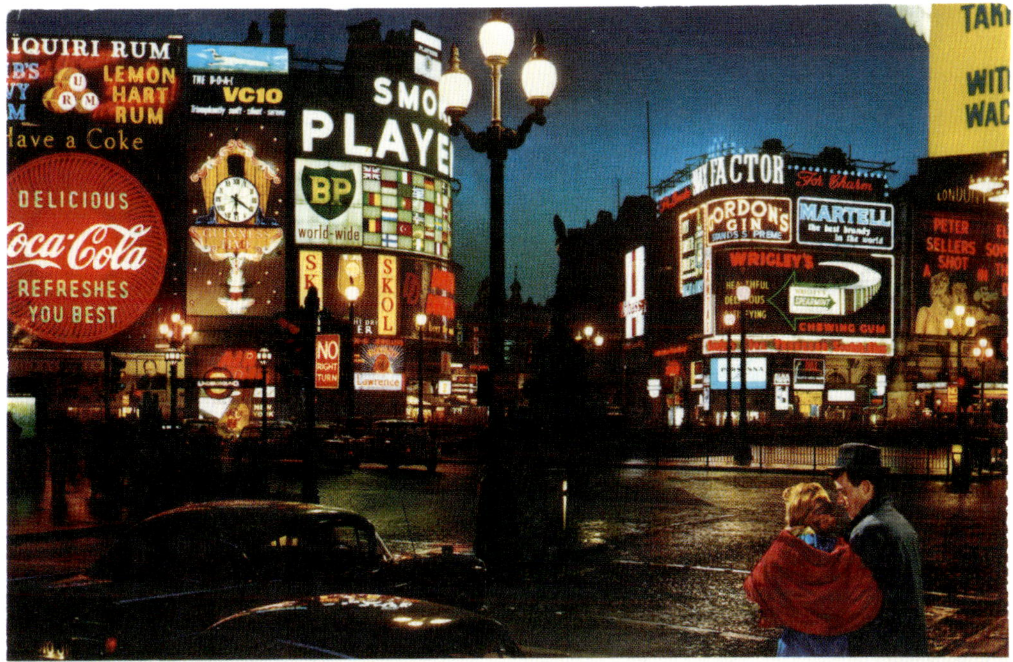

Postcard of *Piccadilly by Night*, c 1965

ELMAR LUDWIG (b 1935); JOHN HINDE STUDIOS

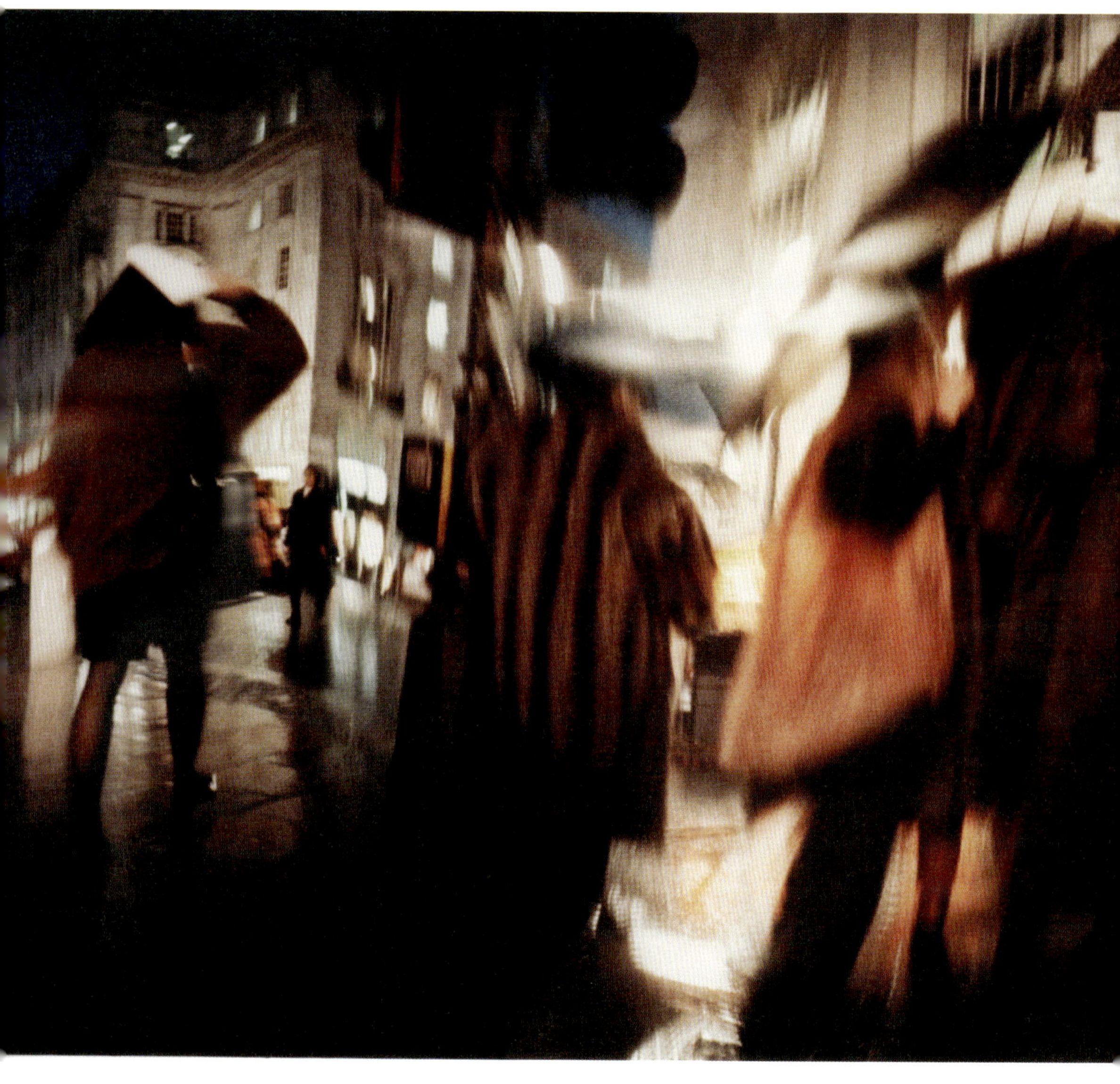

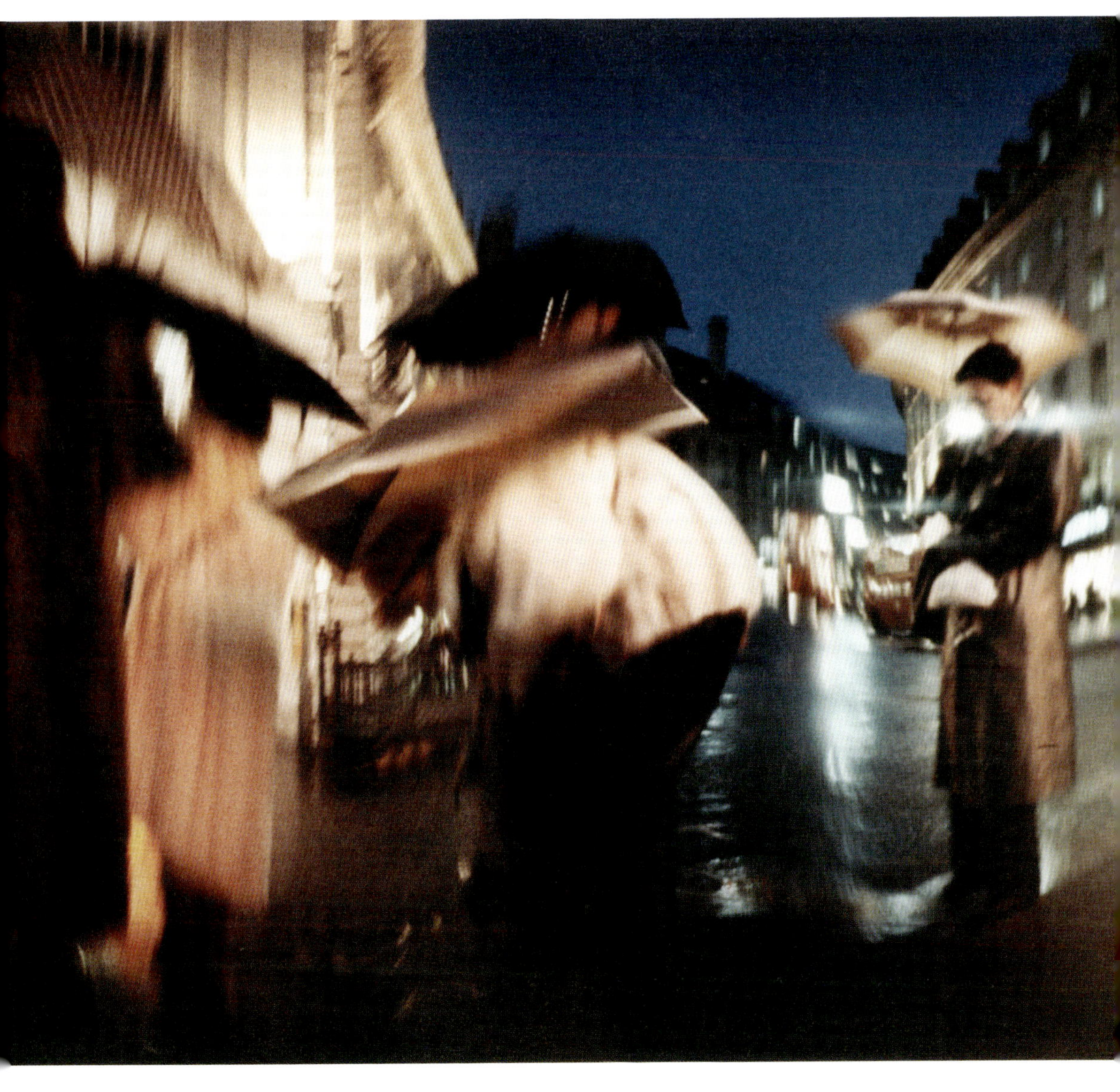

Piccadilly Circus, 1988

JIM FRIEDMAN (b 1959)

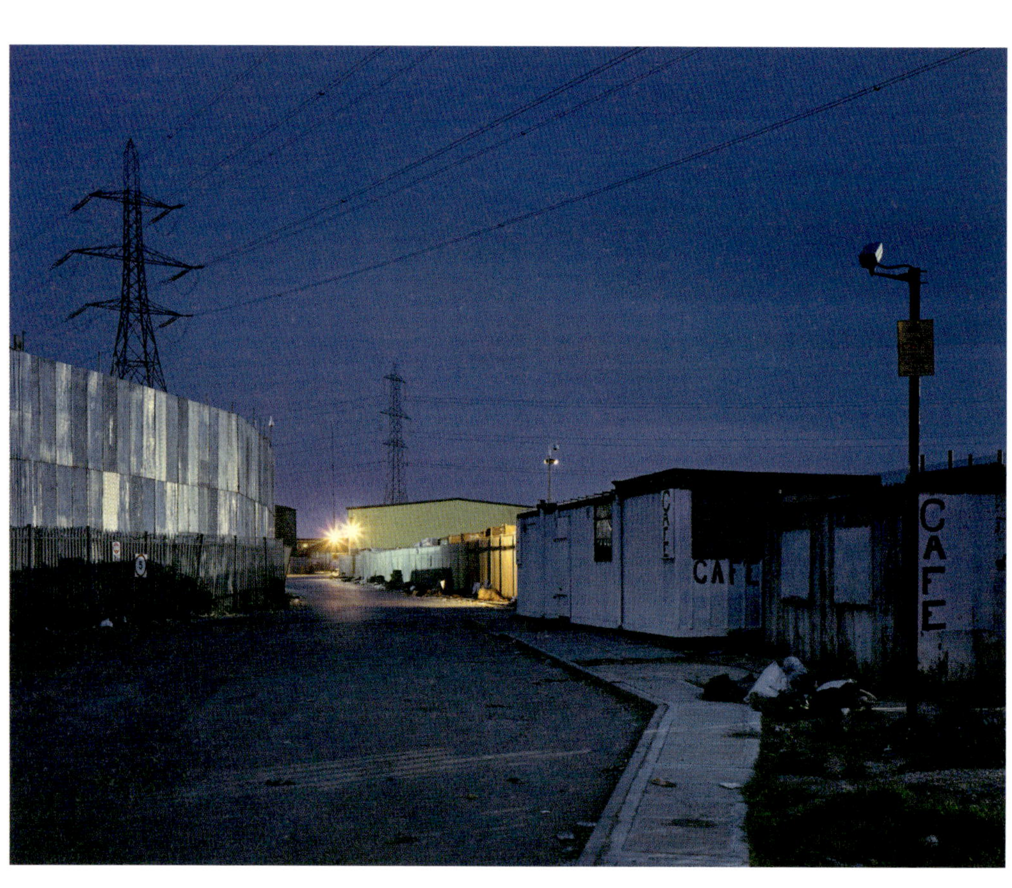
CAFE

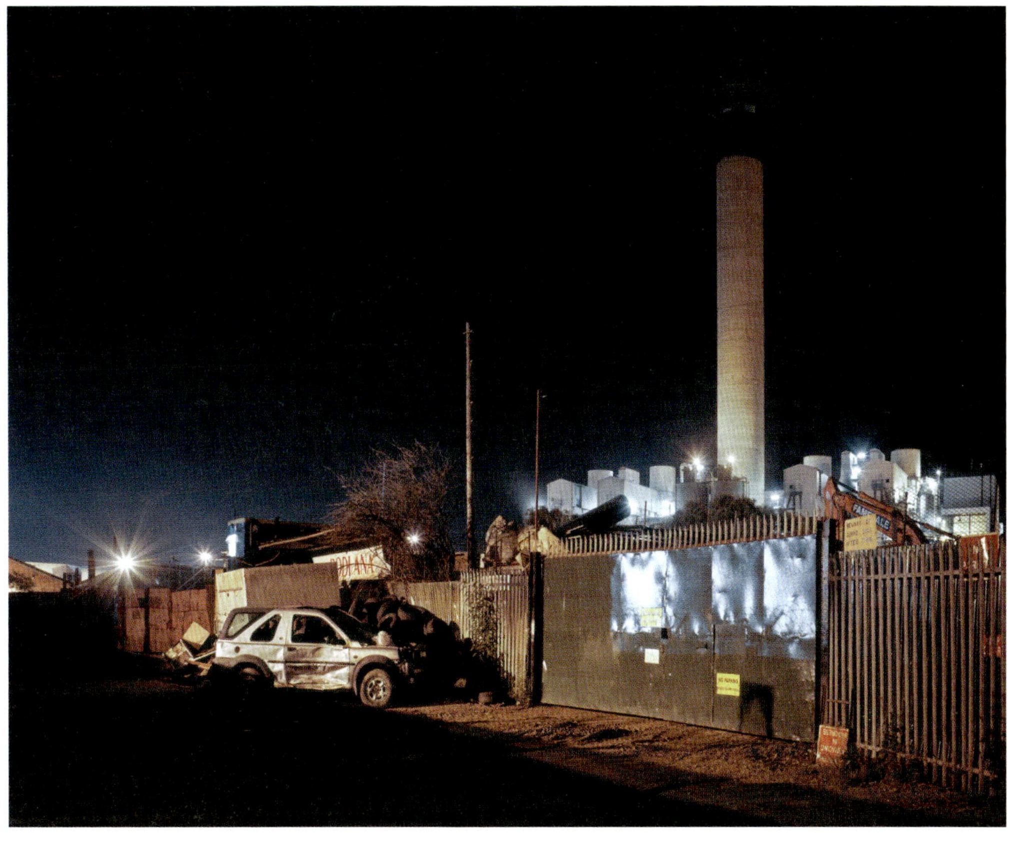

View past café on industrial estate, RM13
Wrecked car on industrial estate, with factory, N18
From the series *Dark City, 2011*

WILLIAM ECKERSLEY (b 1980)

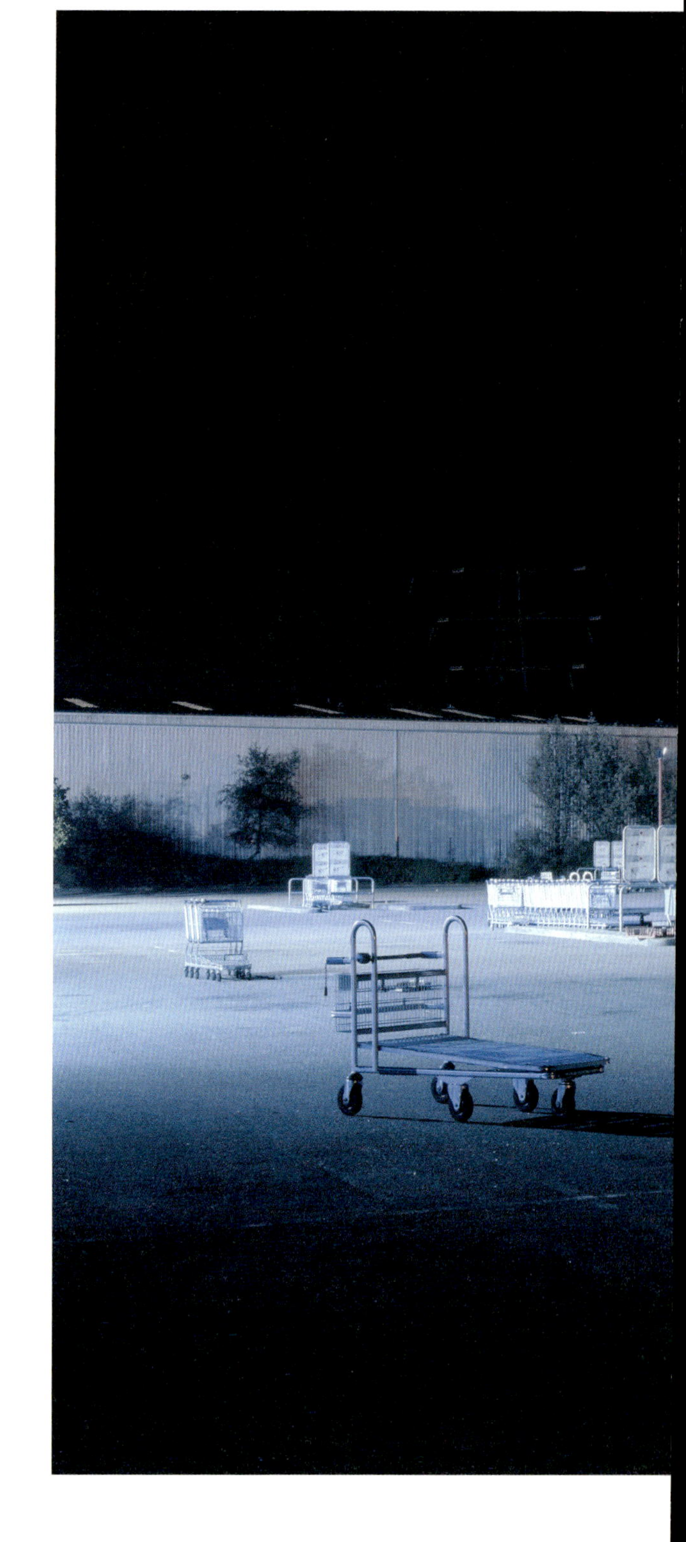

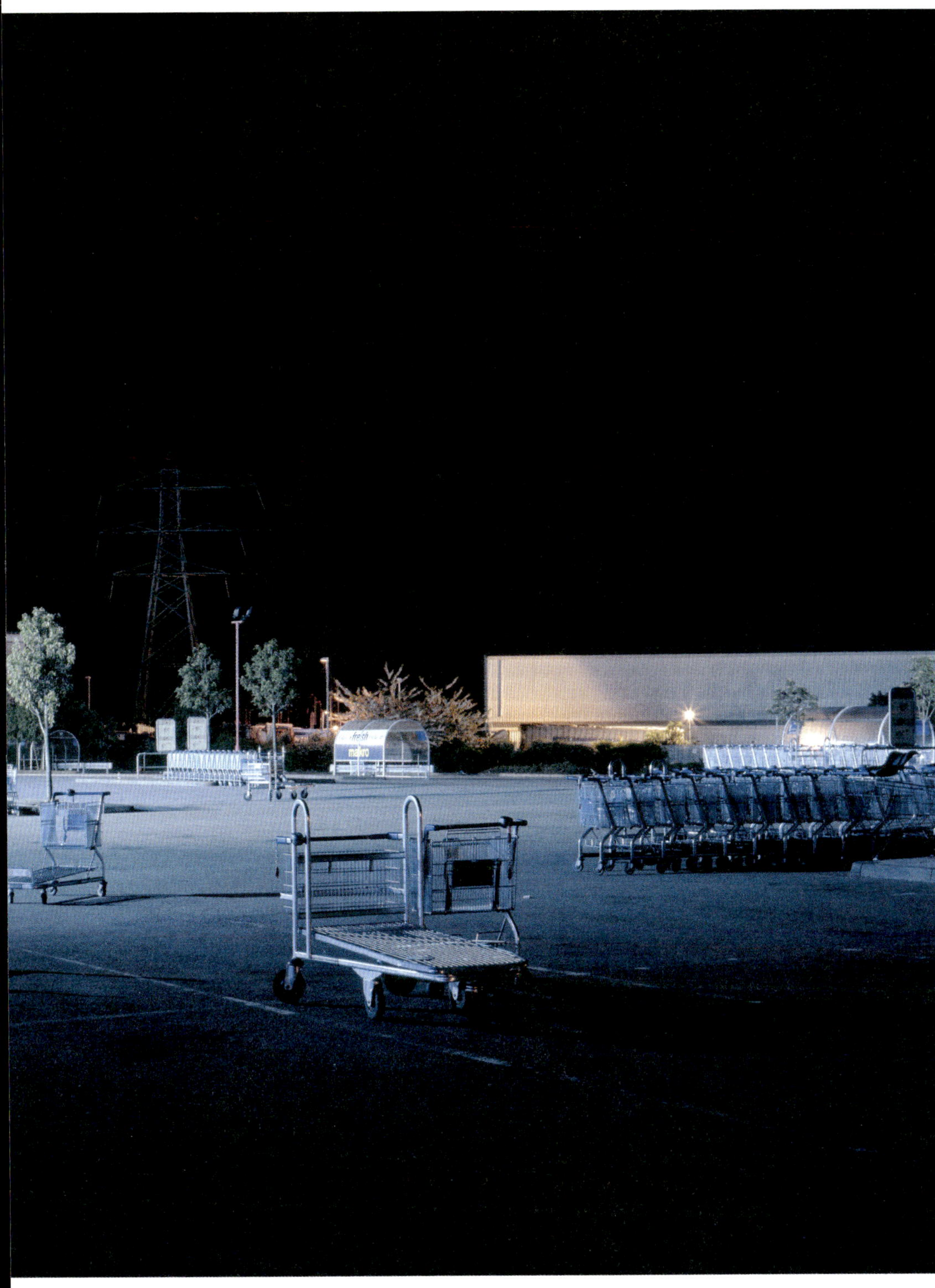
fresh
makro

PREVIOUS PAGES
Trolleys in empty car park, CRO
from the series *Dark City, 2011*

WILLIAM ECKERSLEY (b 1980)

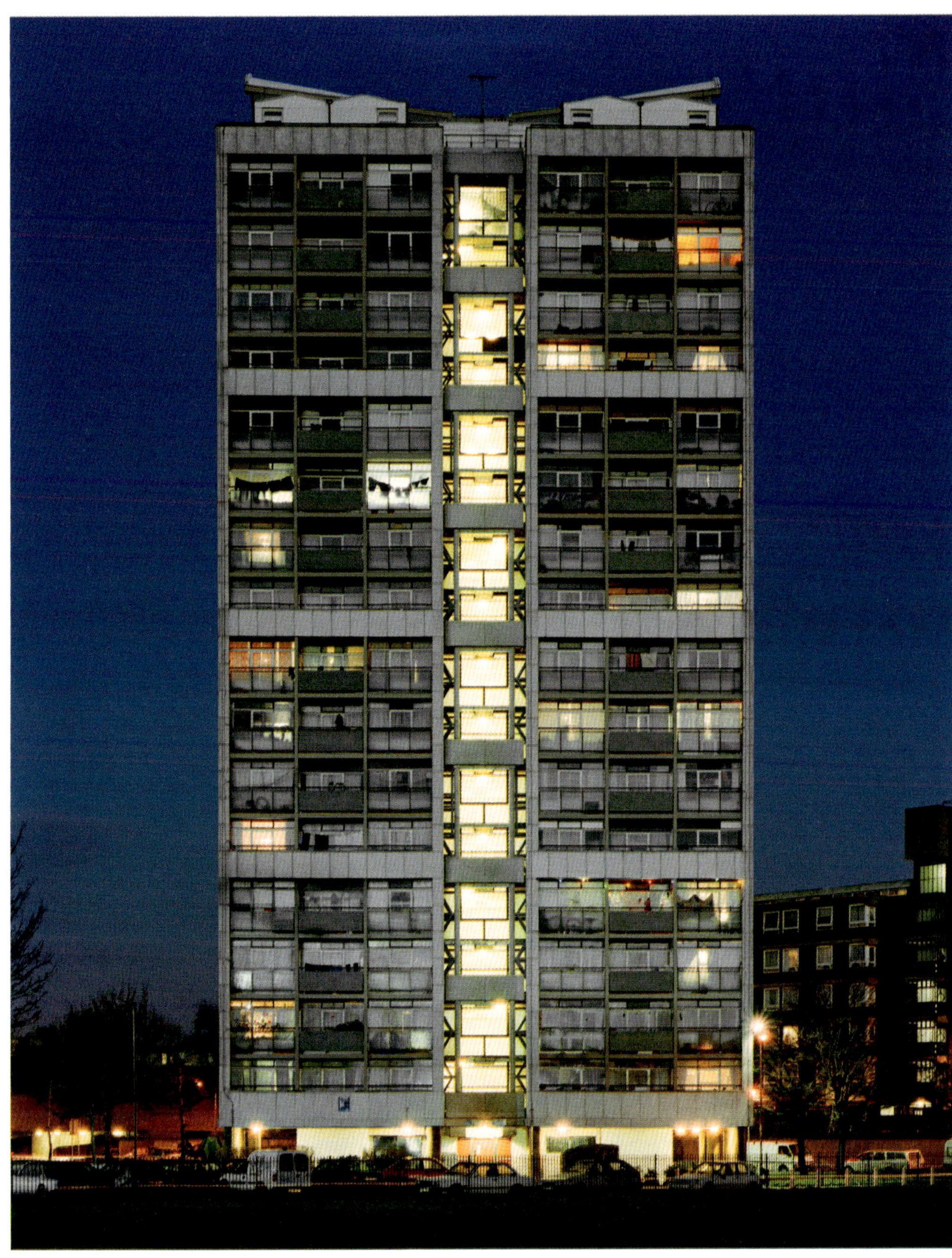

The Brandon Estate, 1999

MIKE SEABORNE (b 1954)

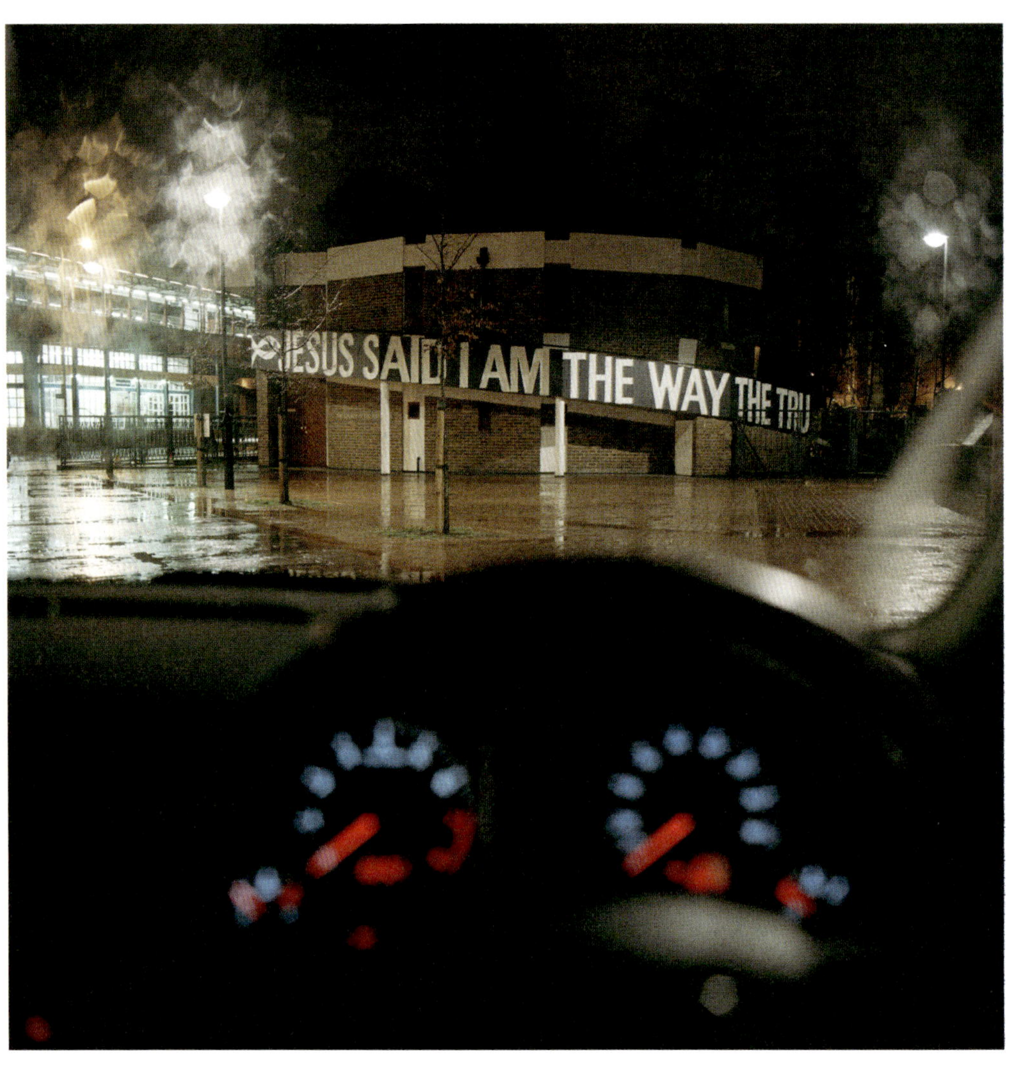
JESUS SAID I AM THE WAY THE TRU

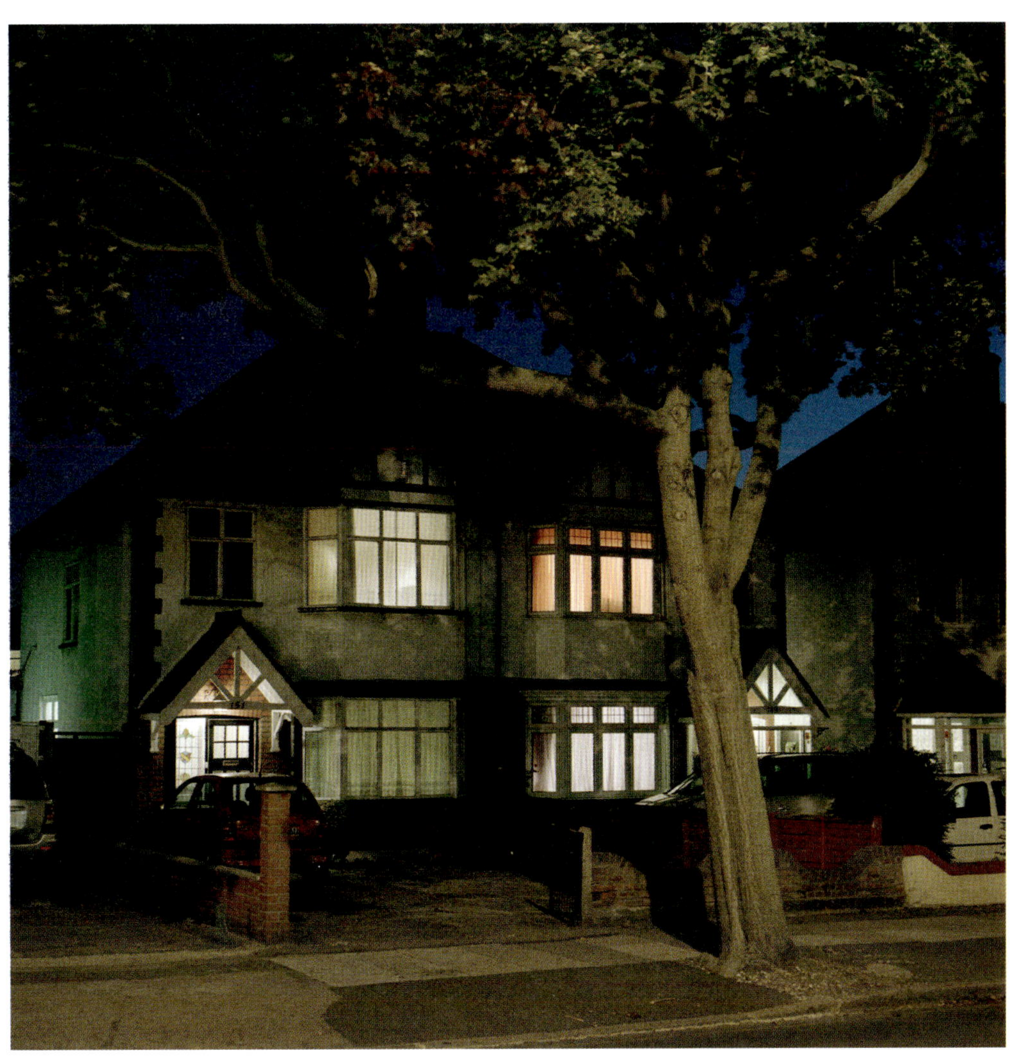

Battersea, 2007
Morden, 2010
From the series *Southwestern*, 2007–10

NIALL MCDIARMID (b 1967)

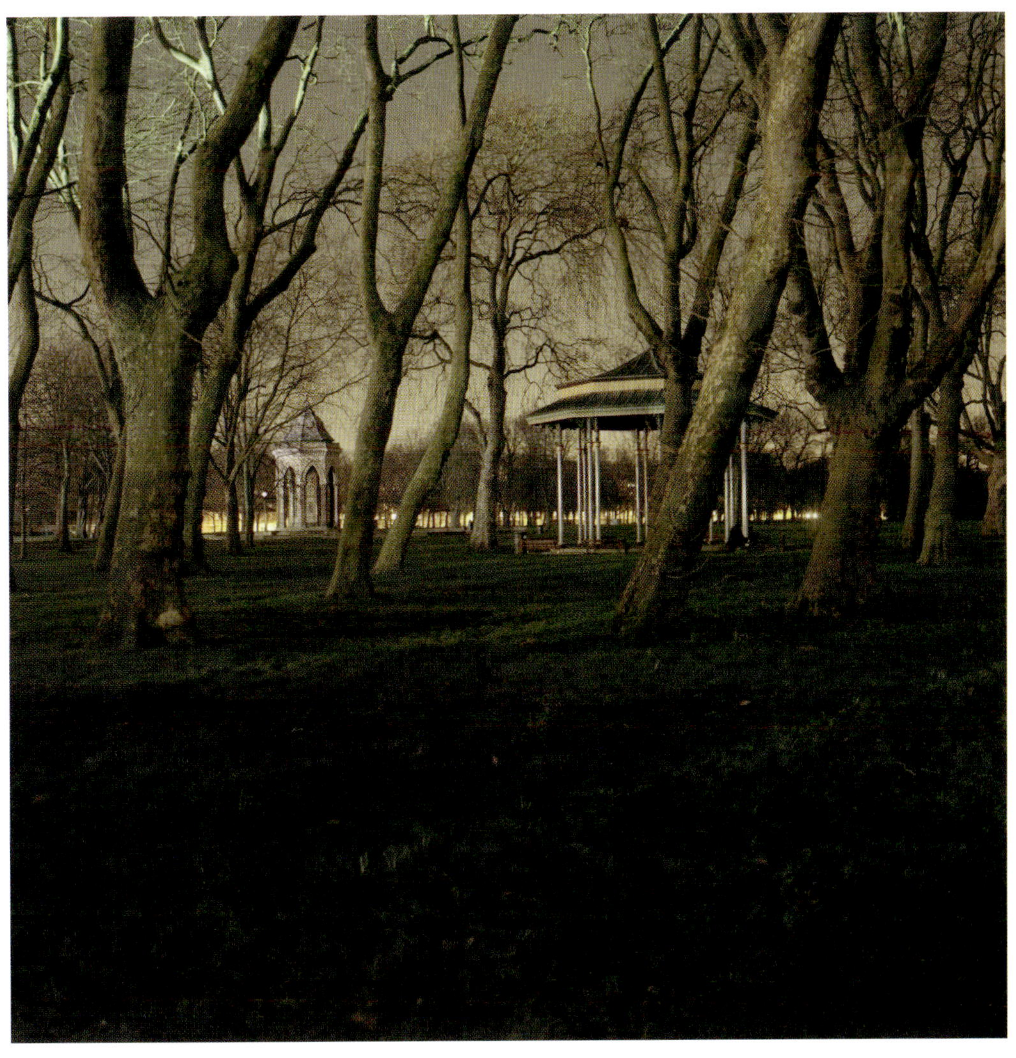

From the series *Hackney By Night*, 2015

DAVID GEORGE (b 1957)

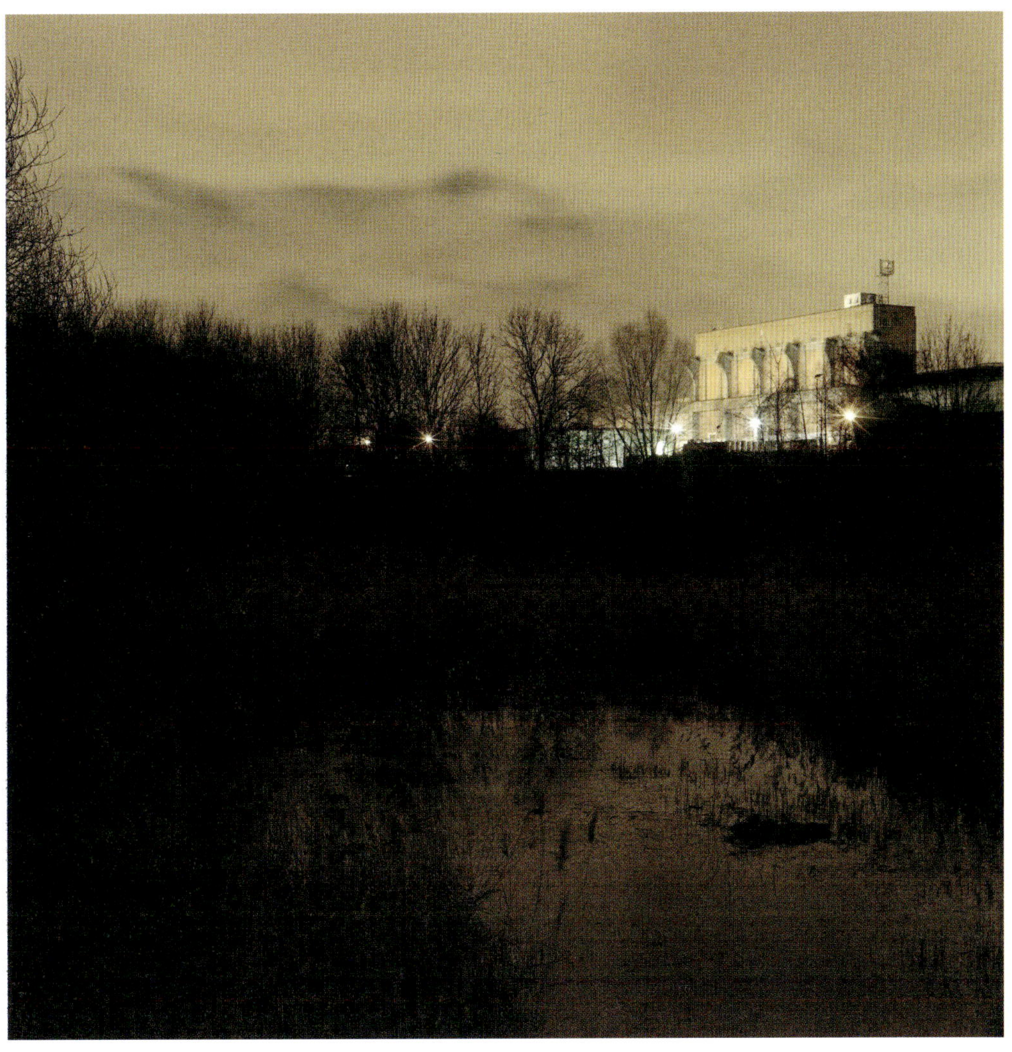

From the series *Hackney By Night*, 2015

DAVID GEORGE (b 1957)

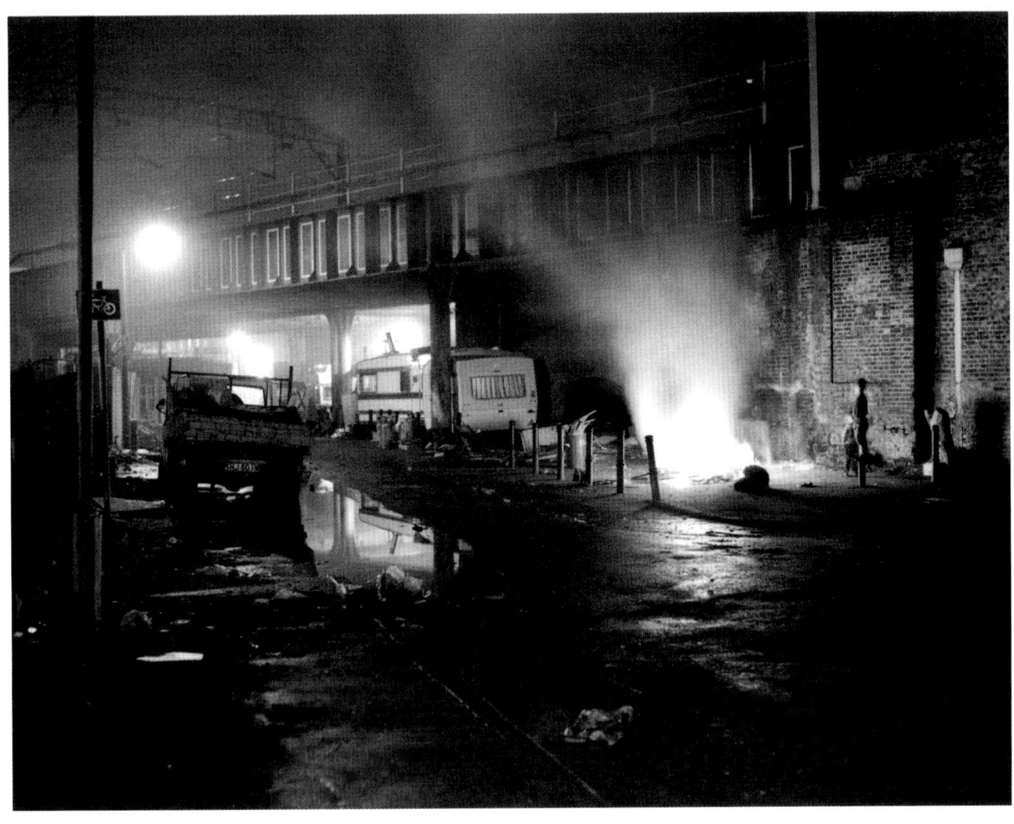

M11 Woodford Green, 1988
Martello Street, London Fields, 1989
From the series *London After Dark*

ALAN DELANEY (b 1958)

Delaney spent ten years on a personal exploration of the urban landscape at night, seeking out the beauty to be found in the available light.

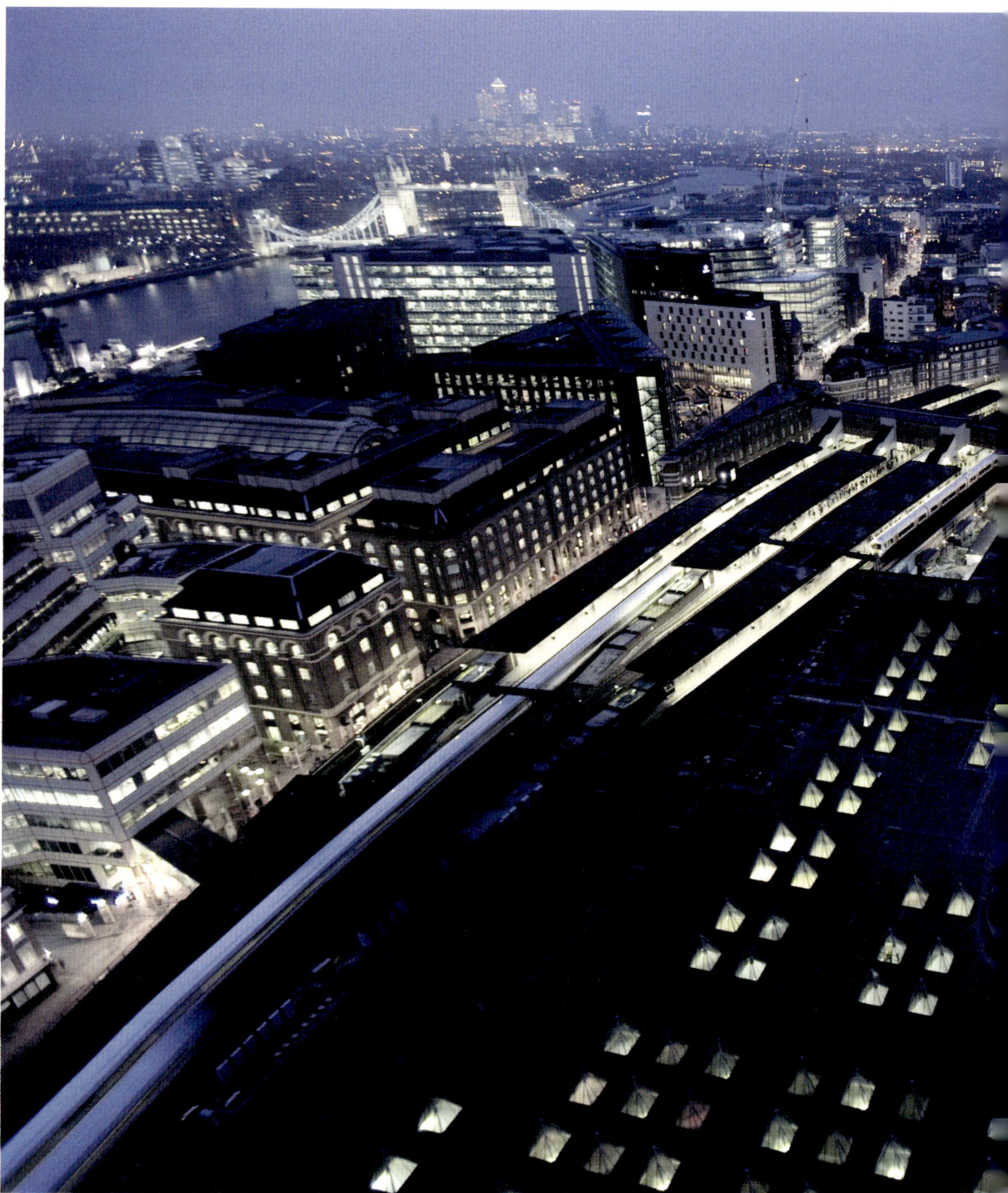

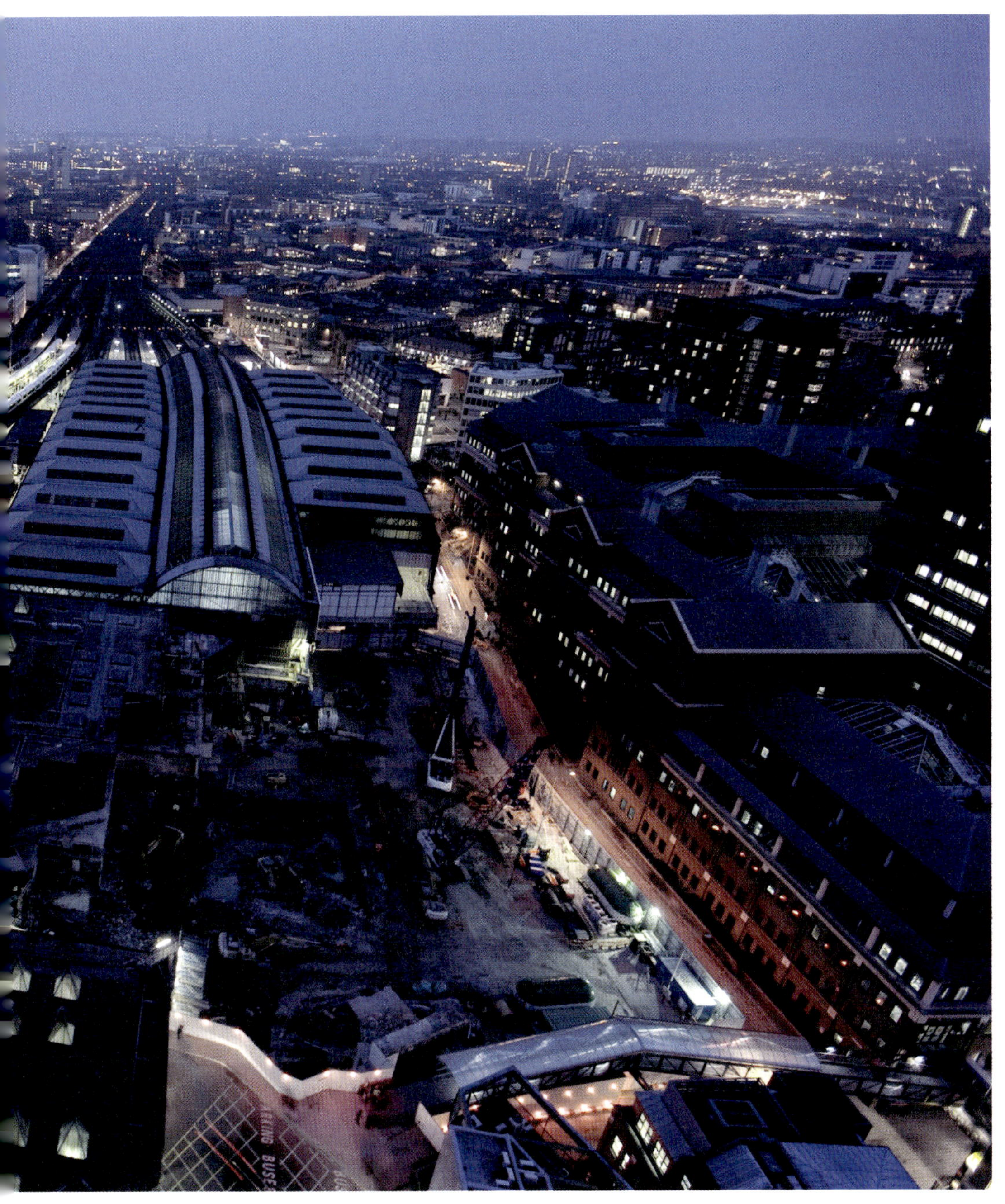

Sleep Walk Sleep Talk: Film Still no. 1308, 2011

SUKI CHAN (b 1977)

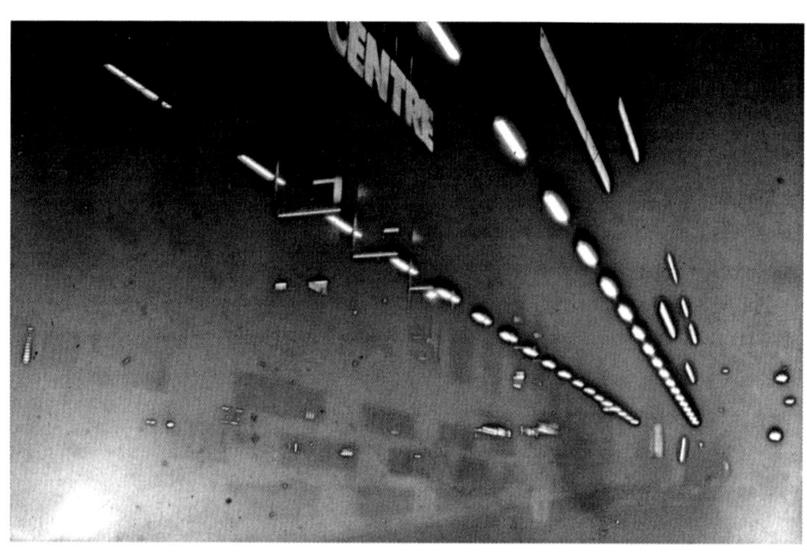
CENTRE

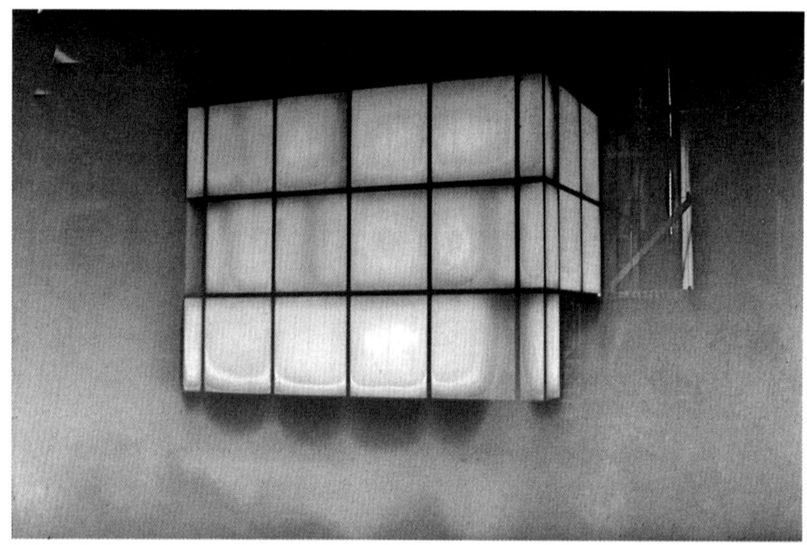

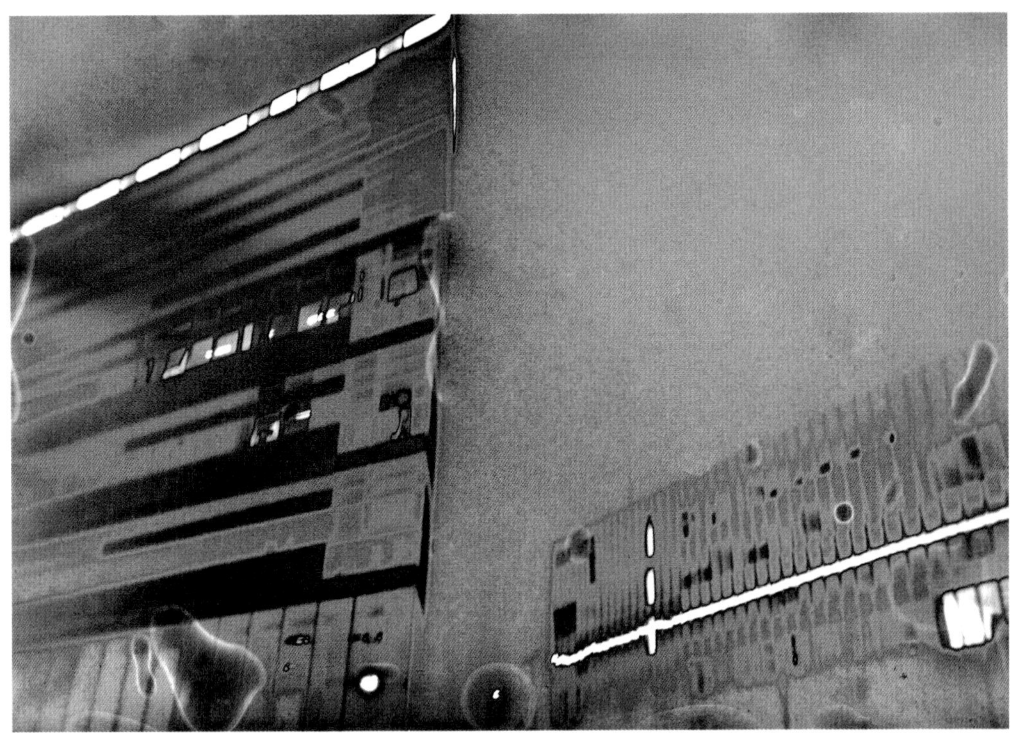

From the series *LDN*, 2015

ANTONY CAIRNS (b 1980)

Pursuing luminous details of the night city in places such as construction sites, underpasses and stations, Cairns fixes the light and dark in abstracted patterns and shapes.

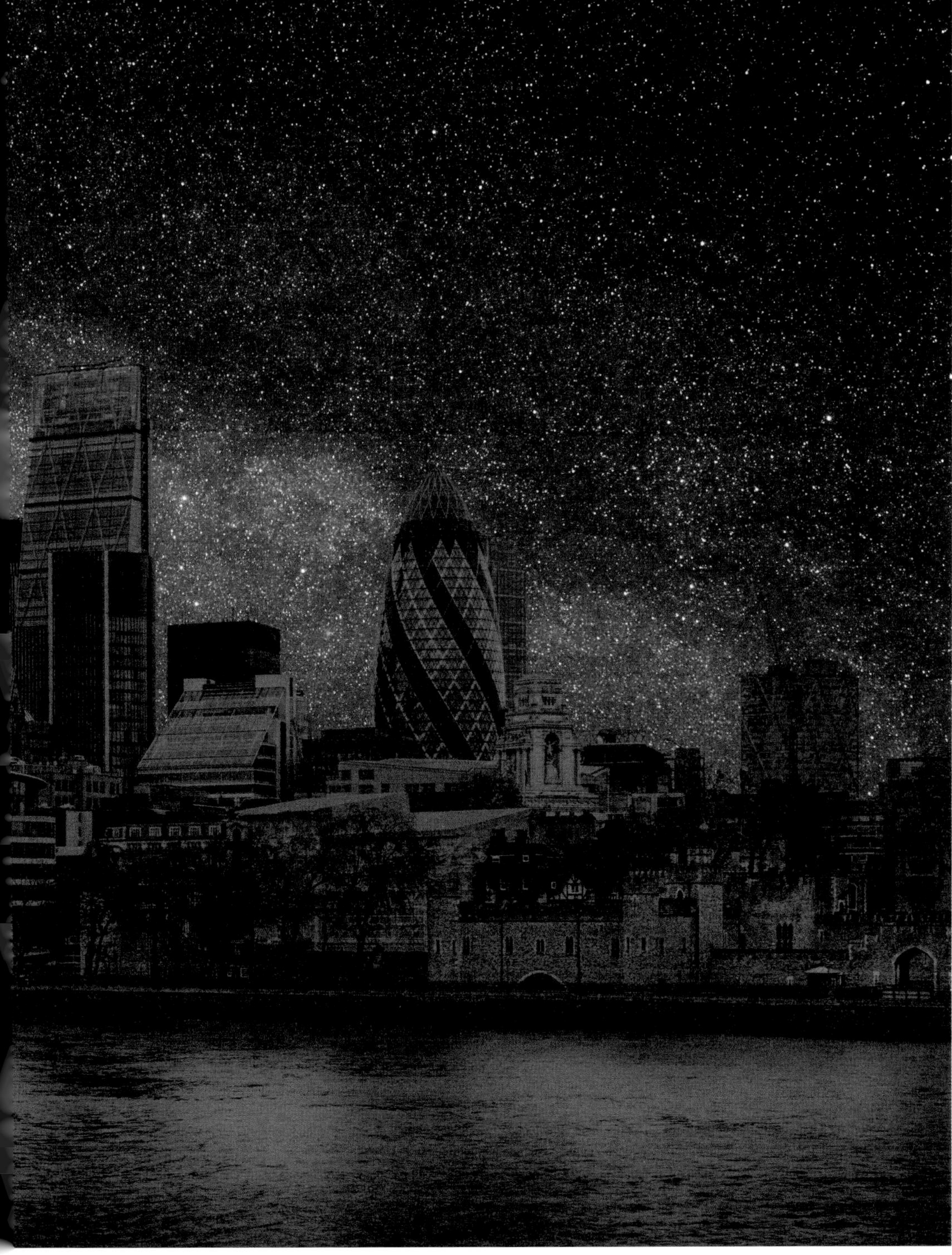

PREVIOUS PAGES

London 51° 30' 17" N 2015-02-17 LST 10:39
from the series *Darkened Cities*, 2015

THIERRY COHEN (b 1963)

London lies beneath a magnificent clear night sky in this crafted landscape; a composite that imagines a starlit metropolis, liberated from artificial light and air pollution.

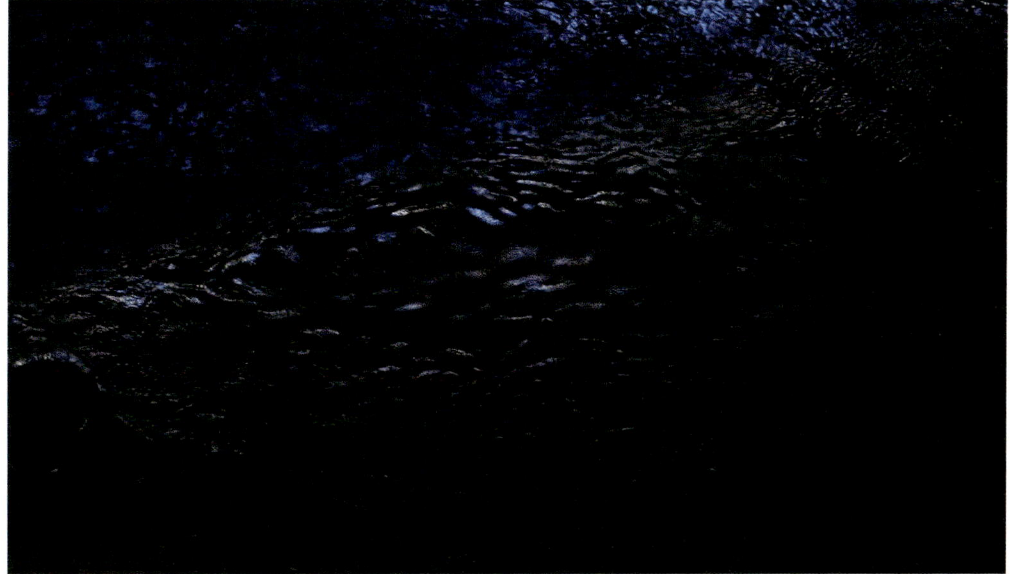

Stills from *London River Burning*, 2017

CHLOE DEWE MATHEWS (b 1982)

Dewe Mathews' film focuses upon the textural surface of the River Thames, morphing in colour and tone as it reflects the lights from the city.

FOLLOWING PAGES
London from the ISS, 2016

TIM PEAKE (b 1972)

From his unique vantage point aboard the International Space Station, astronaut Tim Peake photographed the capital at night, sending his images to Earth via social media.

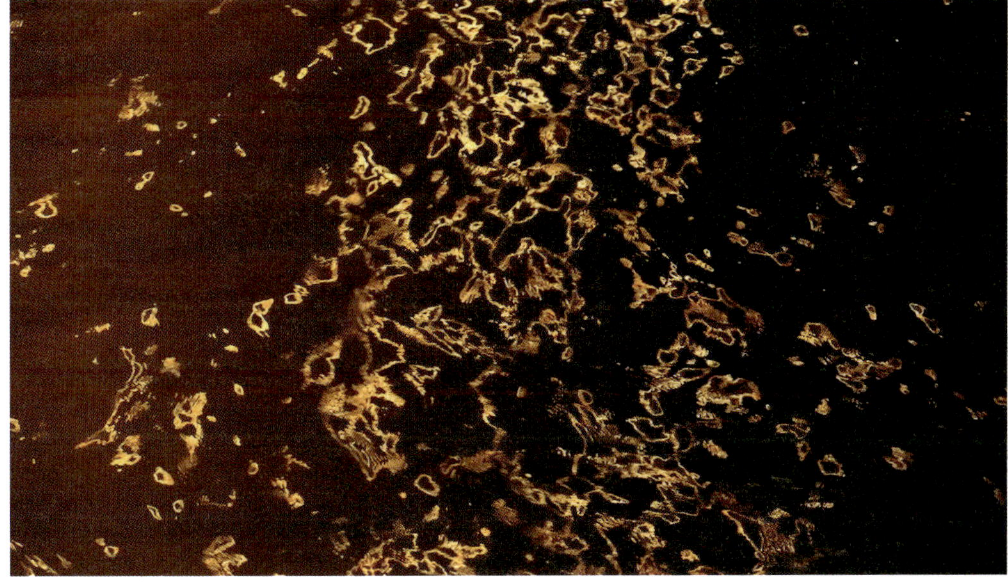

Stills from *London River Burning*, 2017

CHLOE DEWE MATHEWS (b 1982)

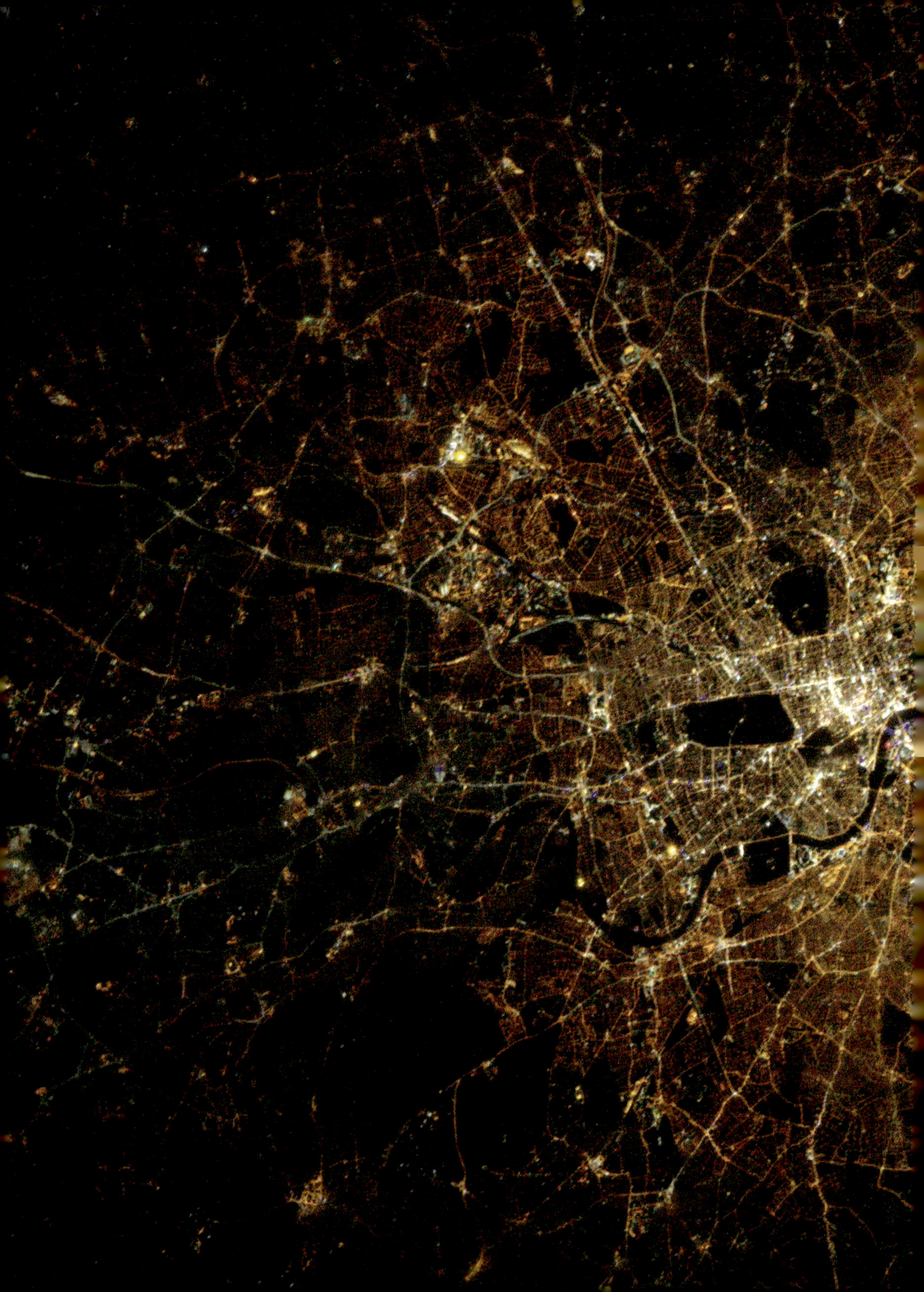

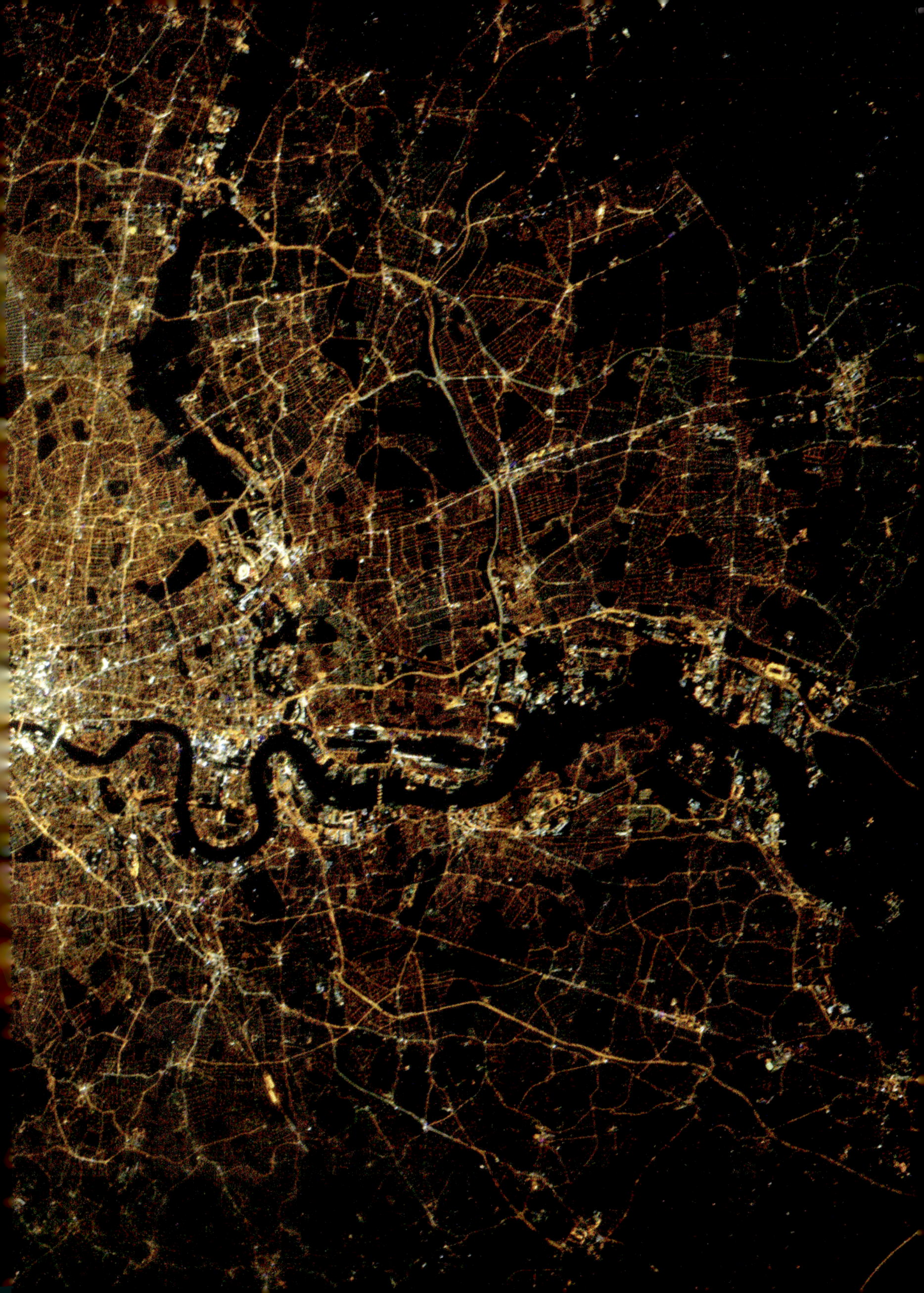

Cave /

Because their engines shredded our skies / we dug
down / we huddled in train tunnels / rocked back
and forth as the city shook

Across the waters / we too poured flames
on their world / shelled it to dust / perforated
their soldiers till streams ran crimson

And whether or not it was the accepted price
of victory / whether earth took blood as sacrifice
or poison / when we surfaced

soot-eyed / cantering like young deer
in the urban morning / something ravenous followed
and remains among us / still

there / in a gargoyle's heart / glinting
from towers / the wild within pets' eyes / tucked
inside car crashes / polishing nightmares / flowering out.

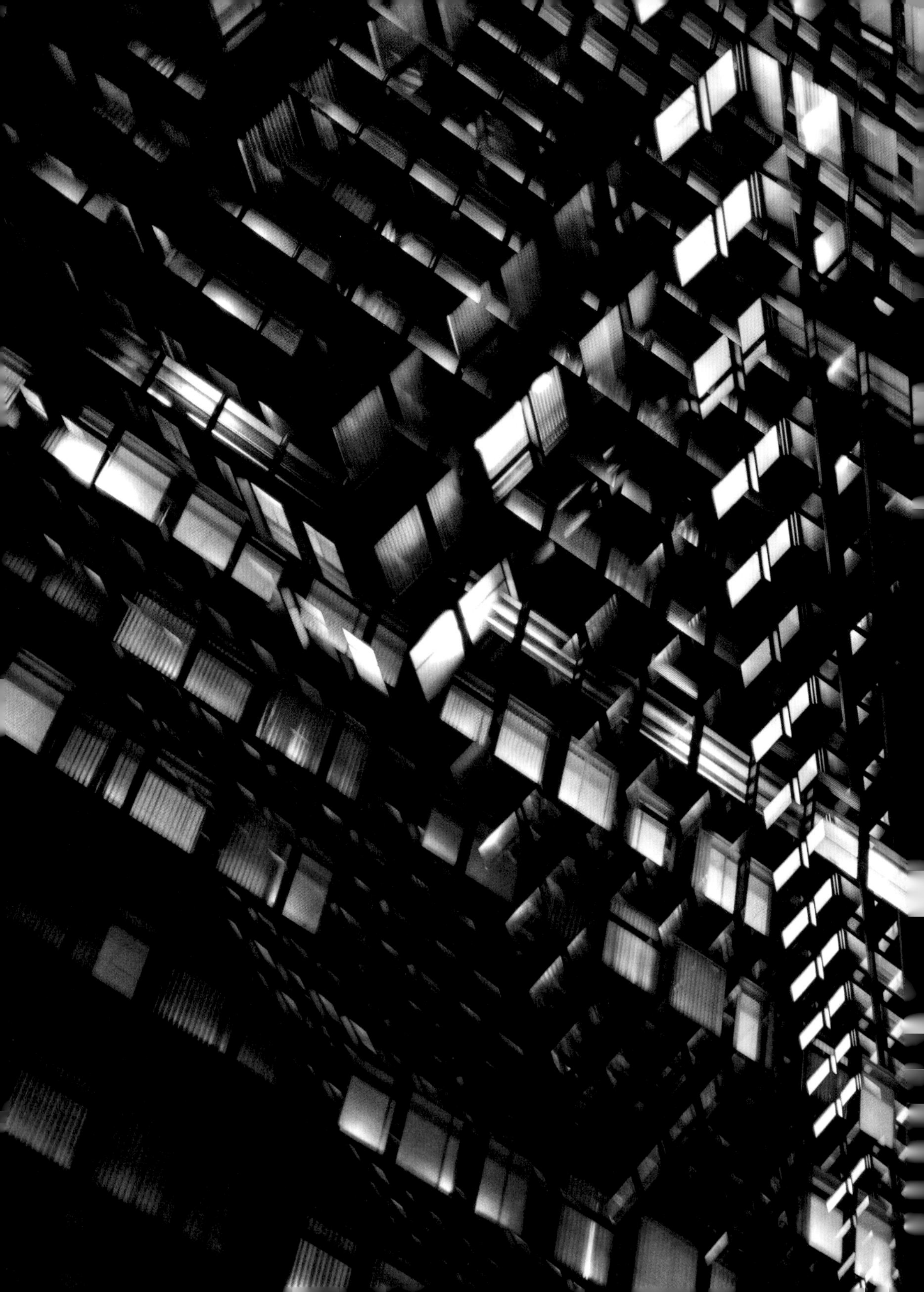

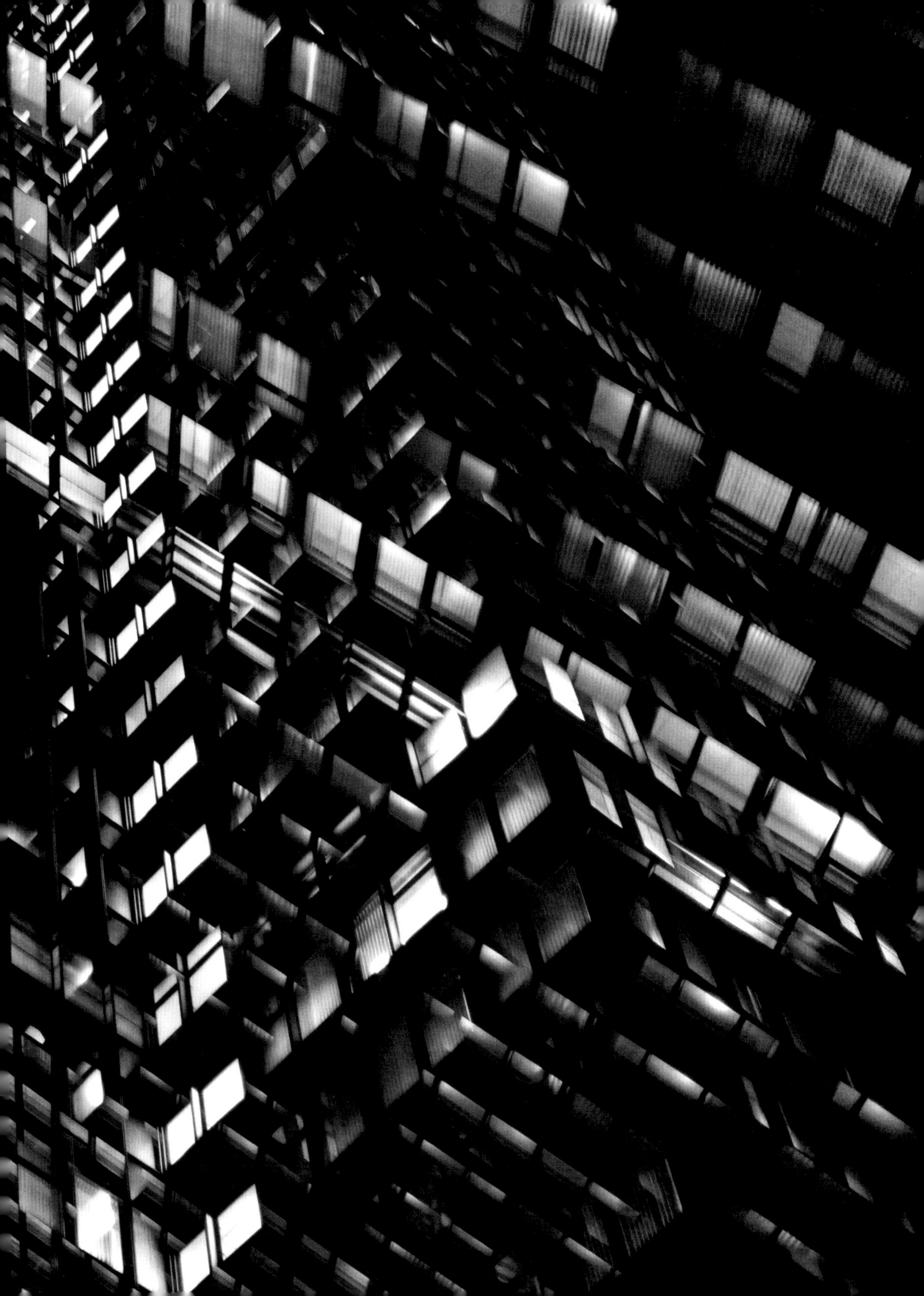

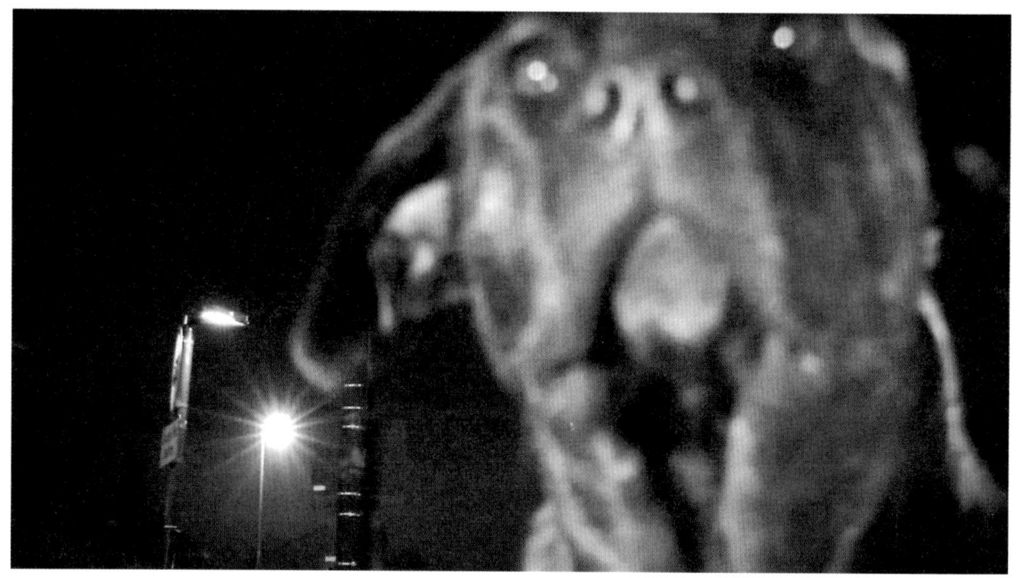

Still from *Lower Street, a Night Journey*, 2016

ANDREA LUKA ZIMMERMAN (b 1969)

Zimmerman's film follows the path of a stray dog on the streets of London and her fight for survival among strange and unsettling nightly encounters.

DARK MATTERS

Despite the enchantment of London under artificial light and moonlight, a literal and metaphorical darker side looms in the urban night. Stepping out from the shadows, notions of threat, vulnerability and fear are never too far away in any city, and London is no exception. While these may manifest in the imagination alone, caught up in association and connotation, they can potentially become a reality, arising through circumstances of crime, accident, mystery or the unknown. 'Dark Matters' addresses such emotions and situations, leaping between the real and the imagined, the documentary and the conceptual.

What greater sense of danger could a whole city face than that which war presents; be it a continually heightened threat level in the face of terrorism, or the directness of attack itself. During the Blitz of the Second World War, Bill Brandt sought to observe London in blackout, stripped back to the bare lighting of the moon (p 89). Such photographs of London destructed through bombing are attractive in their subtle, delicate lighting, yet foreboding because of the damage and violence they represent. 'Moonlit scenes always have a very peaceful if not desolate atmosphere,' Brandt wrote.[18]

Brandt's approach to photographing the underground shelters where people sought refuge from the bombing above also prompts multiple responses. He portrays Londoners sleeping (or posed as such) in the cramped makeshift shelters (pp 90–1). On one hand, they show Londoners at ease, fulfilling the propagandist 'Blitz spirit' purpose of the Ministry of Information that commissioned Brandt to make the work. On the other hand, they convey the harsh realities that Londoners young and old faced, forced to take shelter in uncomfortable conditions night after night. Those photographs depicting people sleeping en masse in dark, confined spaces also carry morbid associations.[19] As biographer Paul Delany writes, Brandt was 'fascinated by an underworld where sleep, dreams and death came together'.[20]

From the reality of the Blitz, an imagined threat is represented in Brian Griffin's eerie *London at Night* (pp 99–101). In a series totalling 33 images, made between 1983 and 1986, Griffin conceived a fictional nuclear attack upon London; the camera 'witnessing' the arrival and destructive impact of an unseen bomb. Long exposure and lens flare add to the surreal nature here, as the sequencing of the photographs builds an ominous narrative.

The city is forever altering and transforming, with whole swathes of the landscape undergoing continual redevelopment. Change is often readily accepted or rejected in equal measure. An unsettling sense of change or loss can be intensified at night, when limited light adds to the drama and tension. Peter Marlow's photography around the derelict Isle of Dogs in 1982 explores the area bereft of the dock industry and poised on the brink of redevelopment, soon to become the financial district of Canary Wharf (pp 104–5). Through minimal lighting, Marlow portrayed an isolated and haunting environment. The compositions are mysterious and charged as they incorporate old and new.[21]

Addressing the loss of diversity and history due to redevelopment today, Lewis Bush embarks on night walks in the city for his series *Metropole* (pp 74–85). Through high contrast and multiple exposure,

Bush layers glass, steel and strips of light as they beam out into the night from corporate office blocks and building sites. The photographs comment on a ubiquitous rise in construction and 'the effect of this capital influx on London'.[22] The sequencing builds in disorientating intensity to emulate the city's overwhelming transformations.

Bush's multi-layering approach expresses what cannot be seen in a single image. Tim Bowditch and Nick Rochowski set out to record what cannot be seen at all. At least not with the naked eye (pp 92–5). Working collaboratively, they ventured on numerous nights to the barely trodden environment beneath the underpasses of the M25, where they were 'fascinated by the voids',[23] making long exposures of these deserted locations orbiting the outer edges of London. Using a camera with a digital achromatic back, which is sensitive to the wider electromagnetic spectrum including infrared, their photographs reveal these hidden, otherworldly and isolated details of London at night.

The imagination can play wildest in solitary, darkened spaces, allowing trepidation and feelings of threat to take hold. This can be seen in Bill Brandt's seminal 1938 publication, *A Night in London,* in which some of the scenes he documented or constructed to appear so are layered with ambiguity and suggestion. Through staged setting and deliberate angle, *Footsteps Coming Nearer* (p 113) carries the weight of the female subject's vulnerability, with various connotations that could imply several impending outcomes.

Alexis Hunter's compelling and provocative work *Dialogue with a Rapist,* 1978, based on a real-life encounter, strikes the viewer on numerous levels (p 112).[24] Her sequenced combination of words and constructed imagery draws a vivid narrative, portraying a late-night scenario of attempted rape upon herself by a black man in Bermondsey. This still challenging work can be contextualised amidst surging racial tension and radical feminist art and activism in the capital at that time. It addresses issues that continue to perturb since the work's conception: racial prejudice, violent crime, women's conduct and safety on the city's streets after dark. Around the same time, in April 1979, mystery and suspense fiction author Celia Fremlin wrote in the magazine *New Society* about female Londoners' overwhelming fears of going out alone at night. Chris Moyse's photograph (p 109) was reproduced on the magazine's cover to illustrate the article. Despite many women's anxieties, the writer's personal view on the subject was that in fact 'what women should fear most is fear itself'.[25]

Nightly suspense and drama are extended further in the work of Tom Hunter, David George and Rut Blees Luxemburg. Hunter's series *Living in Hell and Other Stories* responded to several fear-inducing and sensationalist headlines he read in his local newspaper, the *Hackney Gazette*. In *Rat in Bed* (p 115) incidental detail and crafted staging encourage the viewer to imagine the potential narrative. At first glance, this nocturnal bedroom appears serene. Then we notice the rats. Hunter's series also echoed famous paintings; in this case, Paul Gauguin's *Spirit of the Dead Watching.*[26]

For his series *Shadows of Doubt,* David George looked to the master of suspense, film director and producer Alfred Hitchcock. Reflecting some of the Hitchcockian aesthetic back upon the man himself, George photographed areas associated with Hitchcock to imagine the geography and topography that he might have encountered during his childhood days growing up in London (p 107). The photographs ask what impact this urban landscape may have had upon Hitchcock's memory and subsequent work.[27]

Blees Luxemburg's *A Girl from Elsewhere* is alluring in abstract detail and glowing, golden hues (p 97). Yet the low-lying angle and ambiguous fluid may imply an unsettling scene. The silky flow of the liquid, tinged red, asks the viewer to question its substance – water, oil, blood?[28] While devoid of people, a darker human engagement is suggested through the simplest of elements and the urban environment.

Vulnerable to the elements and the disquiet of night-time are the countless individuals who face sleeping rough on London's streets. Homelessness and poverty have been constant subjects for many concerned photographers over the decades, and their hardships are accentuated in photographs of their nightly circumstances (pp 118–9). Potential danger on the nocturnal London streets is explored further in *Lower Street, a Night Journey*, in which filmmaker Andrea Luka Zimmerman portrays the fictional experiences of a stray dog (p 76). She imaginatively conveys the creature's resilience and simultaneous helplessness amidst the harshness of life.

The malleability of film and photography lends itself brilliantly to conveying these darker traits of London at night, where fear, threat and suspicion often lead the imagination to blend with reality. Lens-based media rises to the challenge of extending and playing with these emotions, due in part to the intrinsic trust and belief that is placed in the viewing of a photograph.

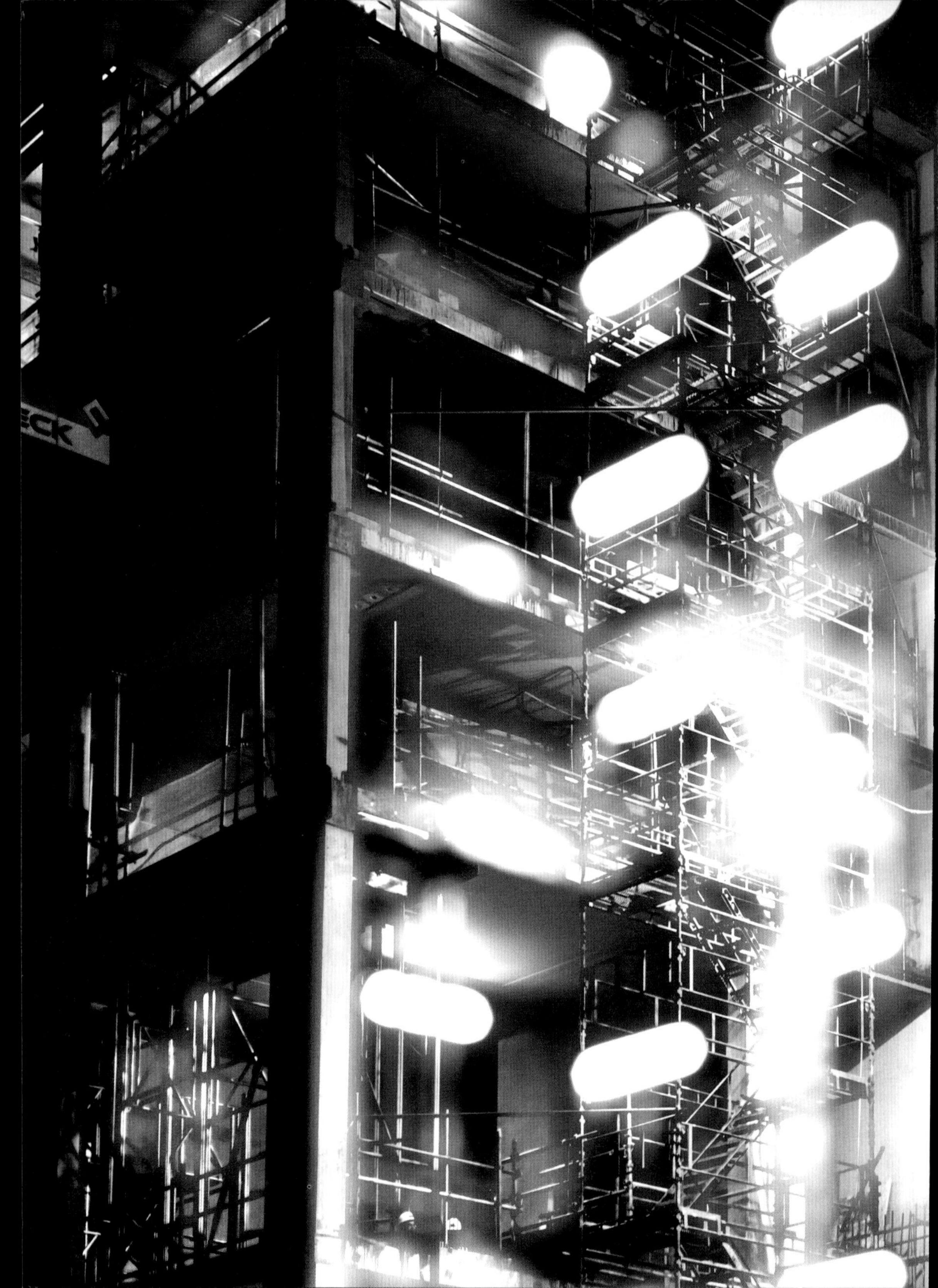

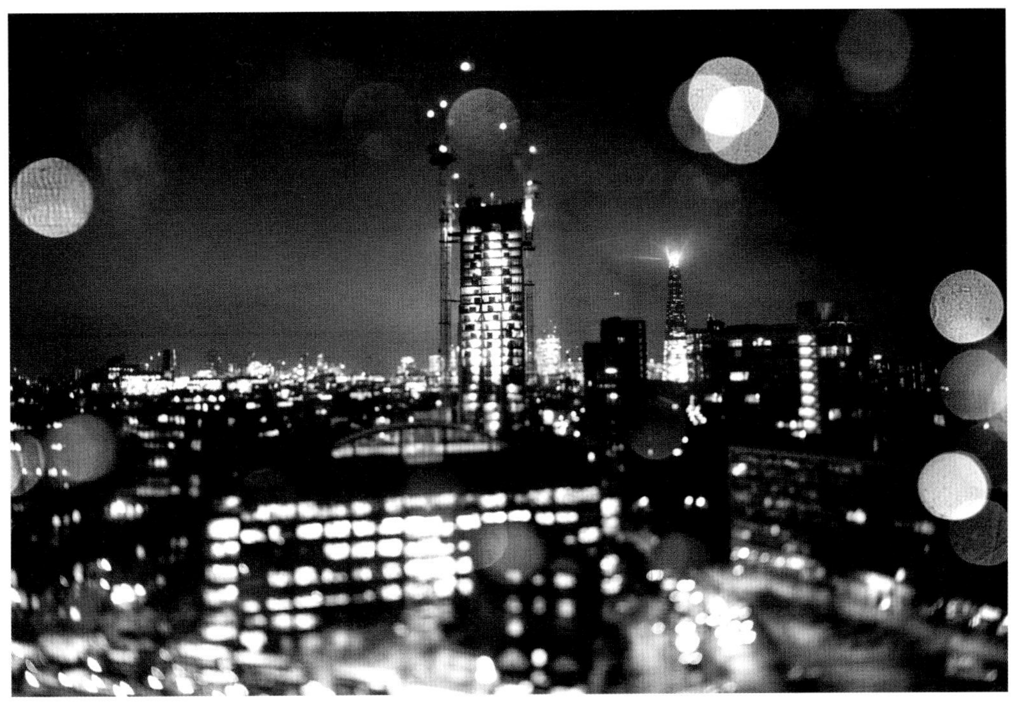

ABOVE AND PAGES 74/75/82/83
From the series *Metropole*, 2015

LEWIS BUSH (b 1988)

In the glare of light emanating from the city's construction sites and high rises, Bush presents a London overwhelmed by the continued impact of redevelopment.

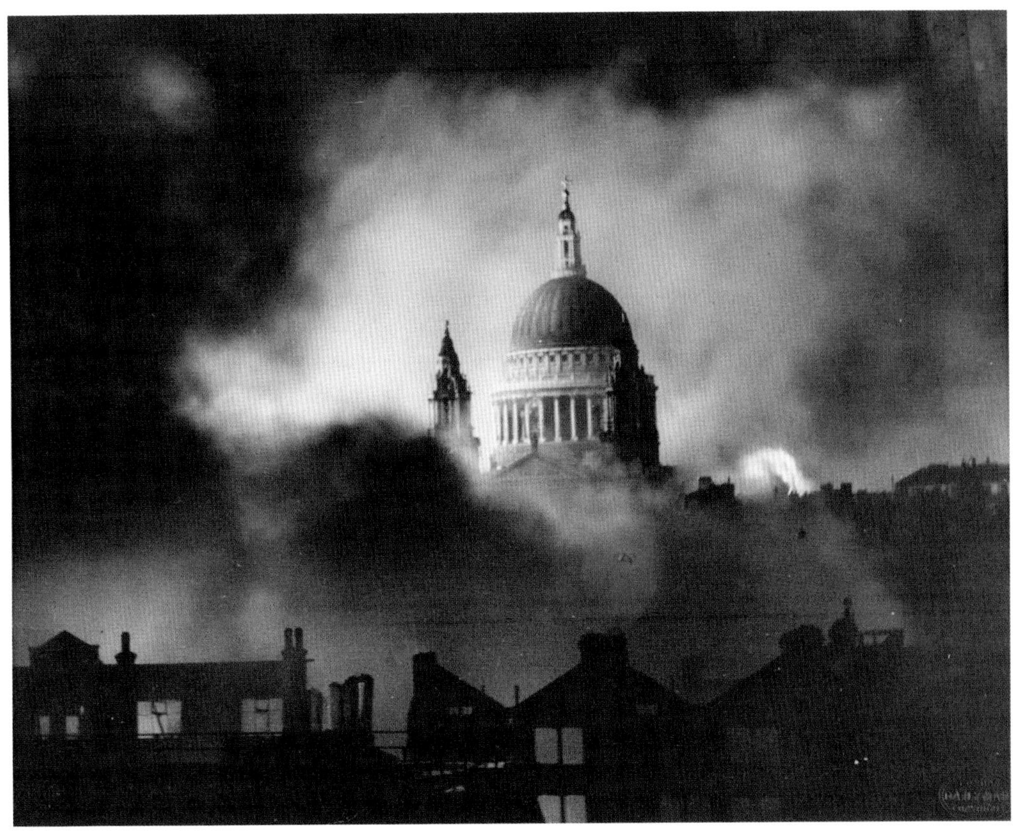

St. Paul's Cathedral During the Blitz, 29 December 1940

HERBERT MASON (1903–64)

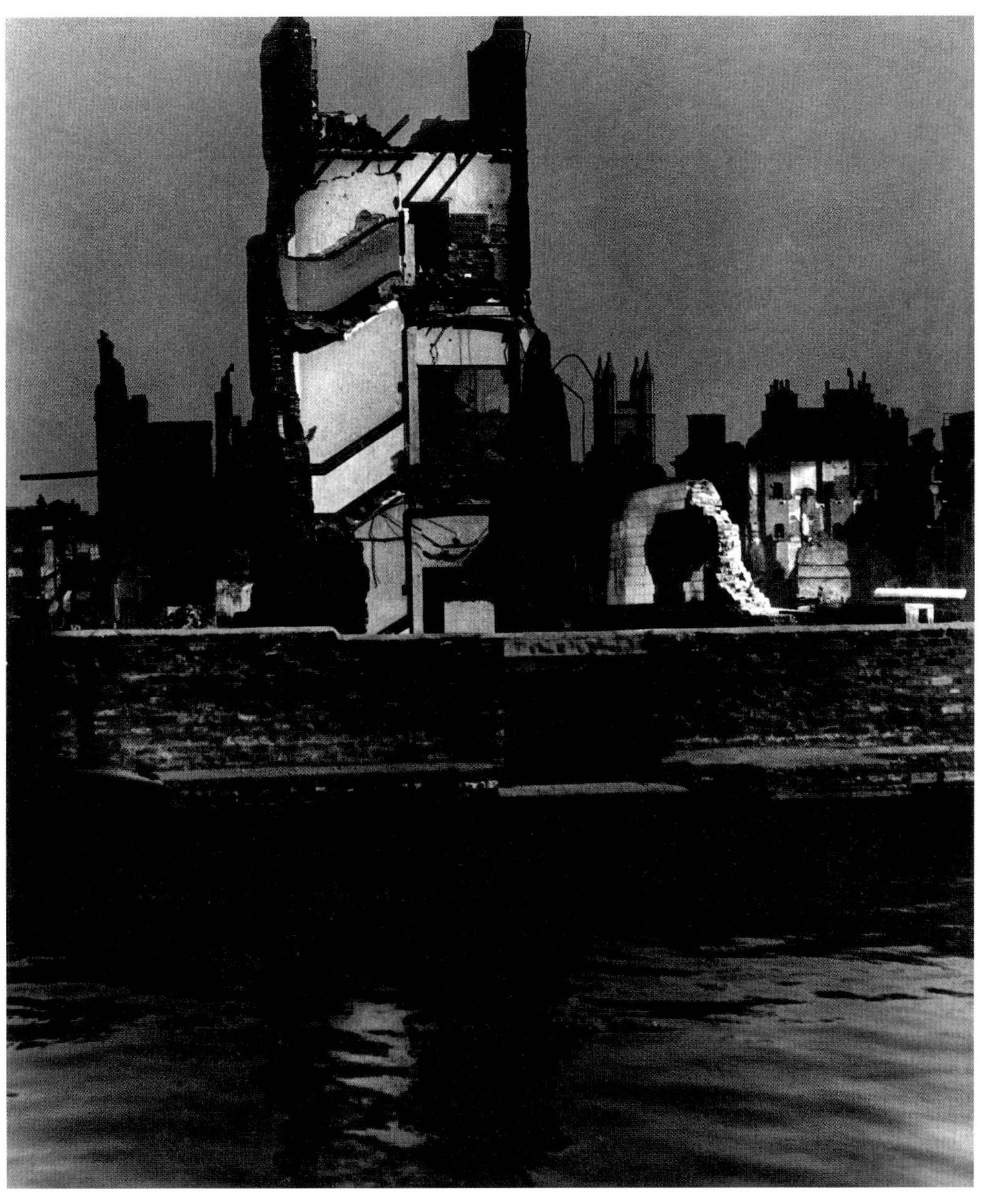

London by Moonlight. The Bombed City, April 1942

BILL BRANDT (1904–83)

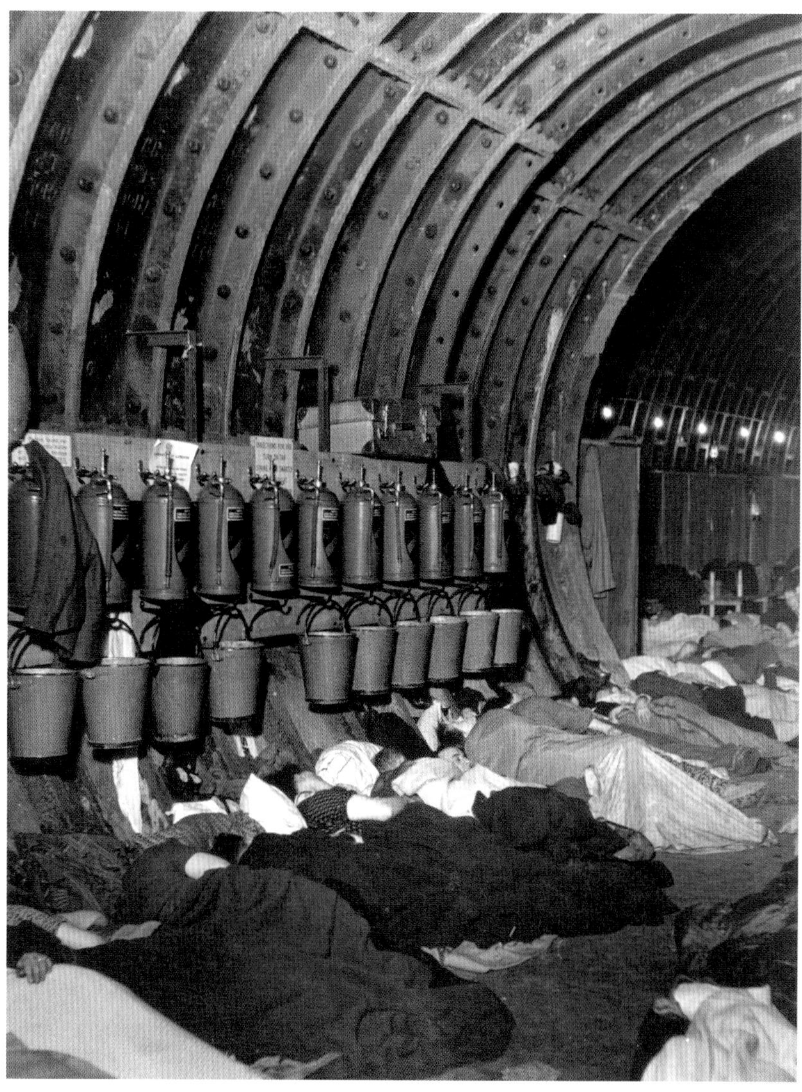

Liverpool Street Station Underground shelter,
November 1940
An East End Underground station shelter,
November 1940

BILL BRANDT (1904–83)

During the Blitz of the Second World War, Brandt was commissioned to document the many Londoners who sought shelter in the Underground stations at night.

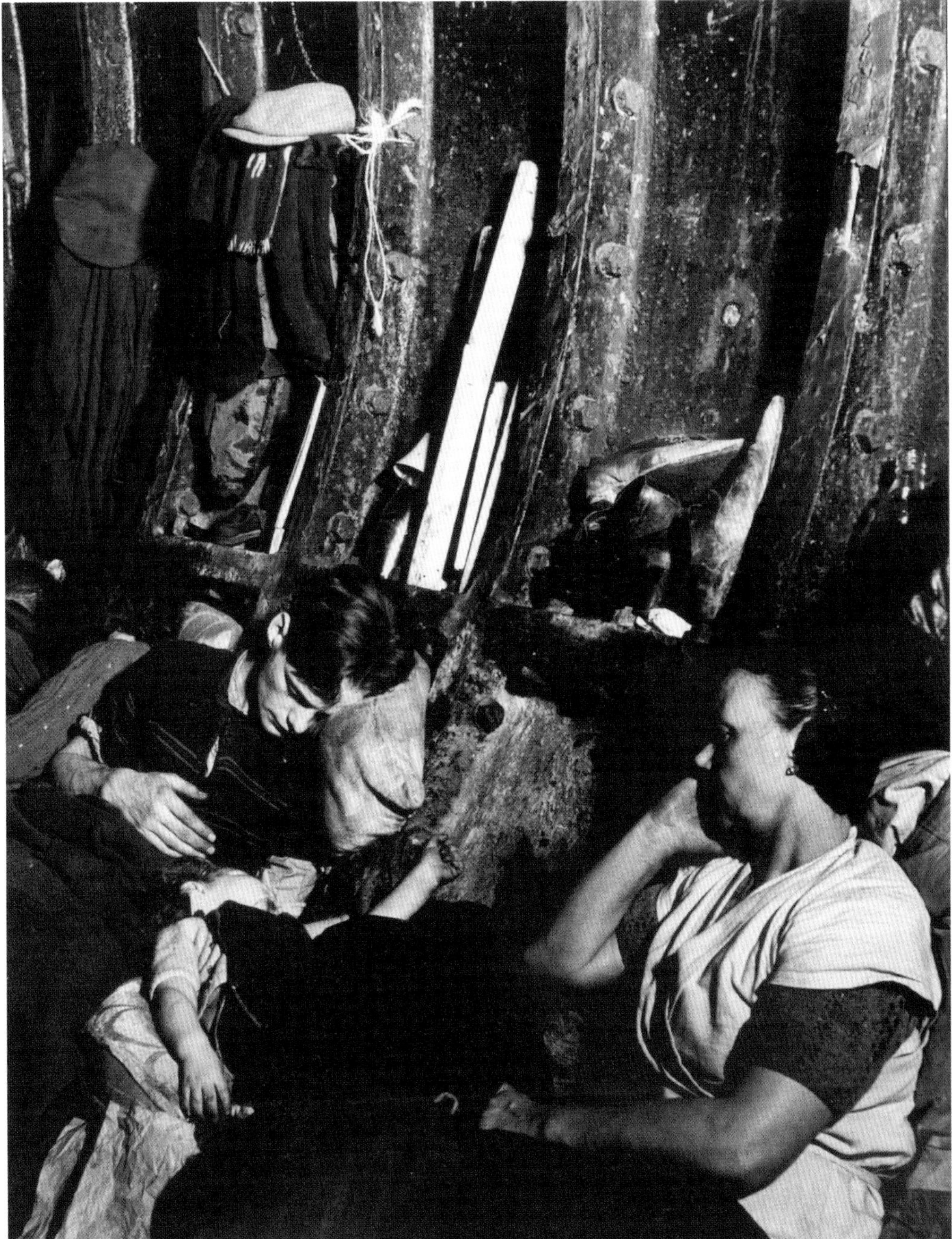

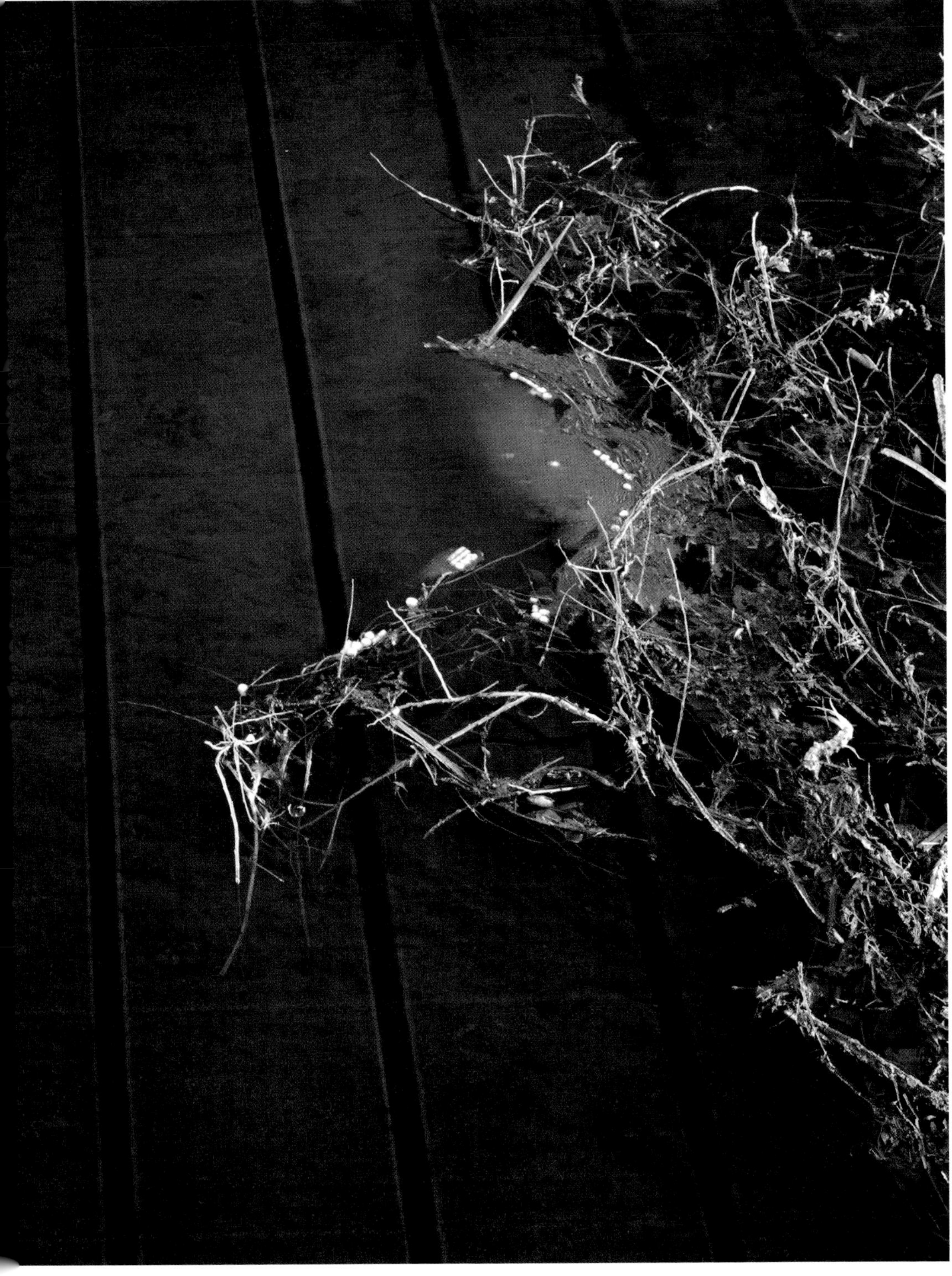

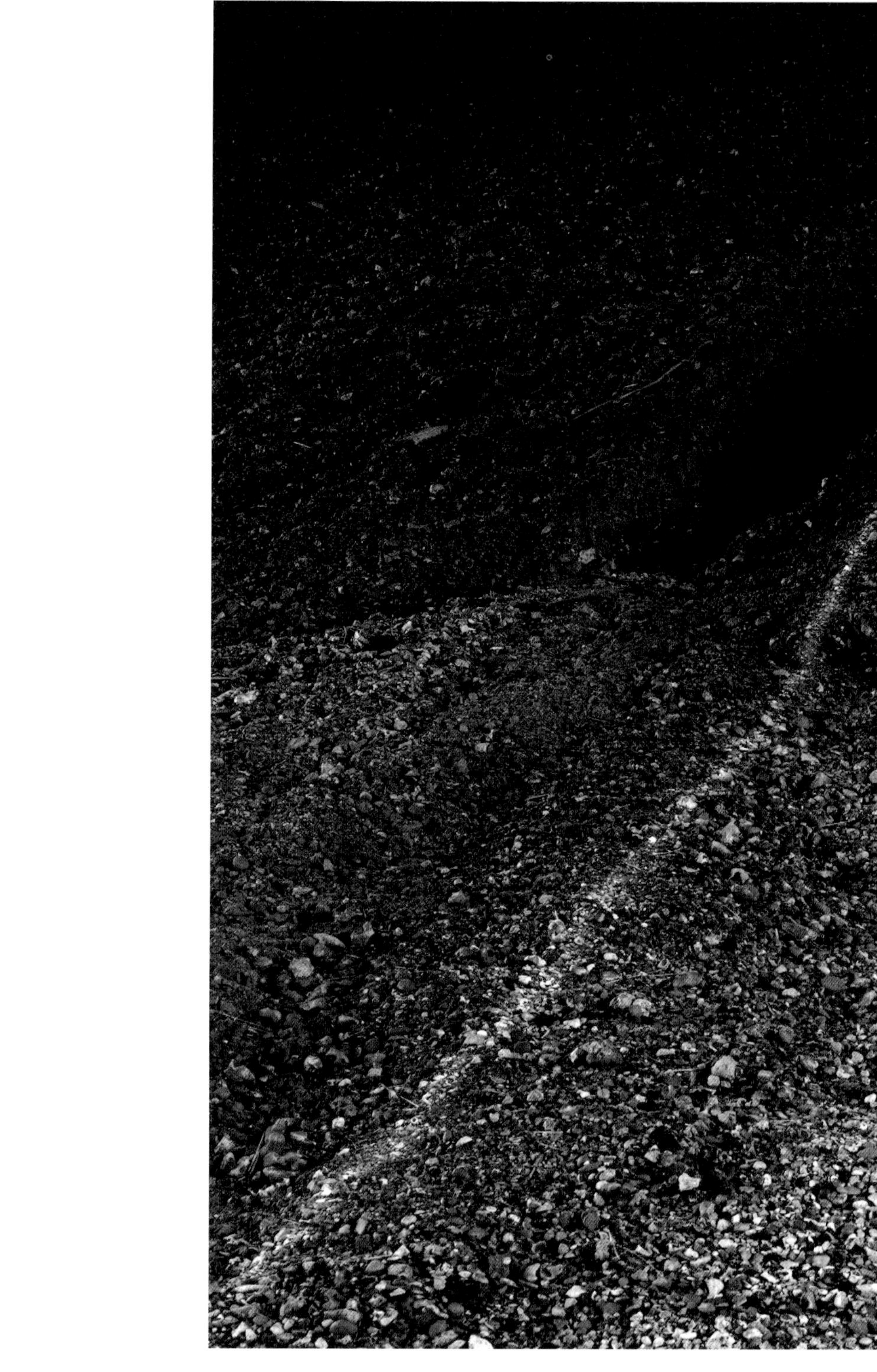

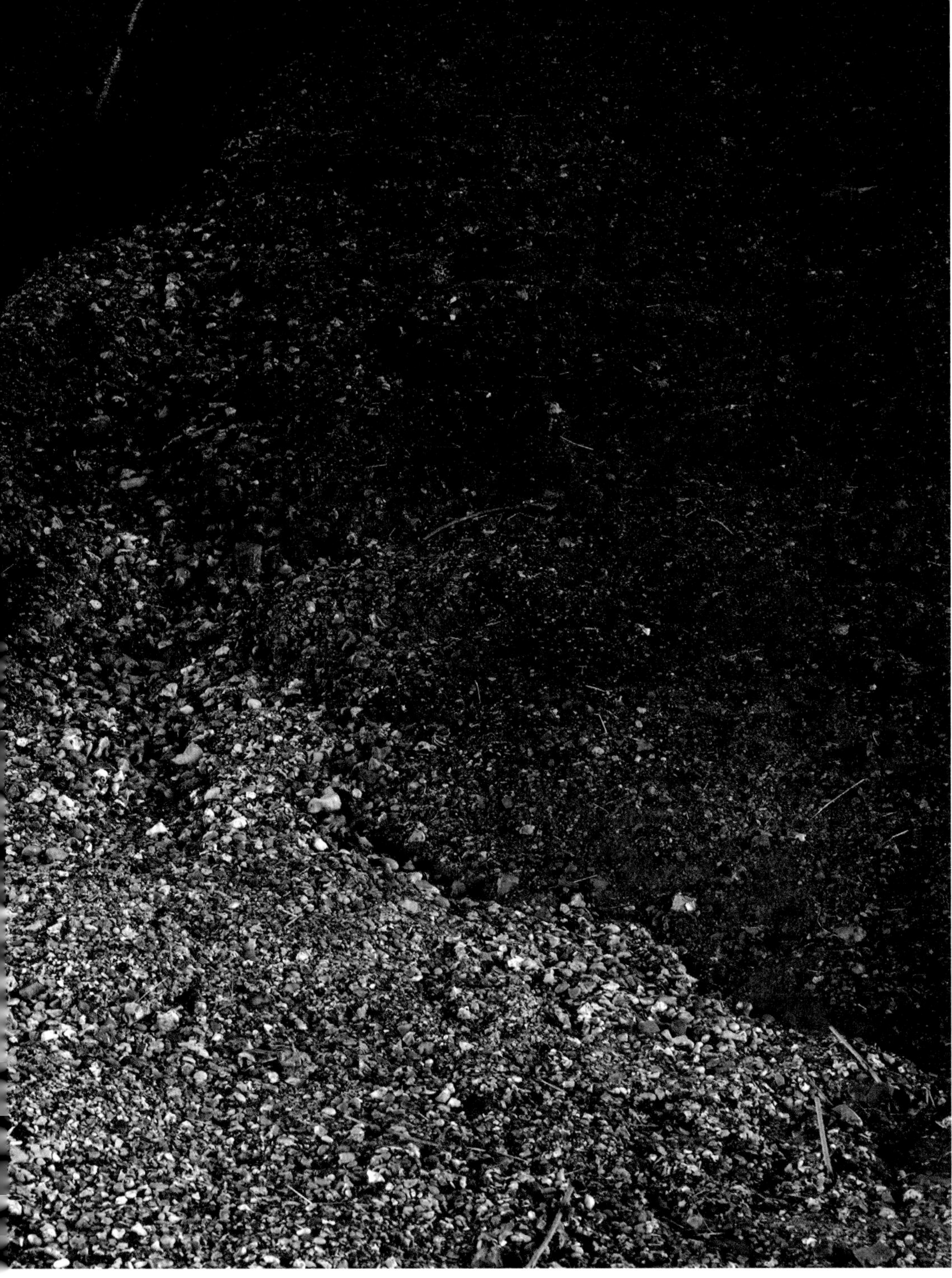

PREVIOUS PAGES
From the series *Hind Land*, 2012

TIM BOWDITCH (b 1986)
NICK ROCHOWSKI (b 1981)

The barely trodden ground beneath the M25 is explored at night to reveal these unknown, curious landscapes orbiting London.

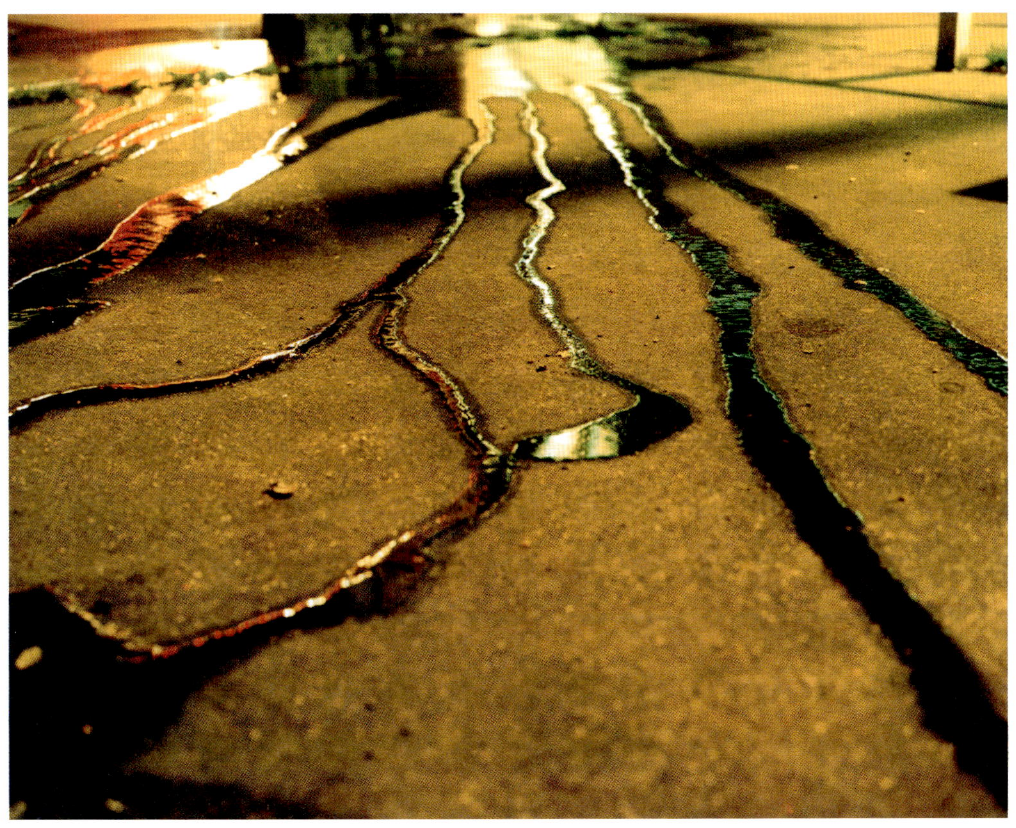

A Girl From Elsewhere
from the series *Liebeslied*, 2000

RUT BLEES LUXEMBURG (b 1967)

Amid the glowing colour a tension exists, created through the ambiguity of the scene and the fluid elements upon the ground.

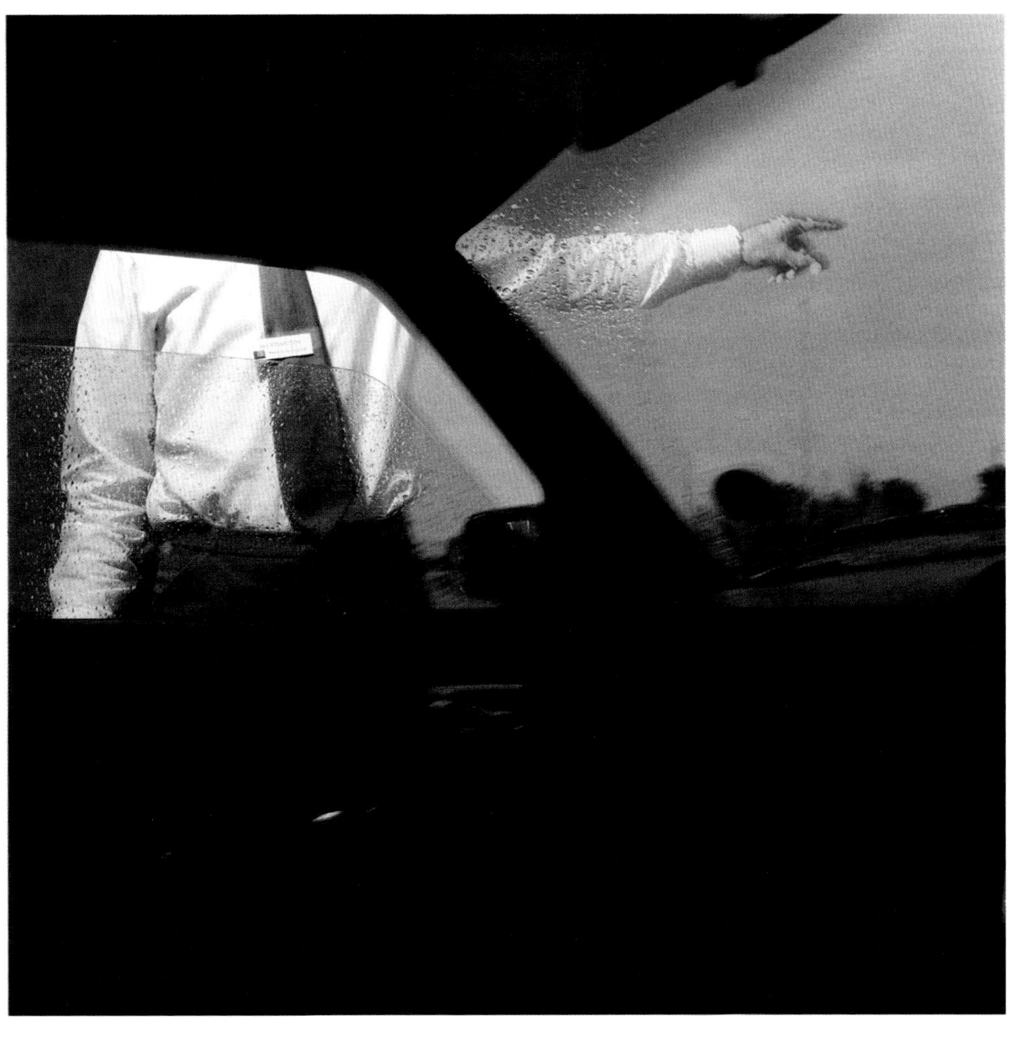

ABOVE AND FOLLOWING PAGES
From the series *London at Night*, 1983–86

BRIAN GRIFFIN (b 1948)

Griffin photographed a dramatic sequence, from which these are selected, portraying an imaginary nuclear attack on London; the threatened impact suggested through actions and play of lighting.

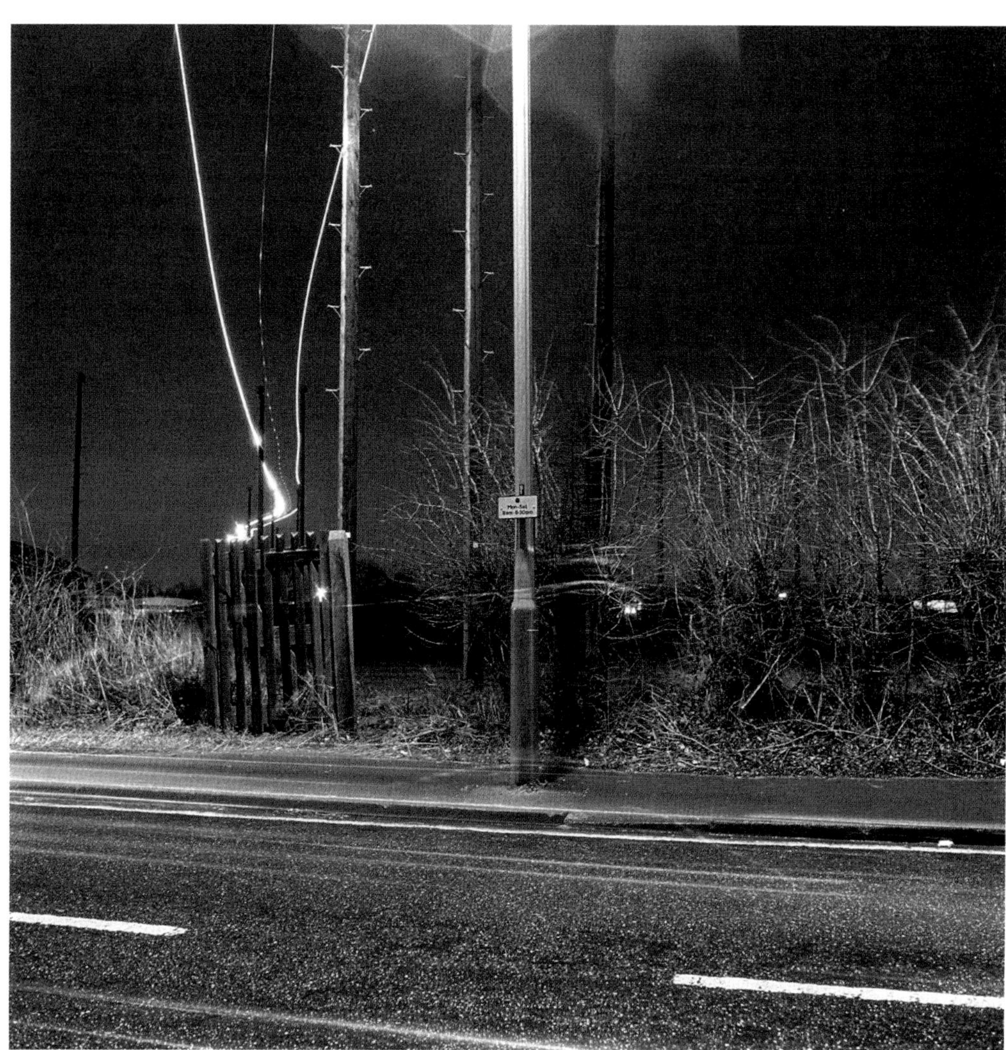
Mon-Sat

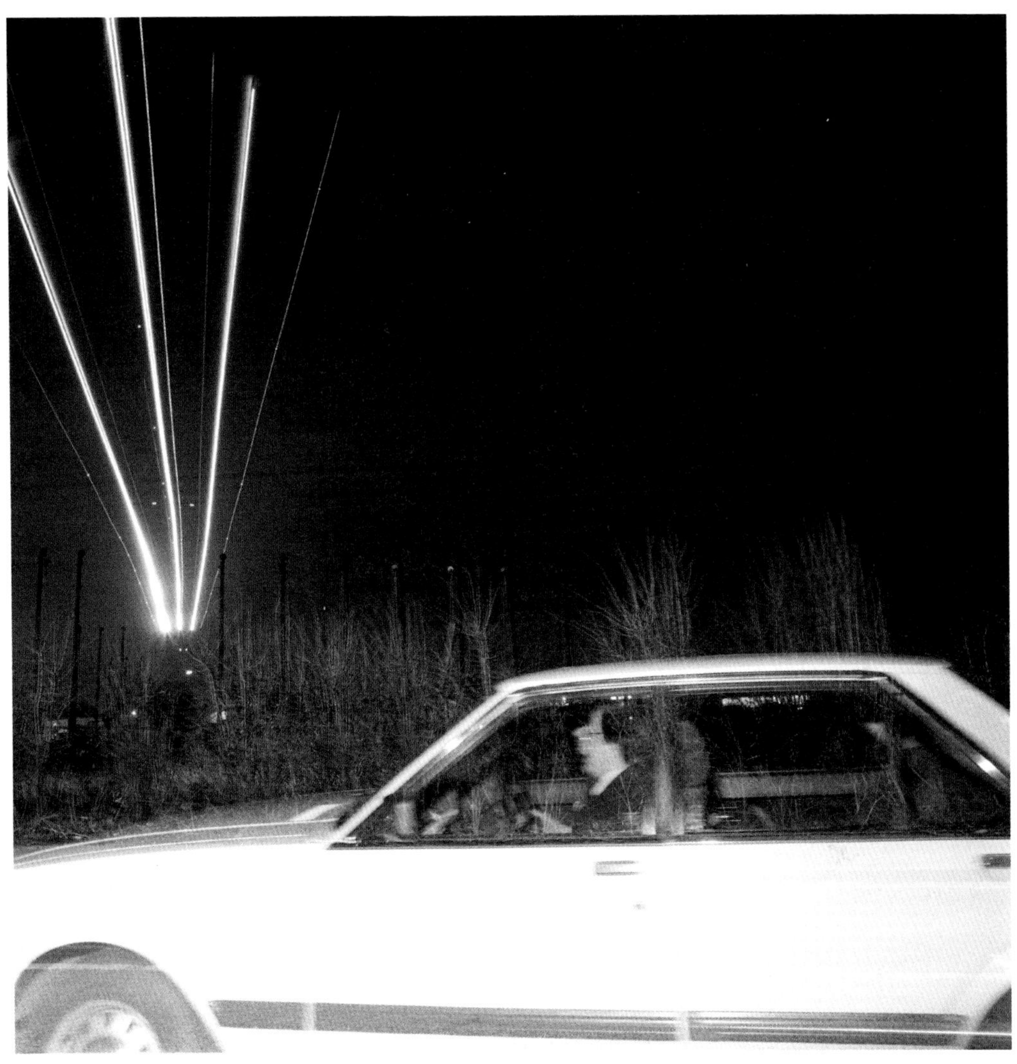

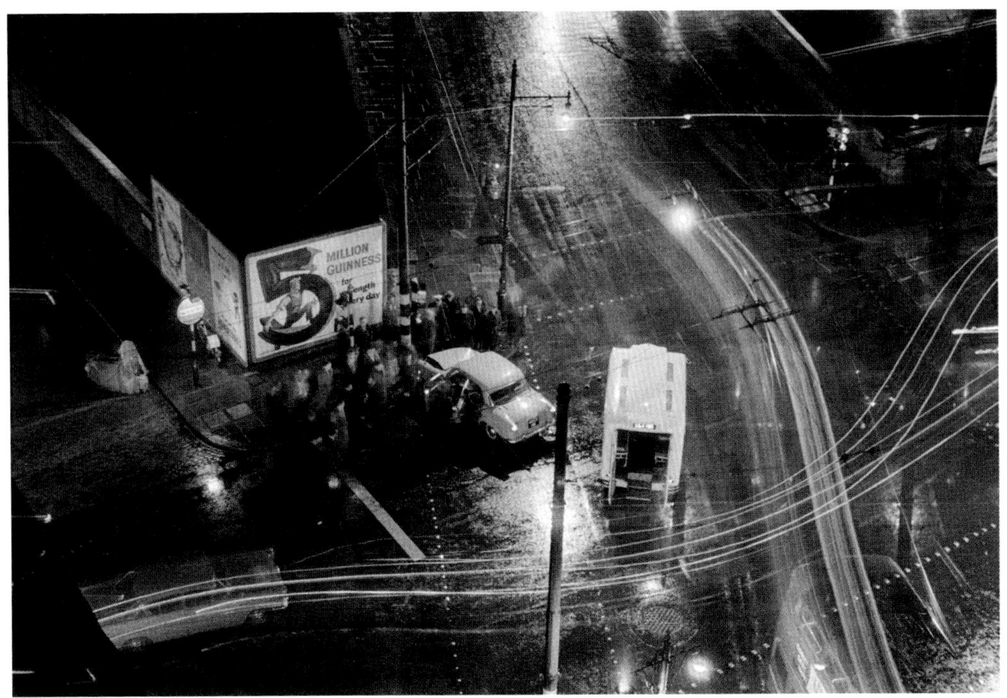

Accident at Night, Clerkenwell, 1959

COLIN O'BRIEN (1940–2016)

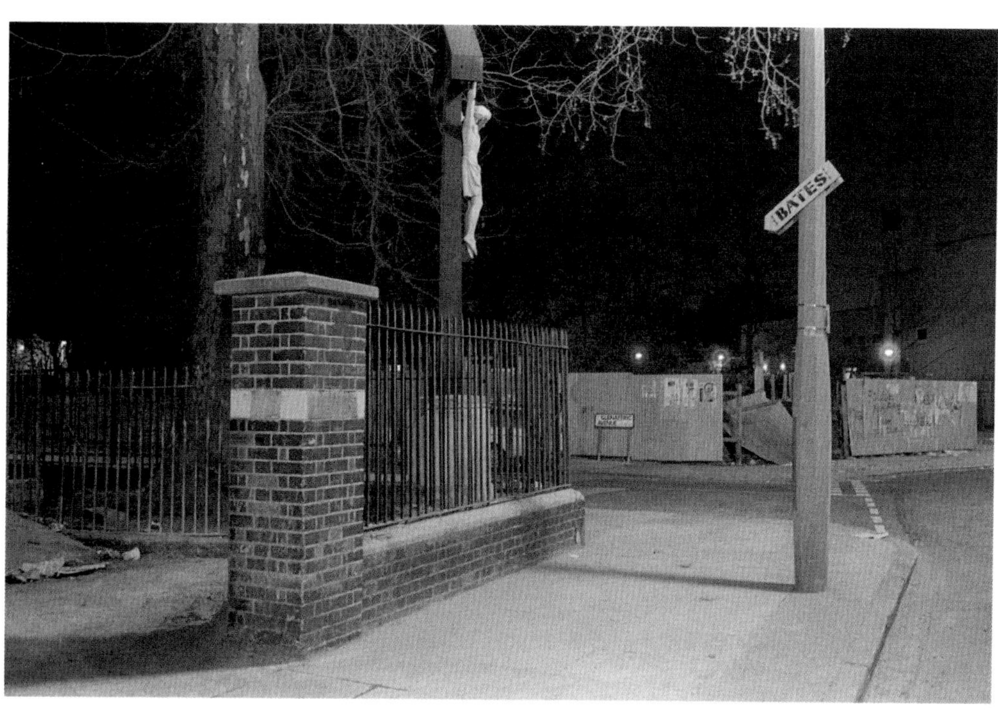
BATES

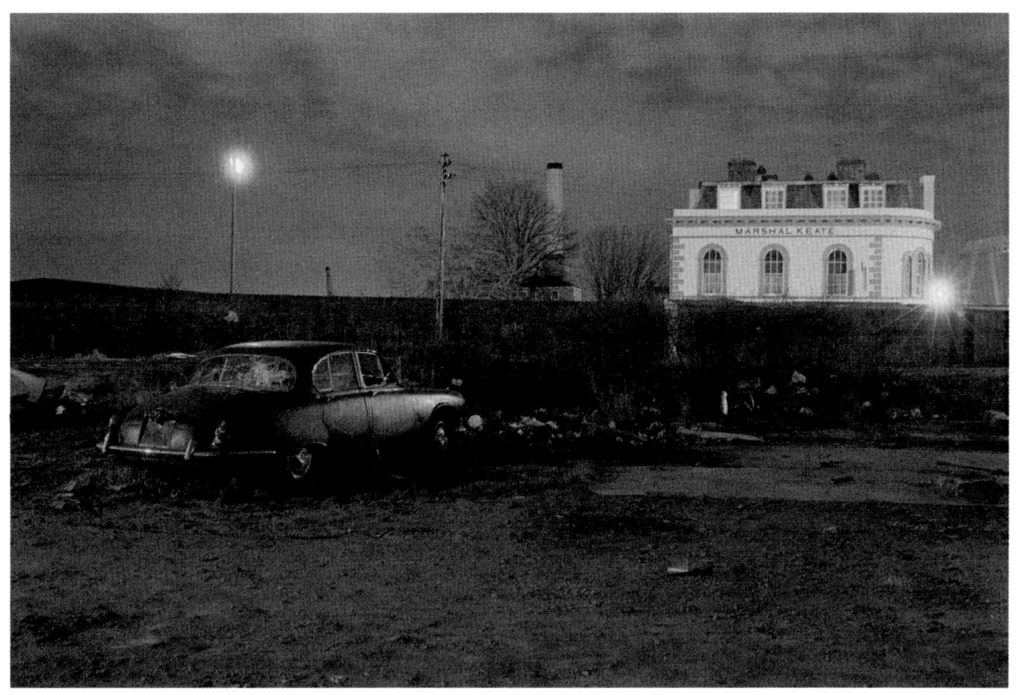

From the series *Isle of Dogs*, 1982

PETER MARLOW (1952–2016)

Marlow observed the night-time landscape of the Isle of Dogs before the area's redevelopment, revealing an isolating and shadowy environment caught between old and new.

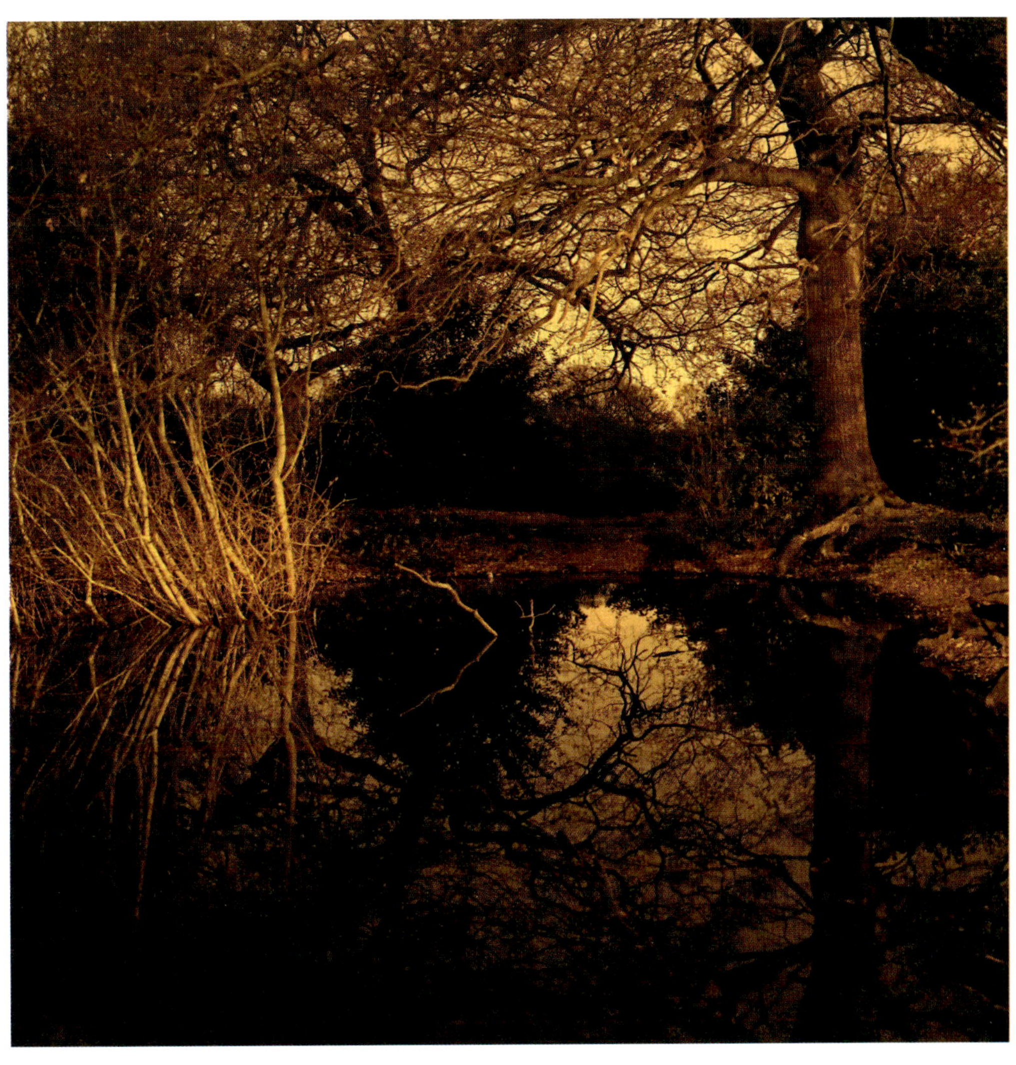

Round Ponds,
from the series *Shadows of Doubt*, 2011

DAVID GEORGE (b 1957)

The film director Alfred Hitchcock's childhood East End was explored to capture the role these environments may have played in informing his later creative sensibilities.

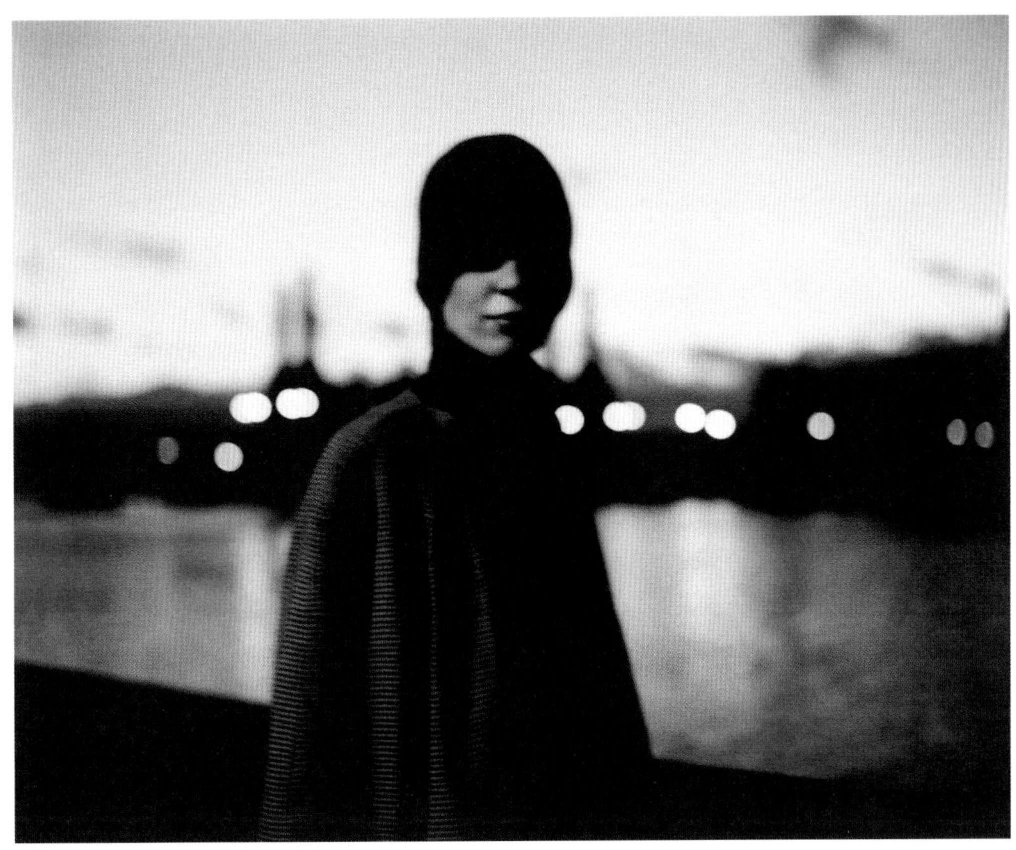

A night walk, 1978

CHRIS MOYSE (b 1949)

From *Life in the Elephant* made for *Picture Post*, 1948

BERT HARDY (1913–95)

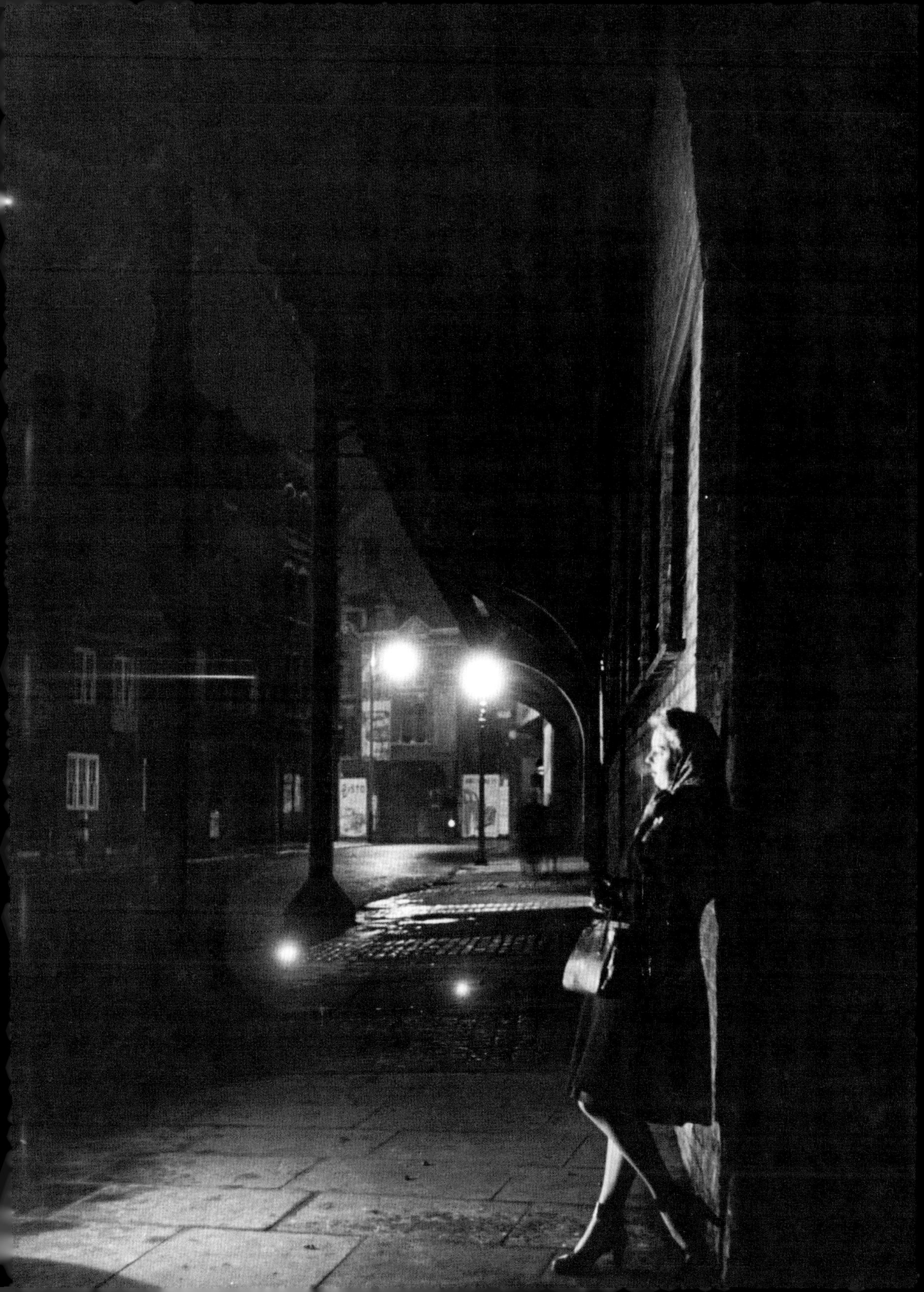

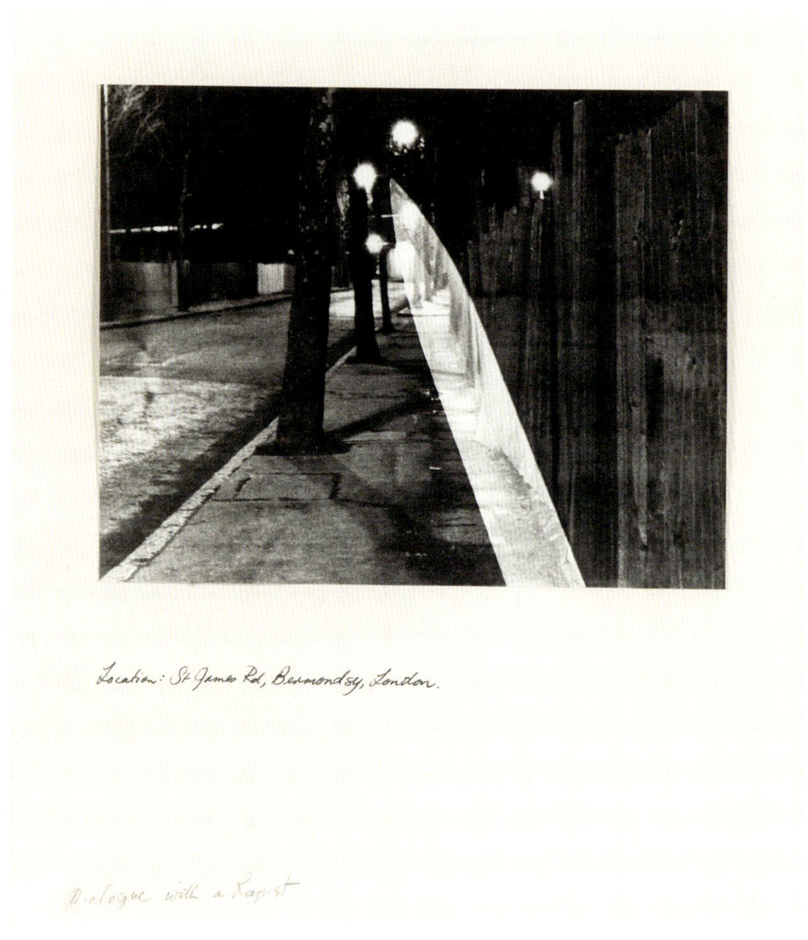

From the series *Dialogue with a Rapist*, 1978

ALEXIS HUNTER (1948–2014)

One of ten sequenced word and image works through which Hunter narrates the dissuading of an intended sexual assault, based on a real-life personal experience.

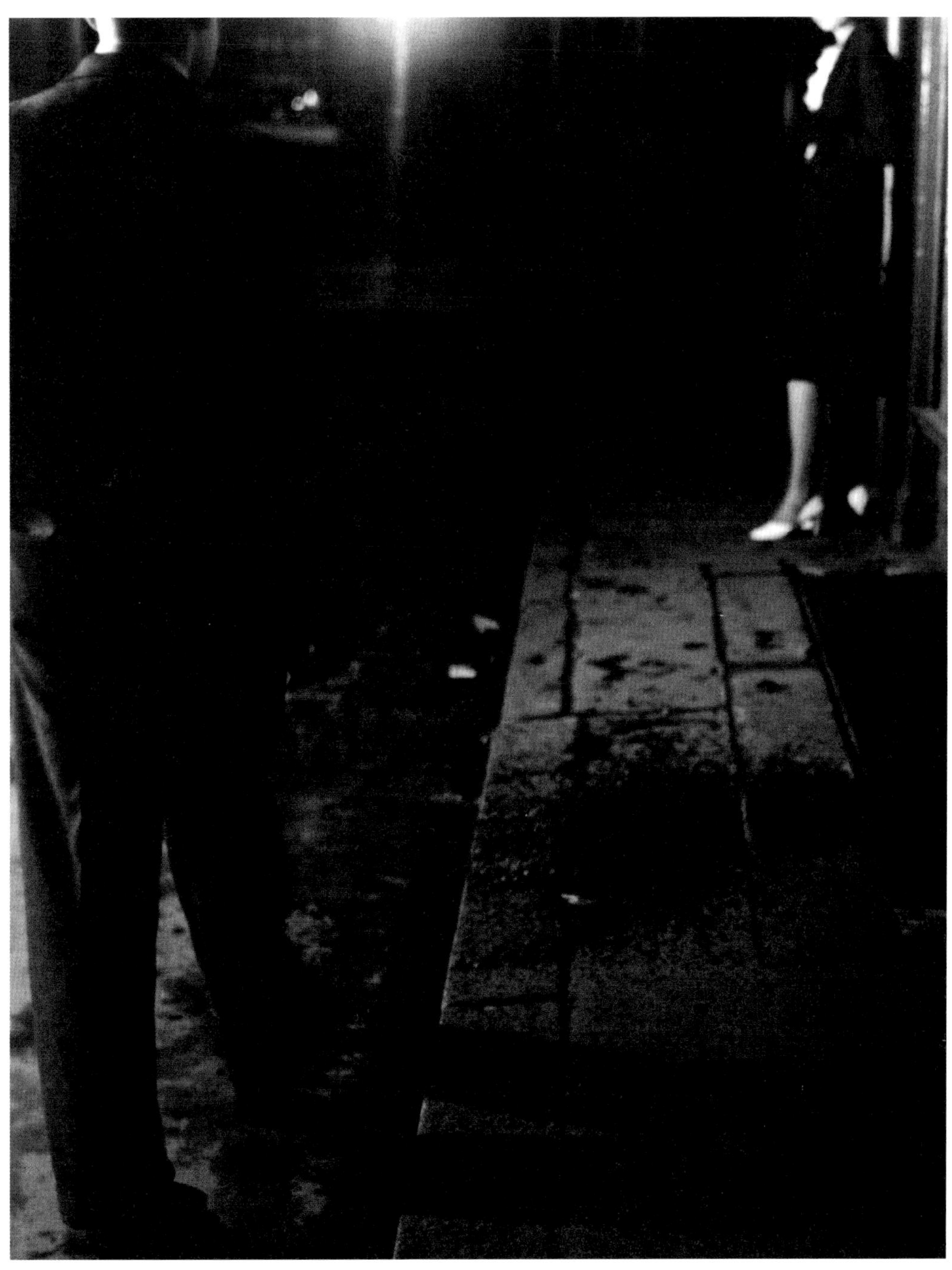

Footsteps Coming Nearer, c 1933–36

BILL BRANDT (1904–83)

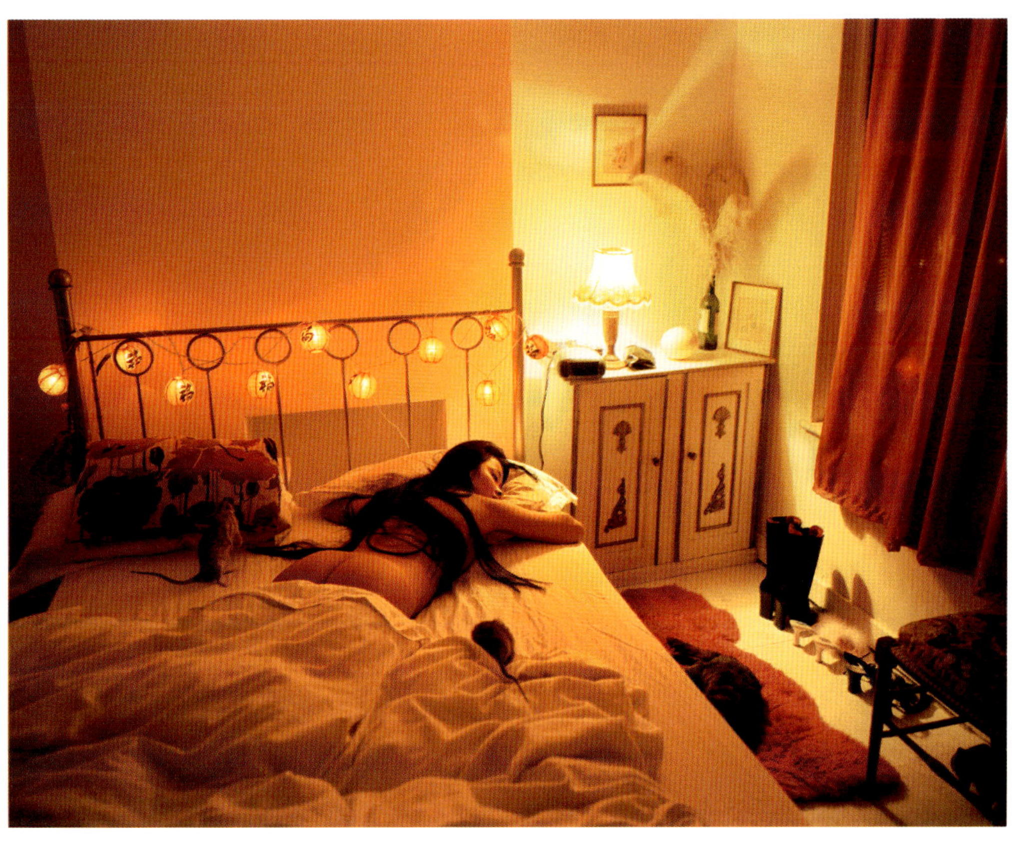

Rat in Bed from the series *Living in Hell and Other Stories*, 2005

TOM HUNTER (b 1965)

Inspired by a local newspaper's sensationalist headline, Hunter constructed an imagined night-time scene that suggests multiple potential narratives.

FOLLOWING PAGES
Night Meeting at the Blackfriars Shelter, c 1902

ANONYMOUS (SALVATION ARMY)

PAGES 122/123
Man holding curry sign, 1960

BRUCE DAVIDSON (b 1933)

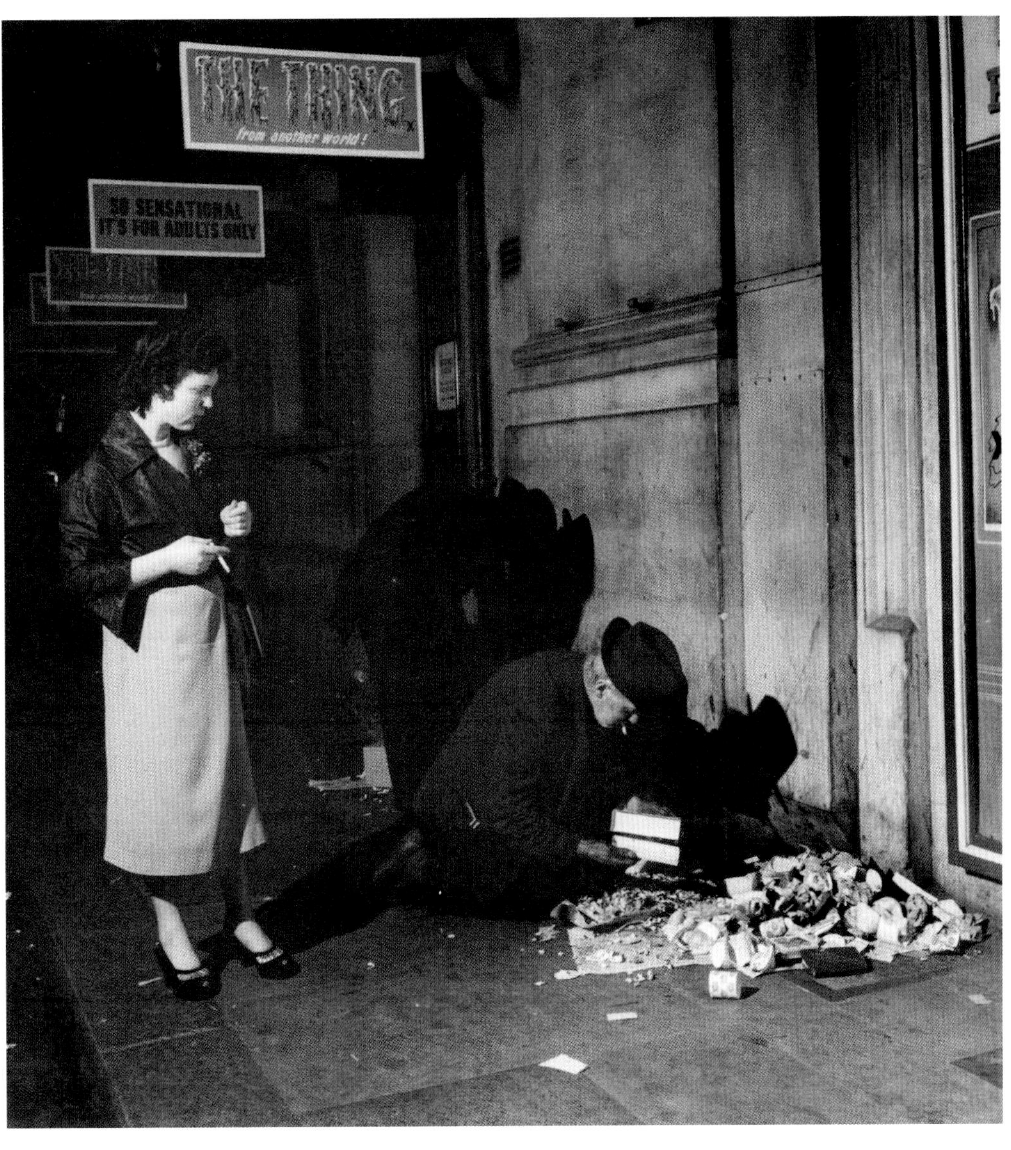

From the feature *What Makes Piccadilly*, *Picture Post*, 4 July 1953

BERT HARDY (1913–95)

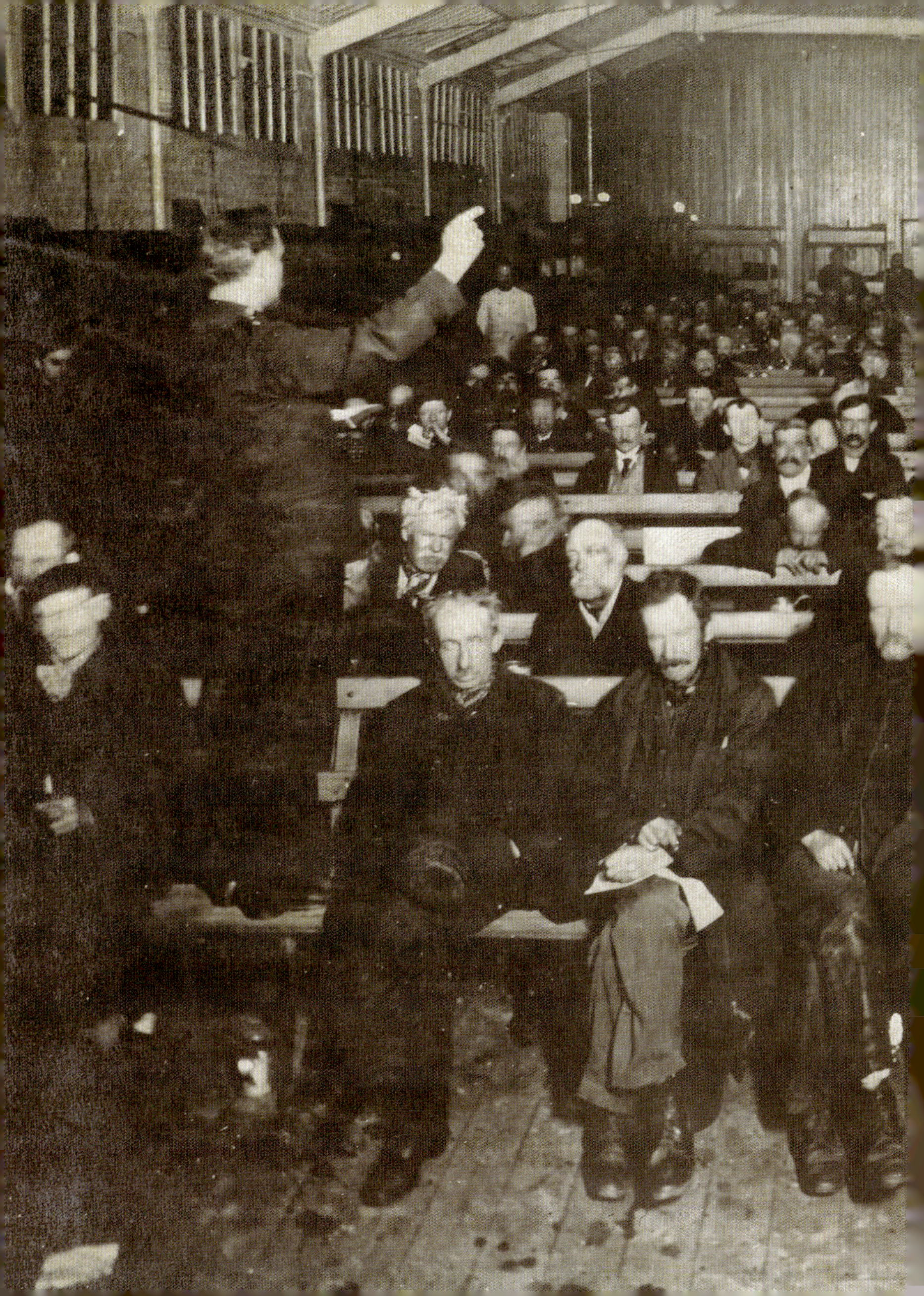

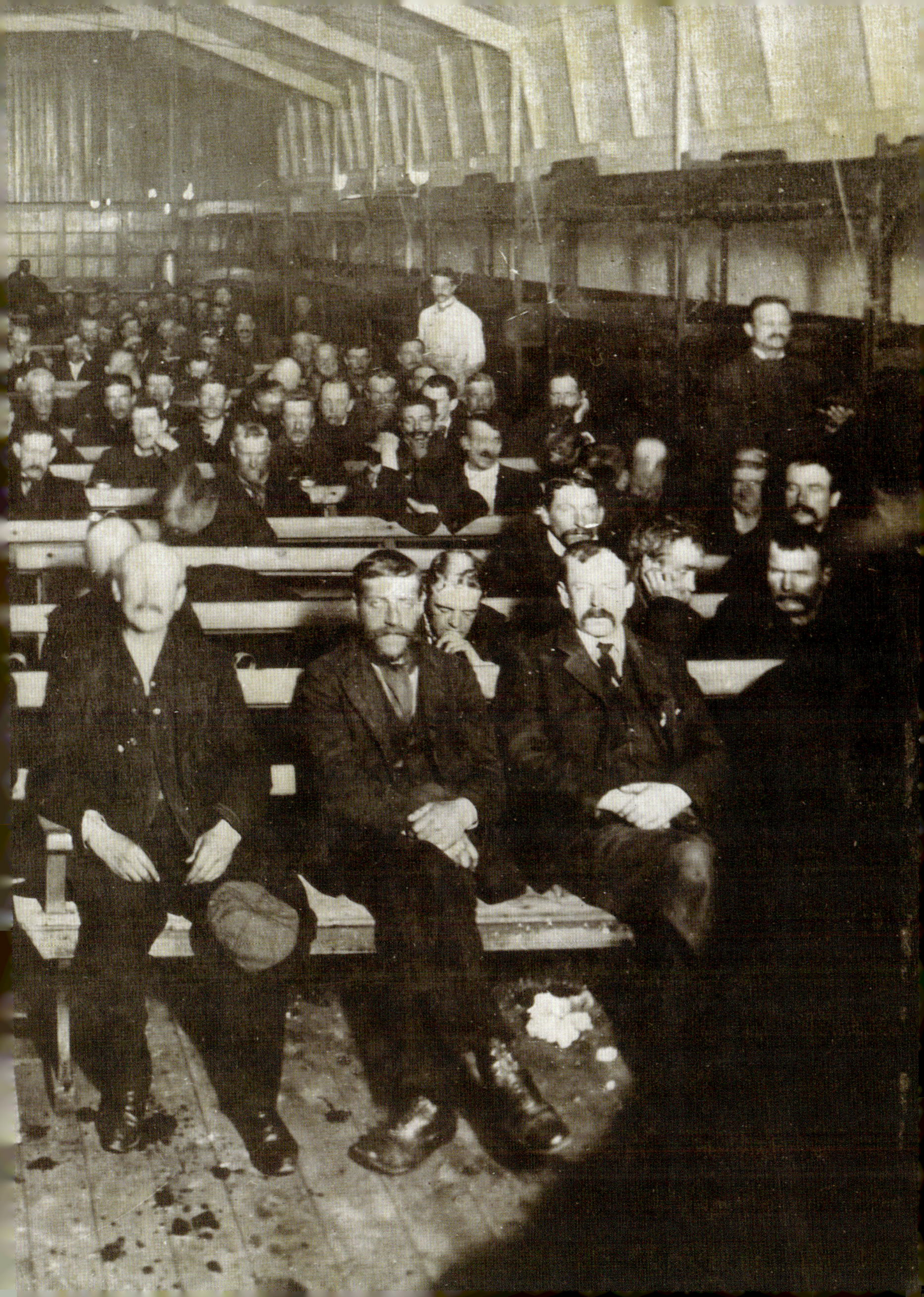

Milk /

Early morning or late night / the milkman hefts the iron cow
of his cart / down the slushy street / past coated pedestrians
queued like nervous children / Four floors up / a night porter
lounges / loose-limbed and lizard-like / On the flip-side
of the wall / tuxedoed Etonians play backgammon / Five floors
down / in a low-lit basement / punters stare / hard
at a dancer's sweaty flesh / Further underground / a commuter
reads a doom-harbouring newspaper / surfaces by a shop front
of fresh fruits bathed in fluorescent light / It's the witching hour
and the wildlife of youth spill out / in feathered head-gear
and white horned tunics / defiant in heels / pissing on bridges
Near by / baseball hatted rappers grip their mics / close
in clenched fists / and if this were a gathering / of humanity
in all its glorious assemblage / they would be the masters
of ceremony / calling us all to heel / to heed the night's sky
peeling back / and watch the morning come / on.

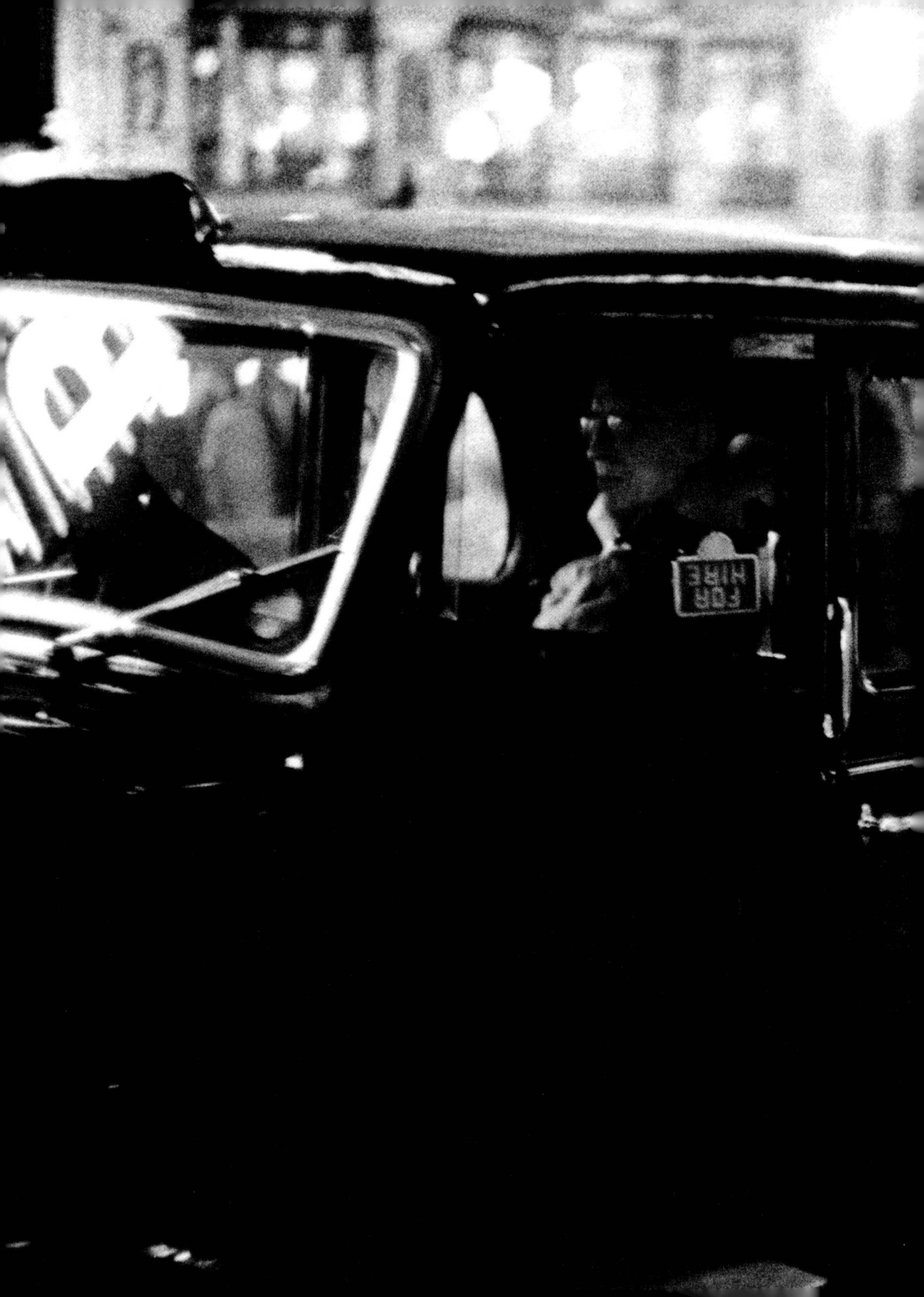

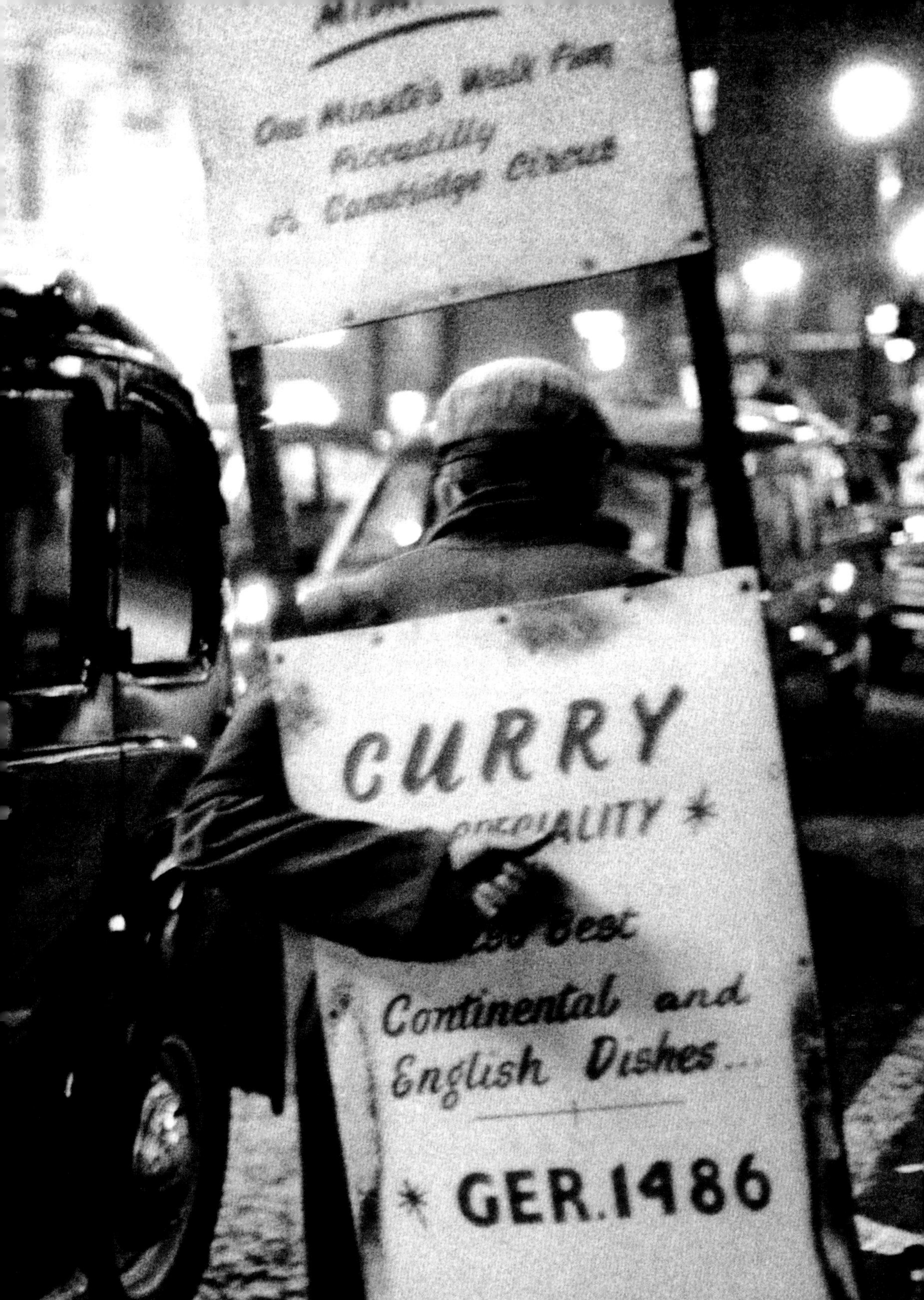
CURRY
Continental and
English Dishes
GER.1486

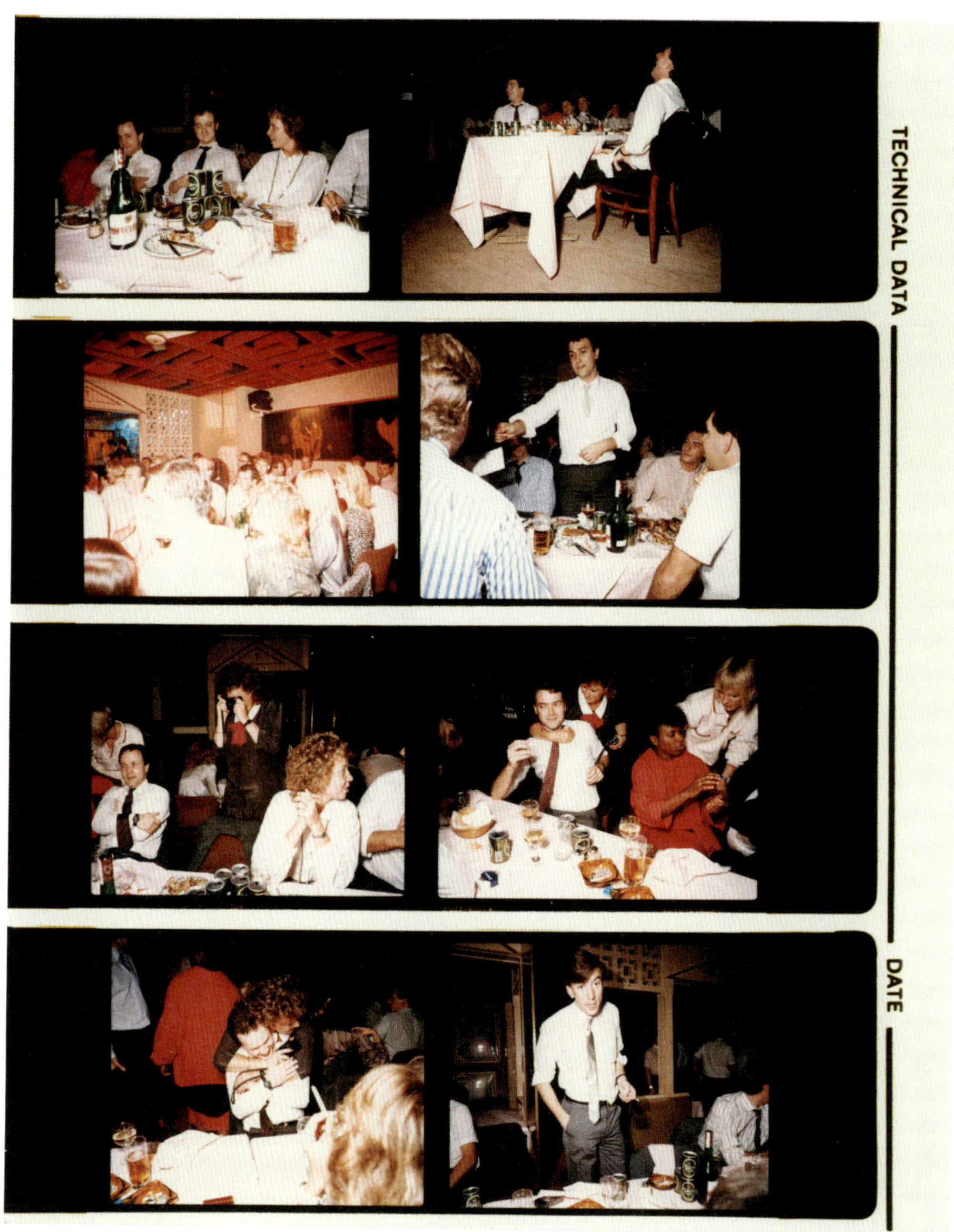

Contact sheet from the series *Workstations*, 1987

ANNA FOX (b 1961)

SWITCH ON SWITCH OFF

London offers endless diverse activity every night of the week. At the end of a working day, many people seek out the capital's vibrant nightlife, contributing heavily to the night-time economy. Others connect with the city in the evening solely via their commute home. And for many more, the night shift is just beginning, with one in eight jobs in London offering work at night, according to the Mayor of London's first 24-hour vision for the capital.[29] A complex network of industries, including hospitality, emergency services, charities, maintenance and transport, envelop and support those looking for a good night out. *Switch On Switch Off* explores such nocturnal pursuits through images conveying work, rest and play – these themes spawning multifarious content for photographers and filmmakers to delve into. Street photography, social documentary, portraiture, constructed imagery and film all provide insight to this participation in the life of the night city.

Work and leisure exist side by side. As London endeavours to be a successful and prosperous 24-hour city, an alert and awake destination like other major world cities, the potential for round-the-clock photography of its citizens increases. The movements and patterns of London's workforce are blending more with those visible during conventional leisure times, due in part to increased flexible working hours and enhanced infrastructure such as the Night Tube. However, inspiration and challenges remain for photographers to make work that captures an aesthetic and characteristic distinct from the diurnal. Even if, in doing so, they also acknowledge this blur that exists between day and night.

Despite the evolving temporal definition of the 'working day', the mass commute at the end or beginning of a work shift is a subject that continues to attract documentation. For example, Nick Turpin's photographs of passengers on the bus travelling through Elephant and Castle at night (pp 142–5), capture that '"no man's land" between work and home'.[30]

Once home at the end of the day, transition to rest would be hoped for, as one closes the door to the city beyond. Yet the domestic environment can indeed still be a place of work. Two photographs that incorporate this are included in Bill Brandt's *A Night in London,* in which he strides through the social classes; from the mother and children in a *West Ham Bedroom* (p 139) to the domestic staff in *Late Evening in the Kitchen* (p 137). While projecting something of the 'rest' that night-time brings, they also address the continuum of work at all hours to meet the demands of London life.

Mitra Tabrizian's *Somewhere in the Night,* from the series *Border,* bridges work and retreat (p 151). The night-shift taxi driver, at work himself, witnesses the lives of his customers heading home from their own jobs or play. Another photograph, *The Long Wait* (p 150) also visits the idea of 'home'. These two constructed photographs reflect on the individual lives of two Iranian migrants. They point to the potential for isolation in the vast metropolis, conveying a sense of longing and contemplation, which at night may be sensed more acutely.[31]

Leaving the home behind and returning to central London again, Chris Shaw's *Life as a Night Porter* plunges into the night shift once more, behind the scenes of hotels in which Shaw was himself employed (pp 130–1). Shaw made his candid, raw photographs to help him stay awake during the long night hours of work. He recorded details from his immediate environment, duties and eclectic encounters in the small hours, from drowsy fellow employees to drunk guests.[32] The surreal circumstances around the nocturnal reception desk and down the not-so-quiet corridors disclose a relatively dysfunctional reality of late-night London.

Many of the vast army of night workers are highly visible where the worlds of work and play cross paths, while some may rarely be seen at all as they go about their tasks. Tish Murtha's photographic exploration of the sex trade in Soho in 1983 reveals this private/public world (pp 168–71). Collaborating with writer and dancer Karen Leslie, the pair befriended sex workers 'on the game, in clip joints, peep-shows and strip clubs'[33] to reveal intimate narratives told through words and images. Murtha wrote, 'To view one aspect without the other limits and distorts the messages involved.'[34]

Voyeurism, privacy and surveillance are concepts that photographers and filmmakers frequently address, sometimes playing with the nature of the medium itself. This is exemplified in Sophy Rickett's provocative series *Pissing Women* (p 183). Assuming a typically male stance as she publicly urinates, Rickett challenges what is deemed acceptable or not, and specifically with regards to gender. The rebellion is amplified by the choice of location, close to the MI6 building (headquarters of the Secret Intelligence Service), hinting further at surveillance in the city at night.

In Marc Vallée's photographs from his series *Vandals and the City*, a graffiti writer observes the city streets below unbeknown to any passers-by (pp 198–9). Although he is certainly aware of it, the writer is then being observed by Vallée, who witnesses his activities and avoidance of identification, under the cover of darkness.

Philipp Ebeling's explorations at night in *London Ends* portray both the extraordinary and familiar in the outer regions of the capital, through the individual activities he documents (pp 160–3). Ebeling's perambulations of the city, by day and night, engaged him with communities from Romford to Hounslow, Bexley to Brent. These images shot after dark offer a broader, ambient picture of the wider capital at night.[35]

When people have a night out, locally or further afield, they might dress for the occasion. The 1920s and 1930s advertisement photographs made by the Bassano Studios illustrate elegant garments that were designed to be worn by women on an evening out in London or elsewhere (pp 176–7). In wonderful comparison, Damien Frost's alluring portraits in *Night Flowers*, made in situ on dark streets or backstage at nightclubs and parties, throw light upon the impressively intricate creations of 'drag queens and kings, club kids, alternative queer, transgender and gender-queer people, goths artists, cabaret, burlesque and fetish performers', visible after midnight (pp 173–5).[36]

Transcending the decades, a visual backdrop of London's subcultural nightlife can be conceived through varied photographic perspectives, from outsider observers, to those personally immersed in a scene. Aside from focusing on sartorial styles, photographers observe the subtleties evident in people socialising. John Goto does so through his intimate portraits of young people at Lewisham Youth Centre, quietly recording the apparent relationships between friends and even the camera (pp 196–7).[37] At altogether different societal events, David Moore cropped his subjects to focus on telling gestures and fragments of clothing, food and drink (pp 184–5).[38] These photographs hold the power to successfully convey the mood and behaviours of the social scenes being observed.

Photography in all its forms is brilliantly suited to portraying the disparate activities taking place in London after dark. The medium succeeds in uniting these eclectic happenings, from work to play, through its innate ability to freeze the moment, yet retain through powerful suspense the energy and restlessness of the nocturnal city.

In 2017, the mayor of London announced his vision to take London 'from good night to great night'.[39] As investment in night-time London unfolds in the future, photographers will continue to be enticed by the urban behaviours, contrasts, familiarities and unrevealed subjects that emerge city-wide and make for such compelling and imaginative photography. On the night bus, at home, in the workplace, street or club, no London night, or emerging dawn, is ever the same.

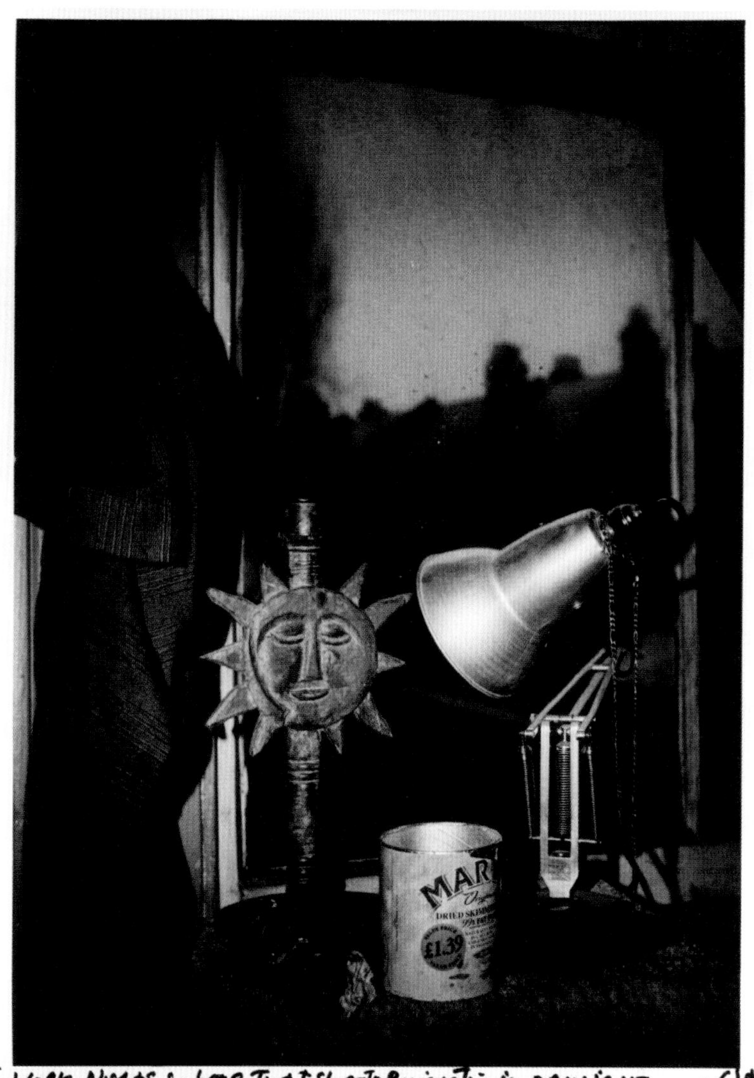

I WORK NIGHTS SO LONG THAT I START TO BELIEVE THIS IS DAYLIGHT

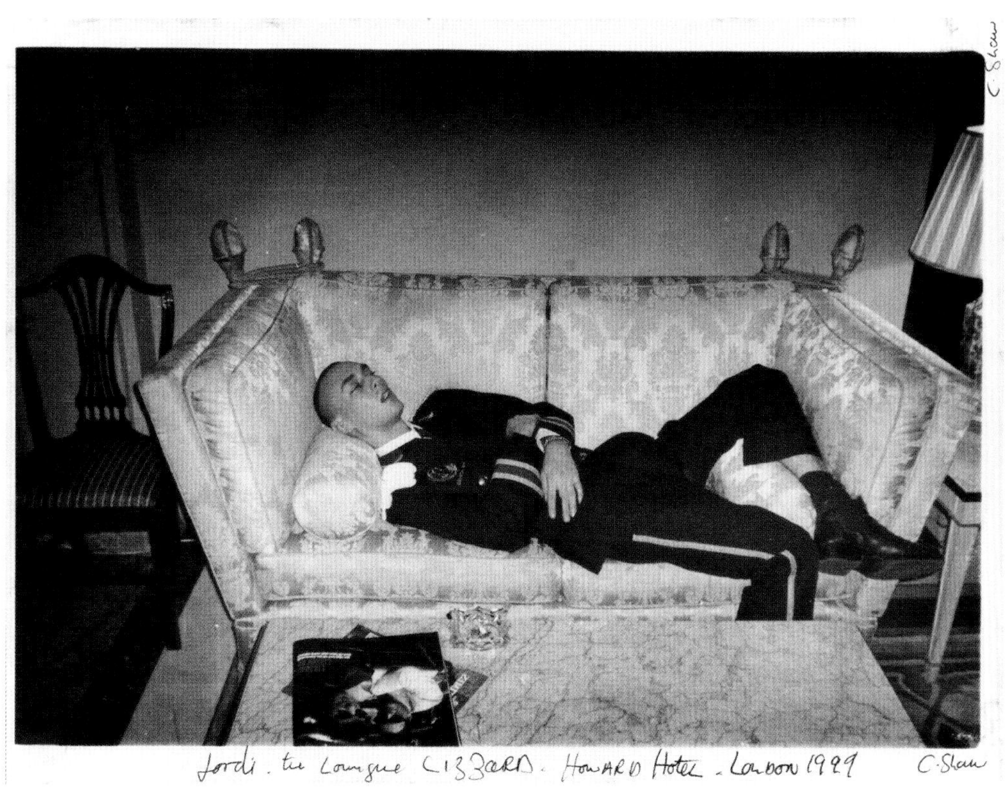

I work nights so long that I start to believe this is daylight, 2003
Lounge Lizzard, 1999

CHRIS SHAW (b 1967)

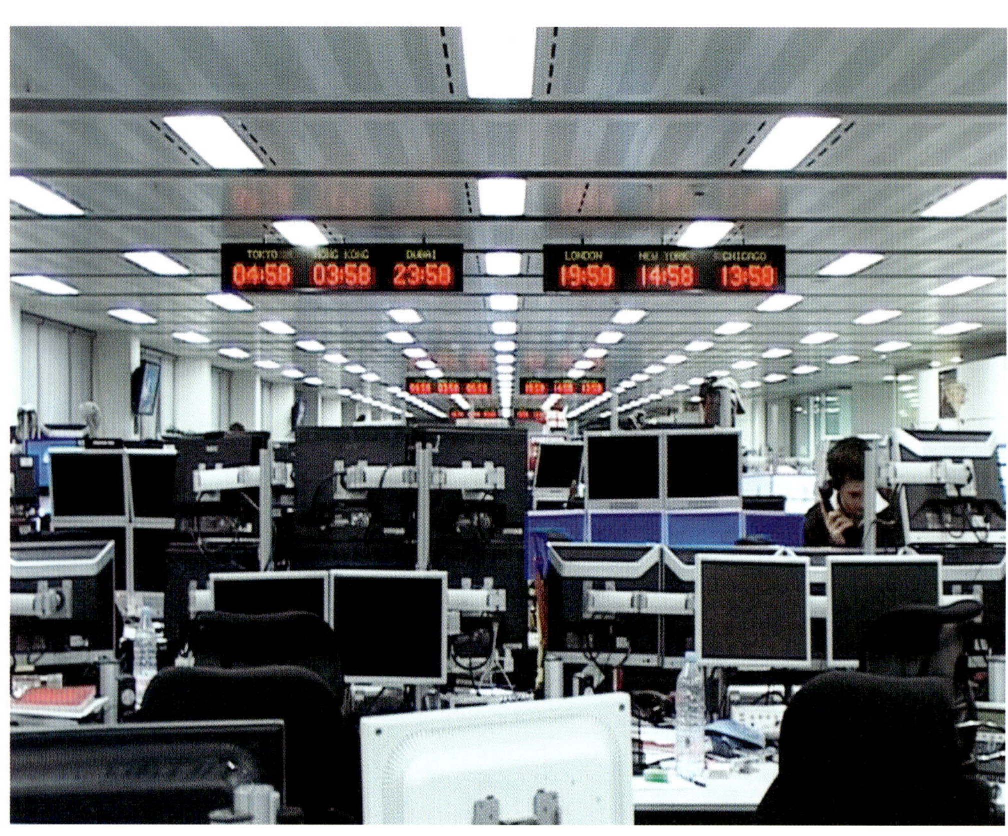
TOKYO
HONG KONG
03:58
DUBAI
LONDON
NEW YORK
14:58
CHICAGO

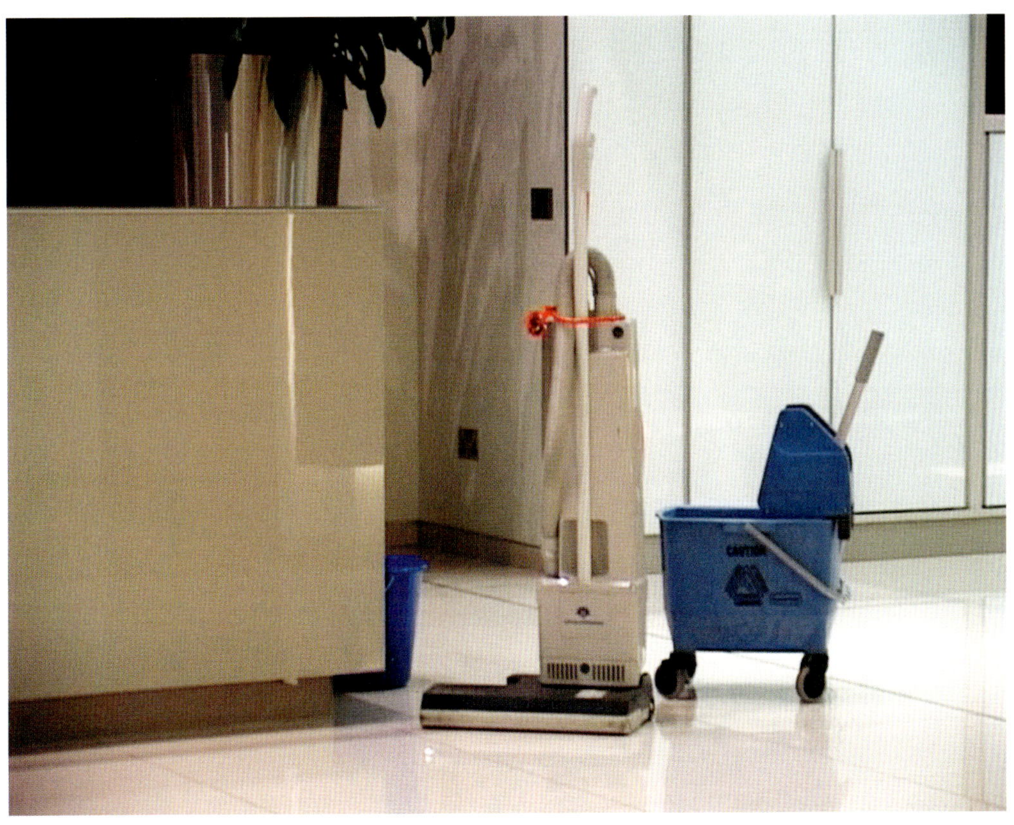

Stills from *After the Bell*, 2009

EMMA CHARLES (b 1985)

Filmed after trading has stopped, cleaners and maintenance staff enter the office environment to undertake their night shift, their interactions with the space largely unwitnessed.

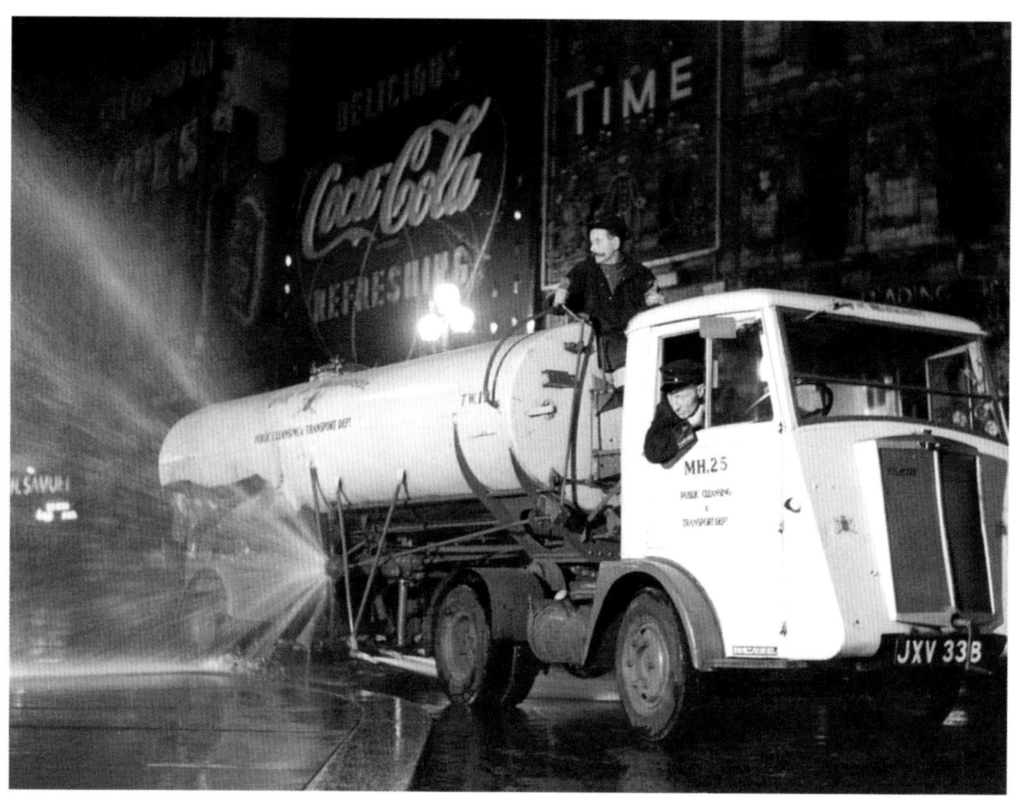

From a feature on London dustmen
for *Picture Post*, 1955

JOHN S. MURRAY (1904–92)

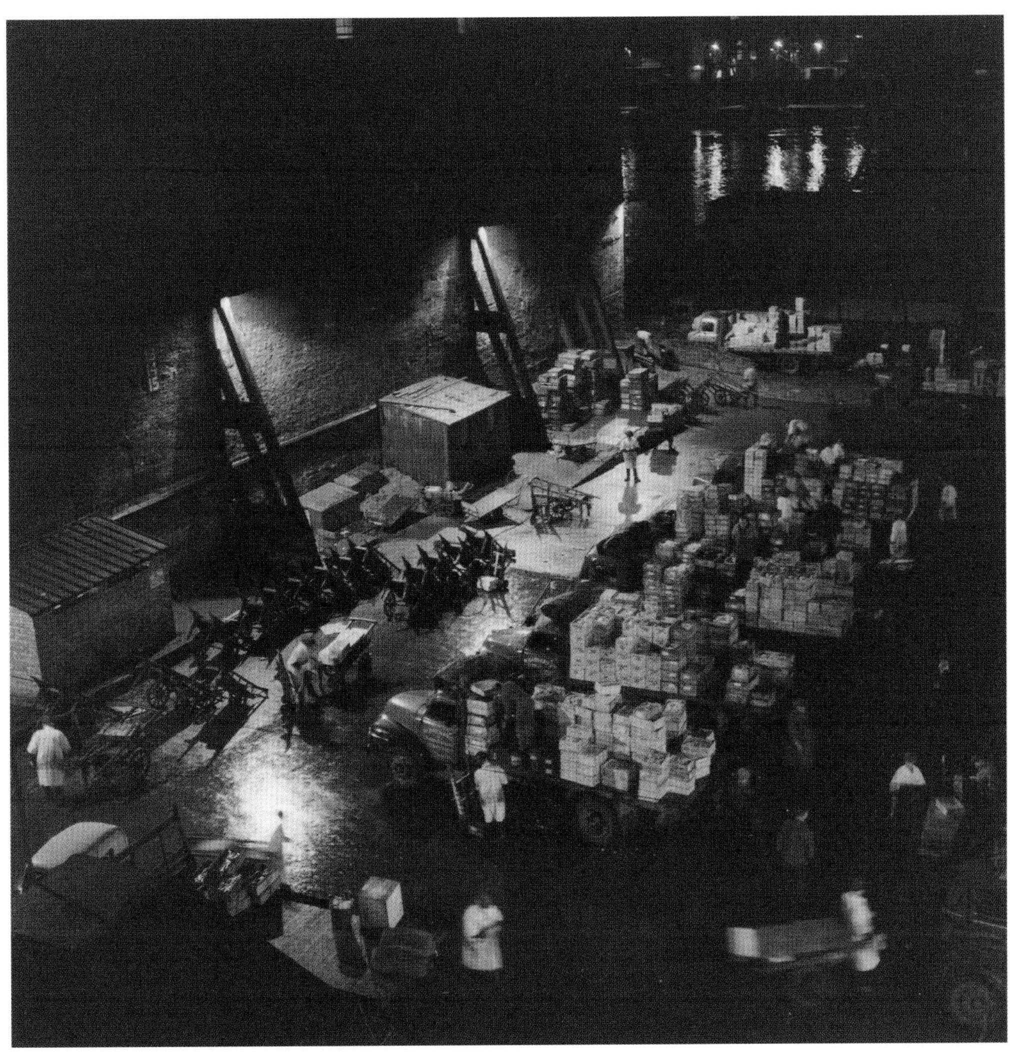

Early morning at Billingsgate Market, 1958

BOB COLLINS (1924–2002)

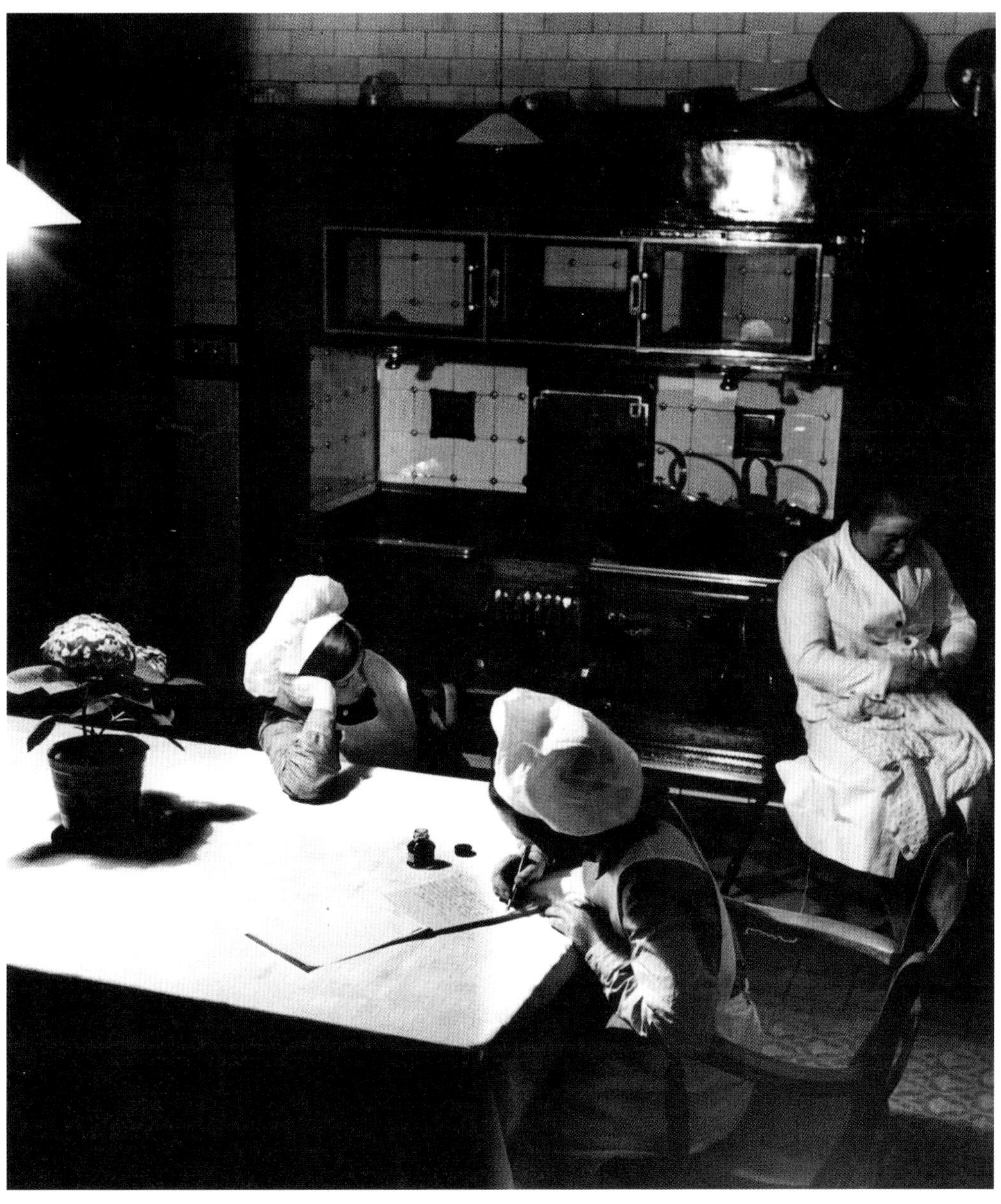

Late Evening in the Kitchen, early 1930s

BILL BRANDT (1904–83)

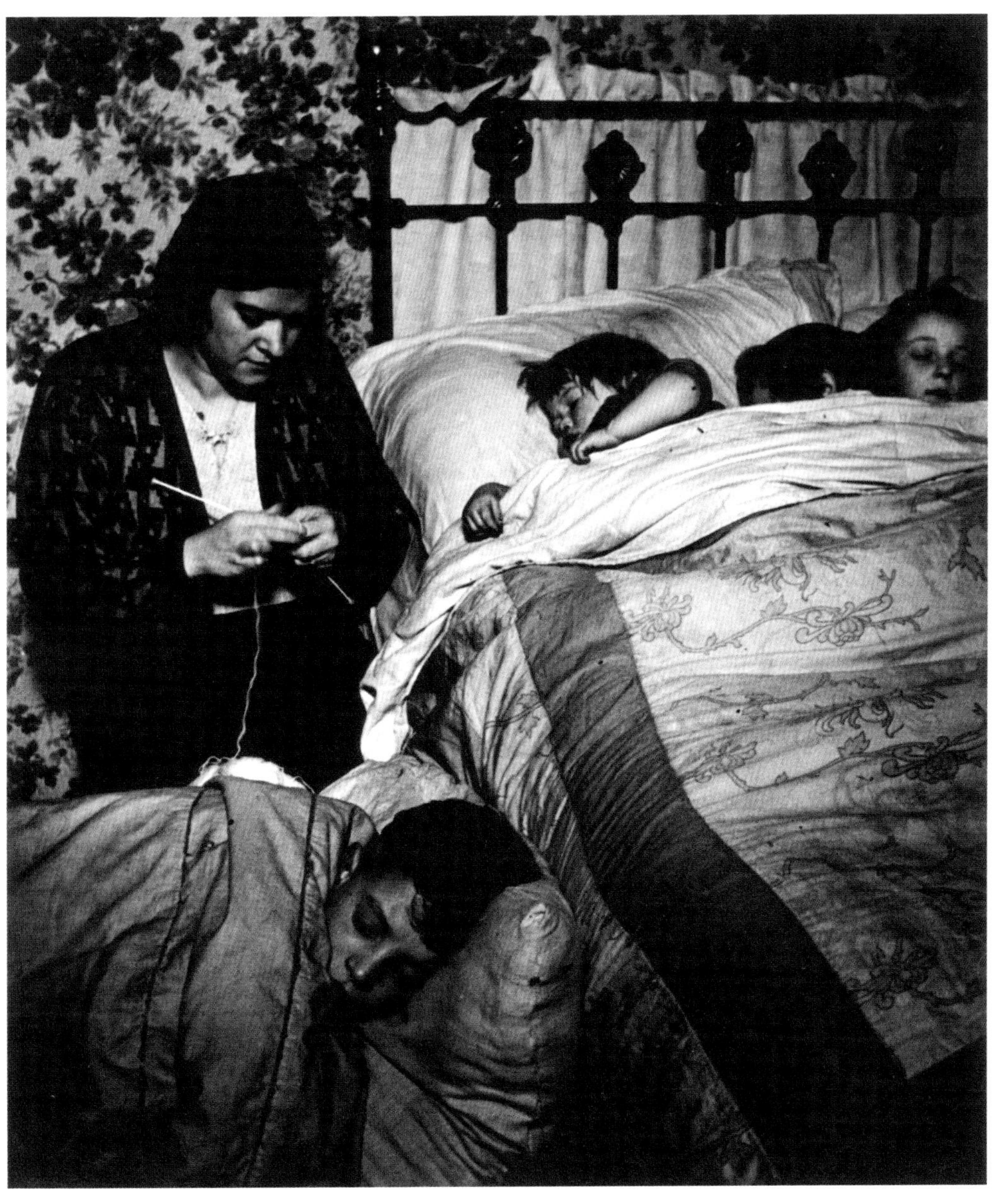

West Ham Bedroom, 1937

BILL BRANDT (1904–83)

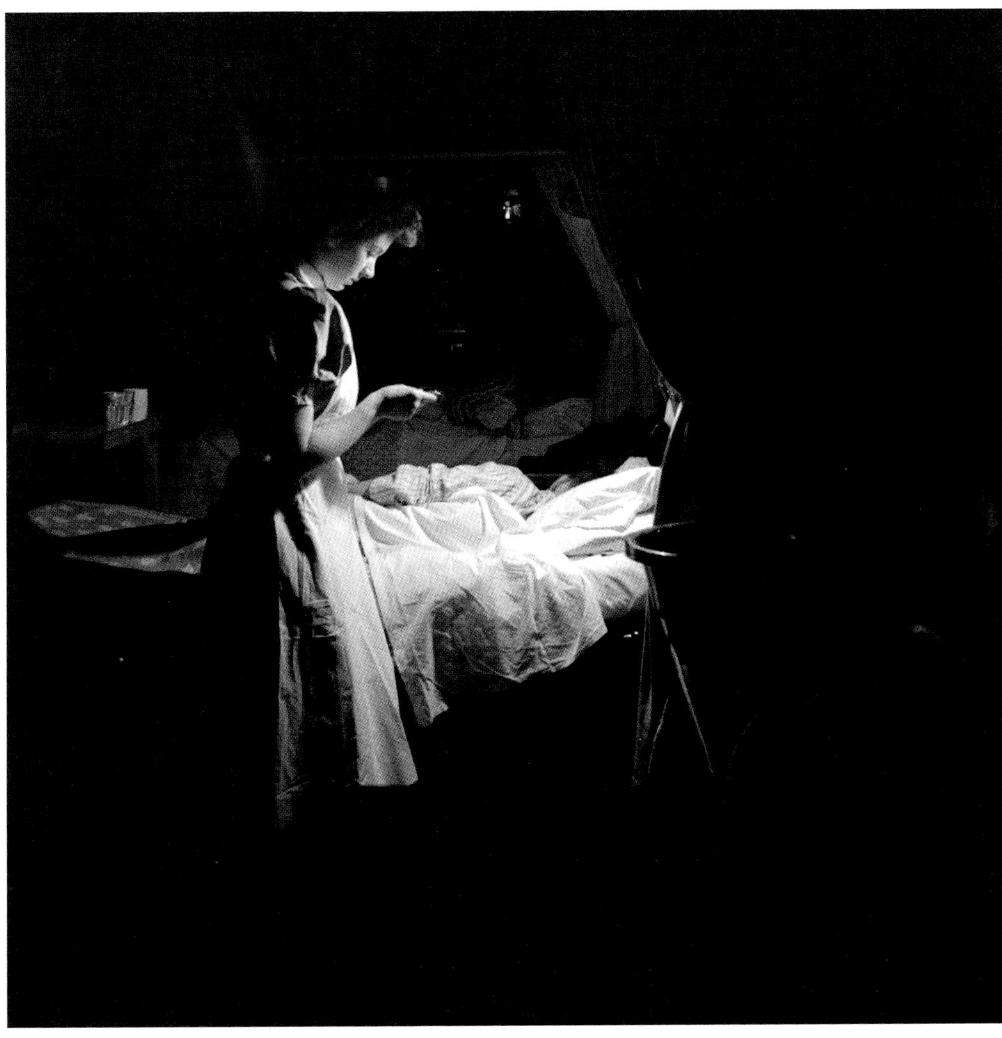

From the feature *I Want to be a Nurse*,
Picture Post, 31 October 1953

BERT HARDY (1913–95)

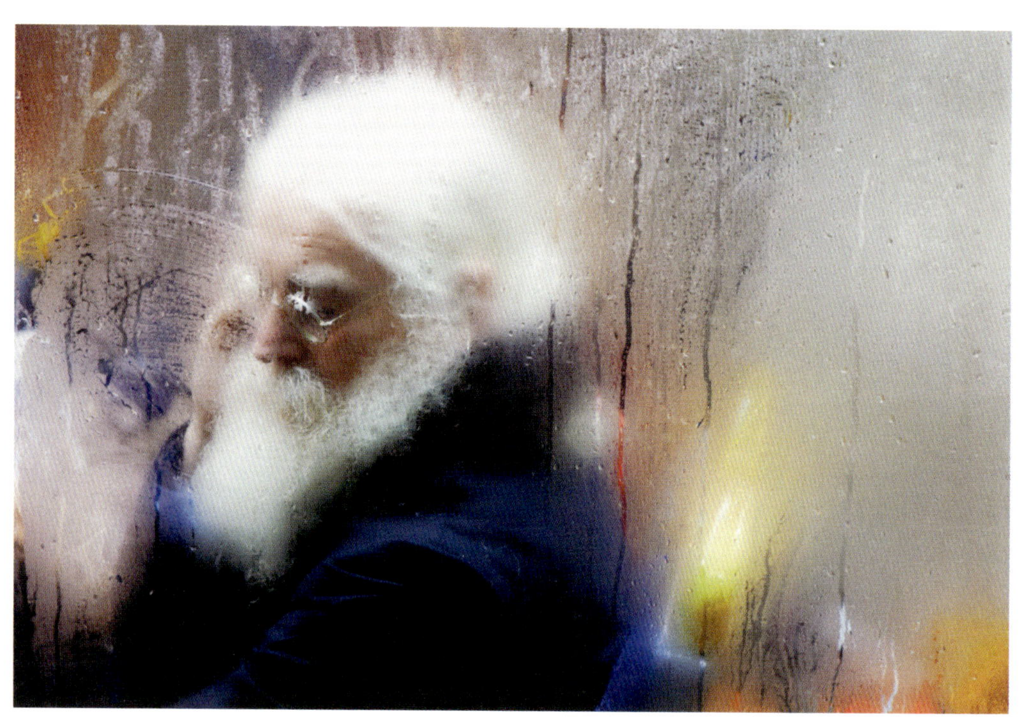

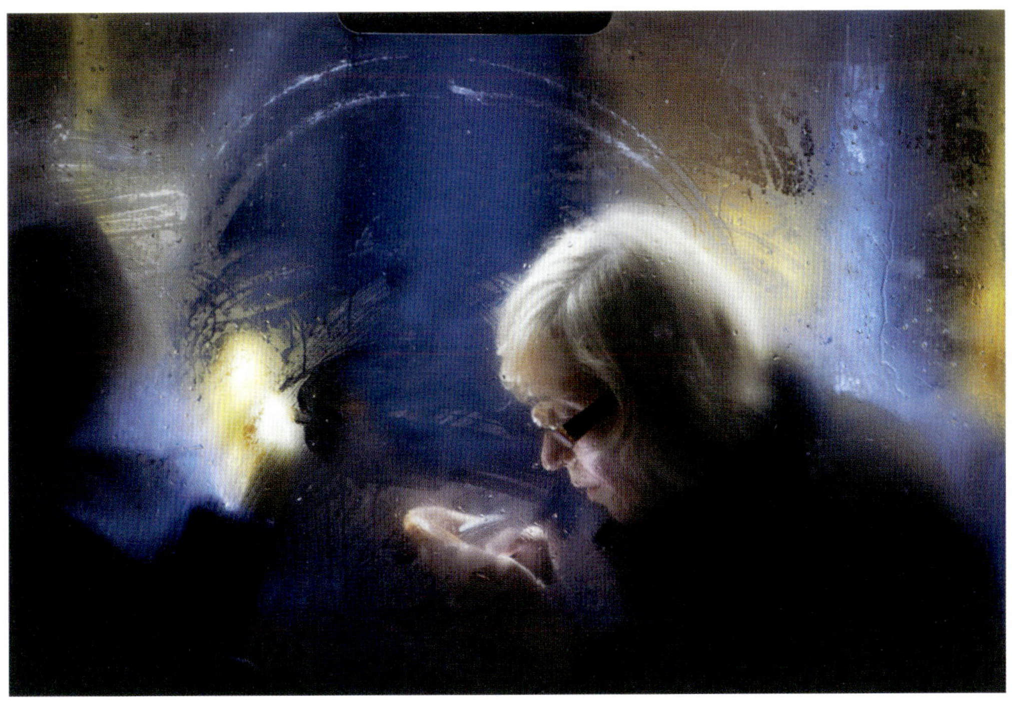

On the Night Bus #28
On the Night Bus #23
On the Night Bus #34 (FOLLOWING PAGES)

NICK TURPIN (b 1969)

Photographed through windows of buses passing through Elephant and Castle, passengers are captured in their own worlds, journeying away from the city for the night.

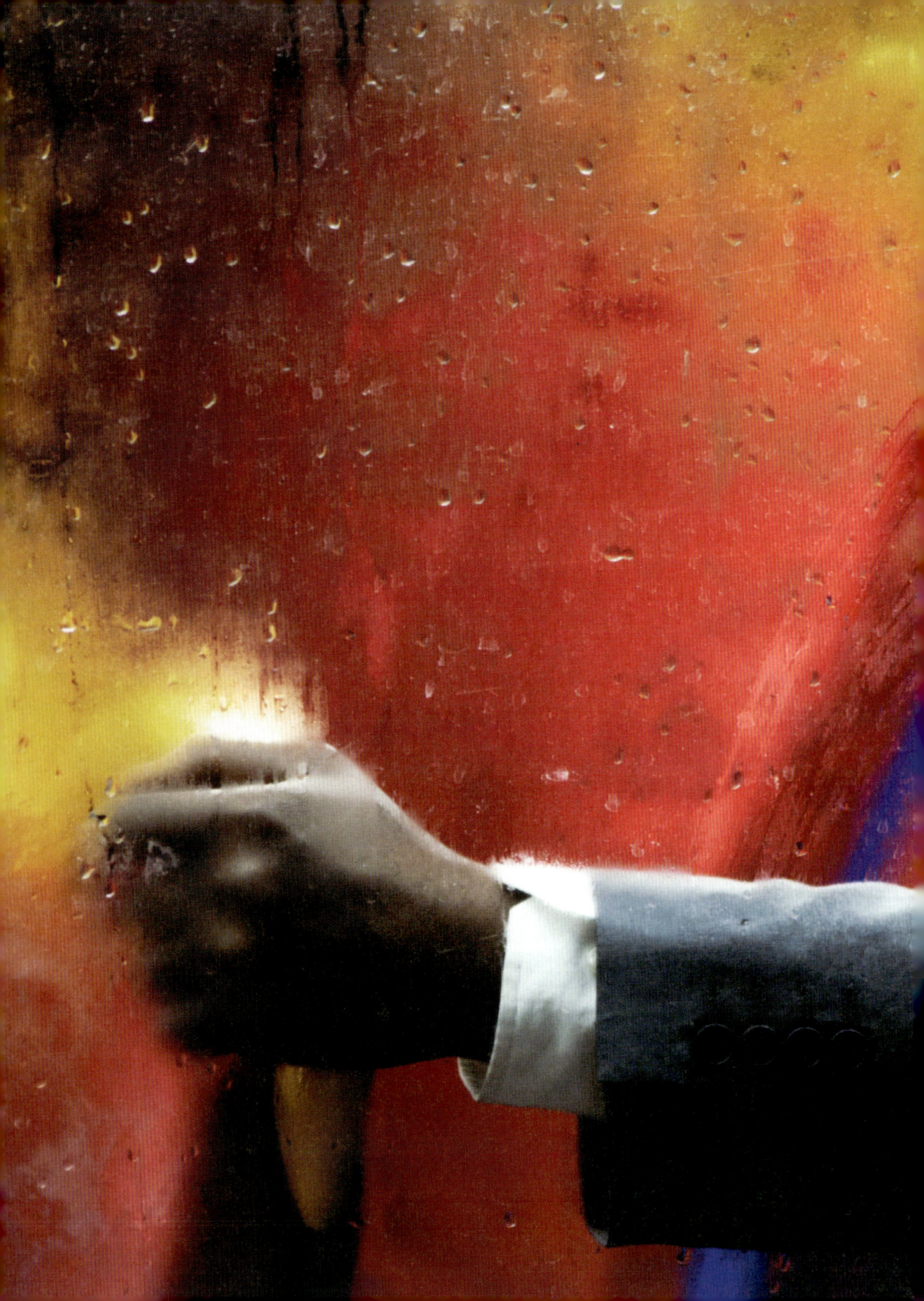

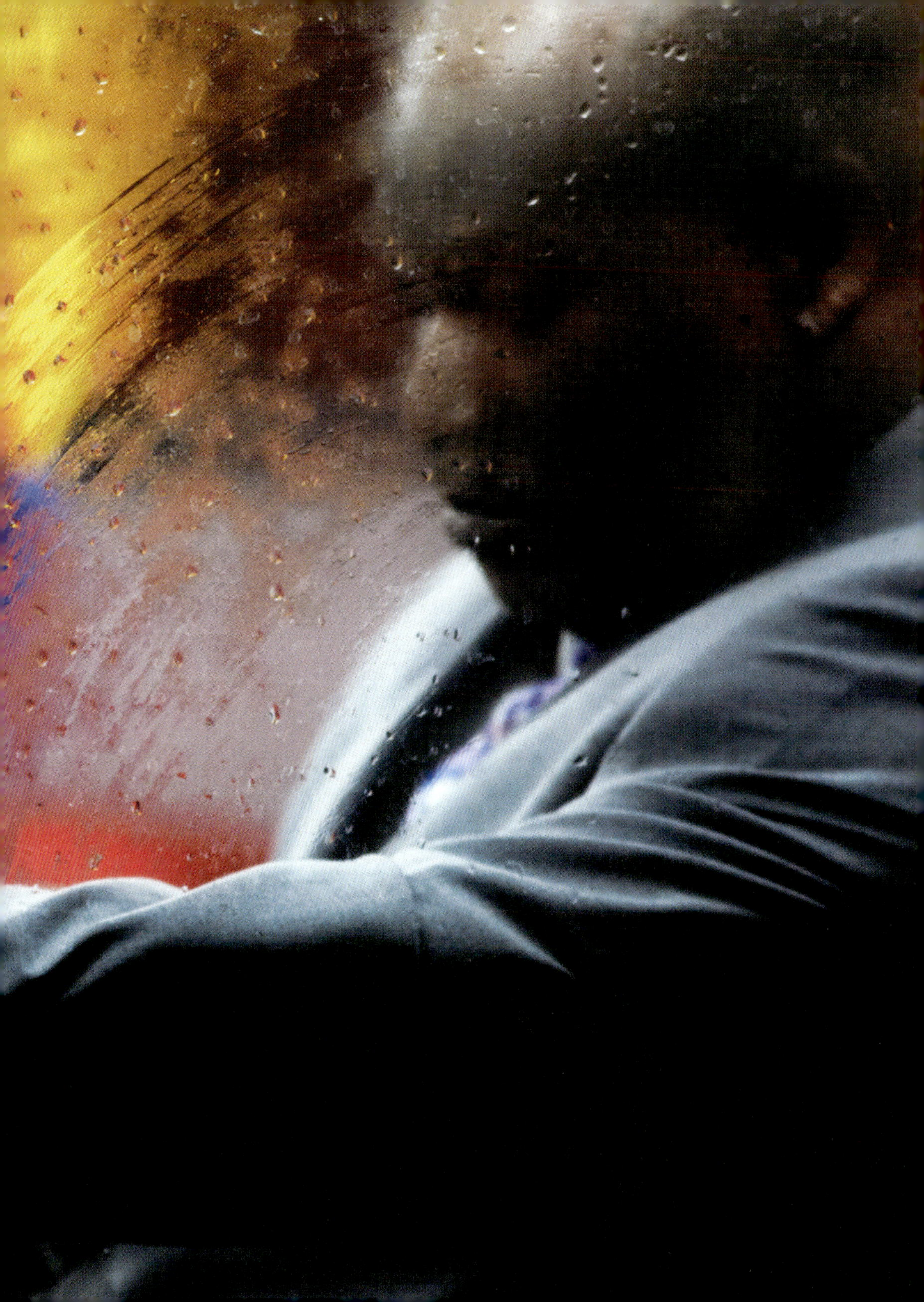

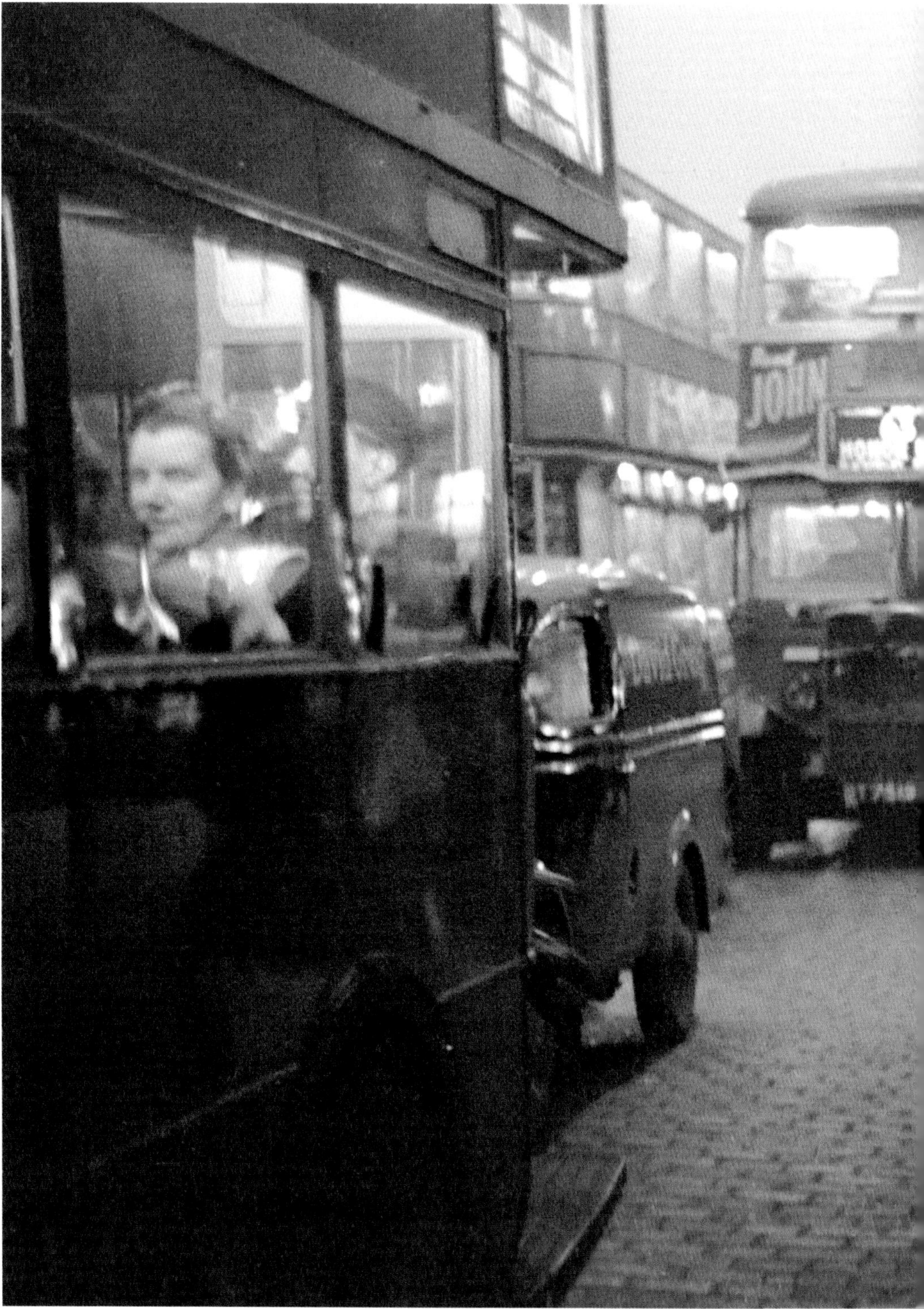
JOHN

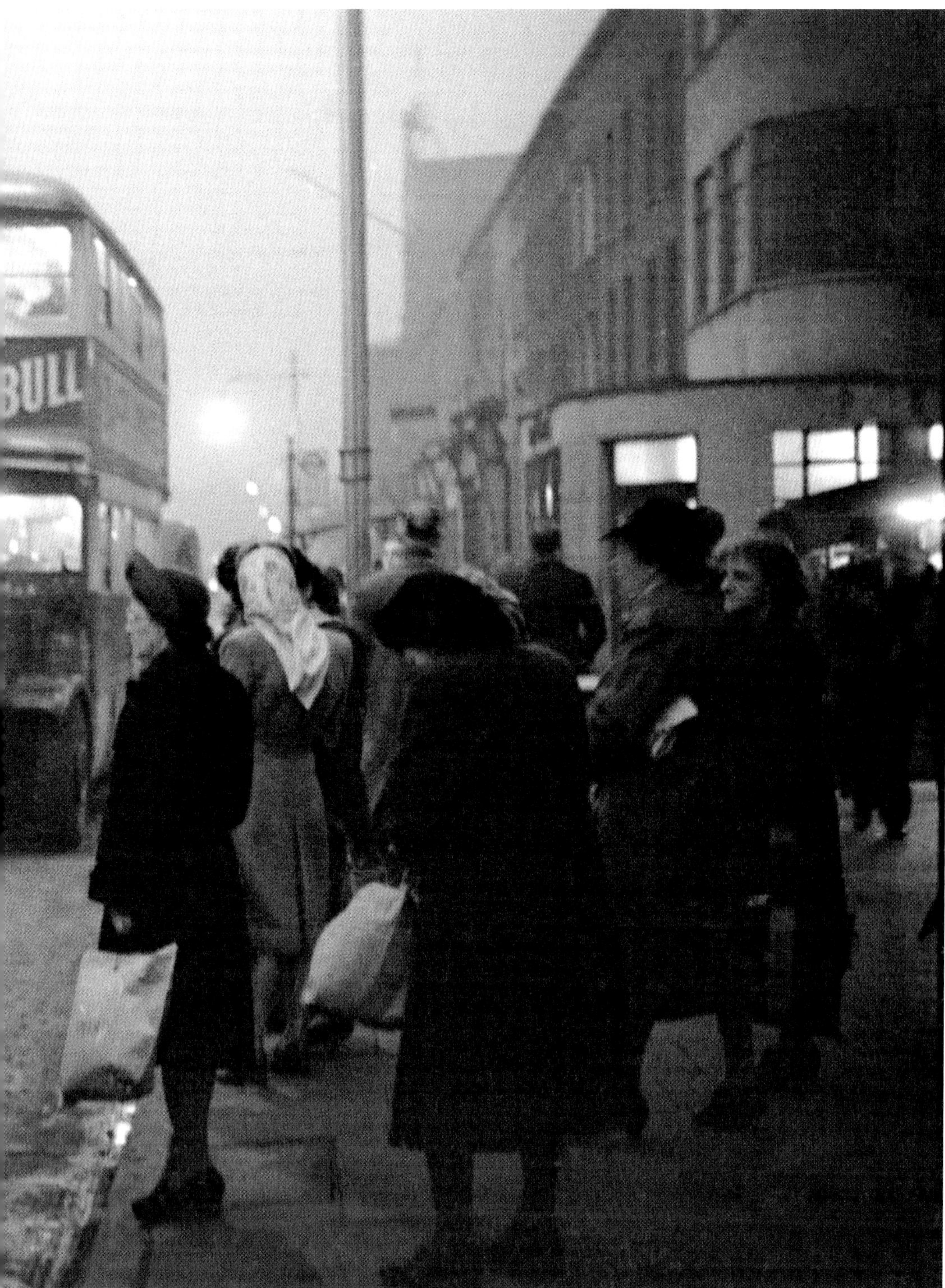
BULL

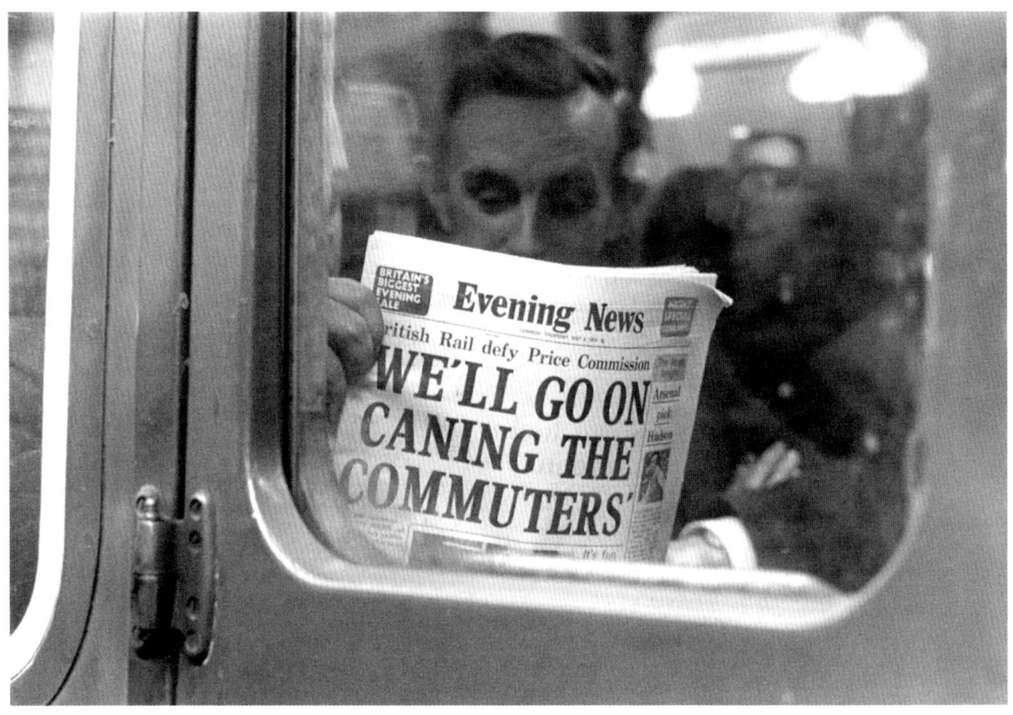

PREVIOUS PAGES
Night Buses, London Road (Elephant and Castle), 1948

BERT HARDY (1913-95)

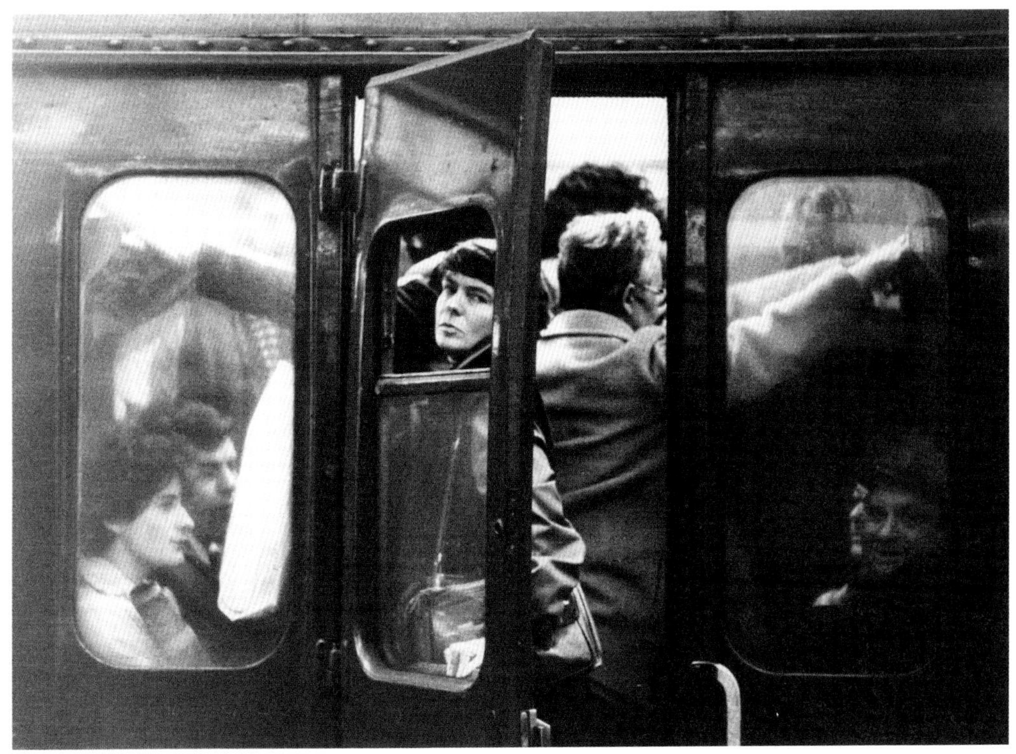

OPPOSITE AND ABOVE
From the series *Coming and Going*, 1977

BARRY LEWIS (b 1948)

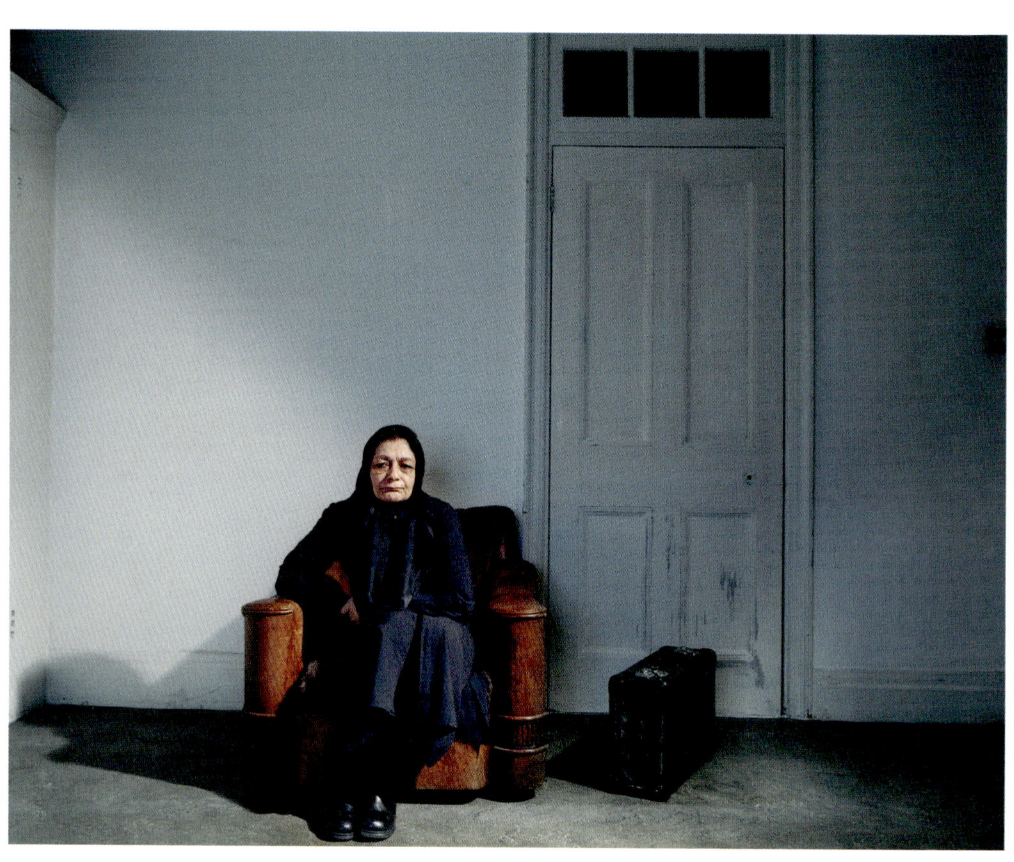

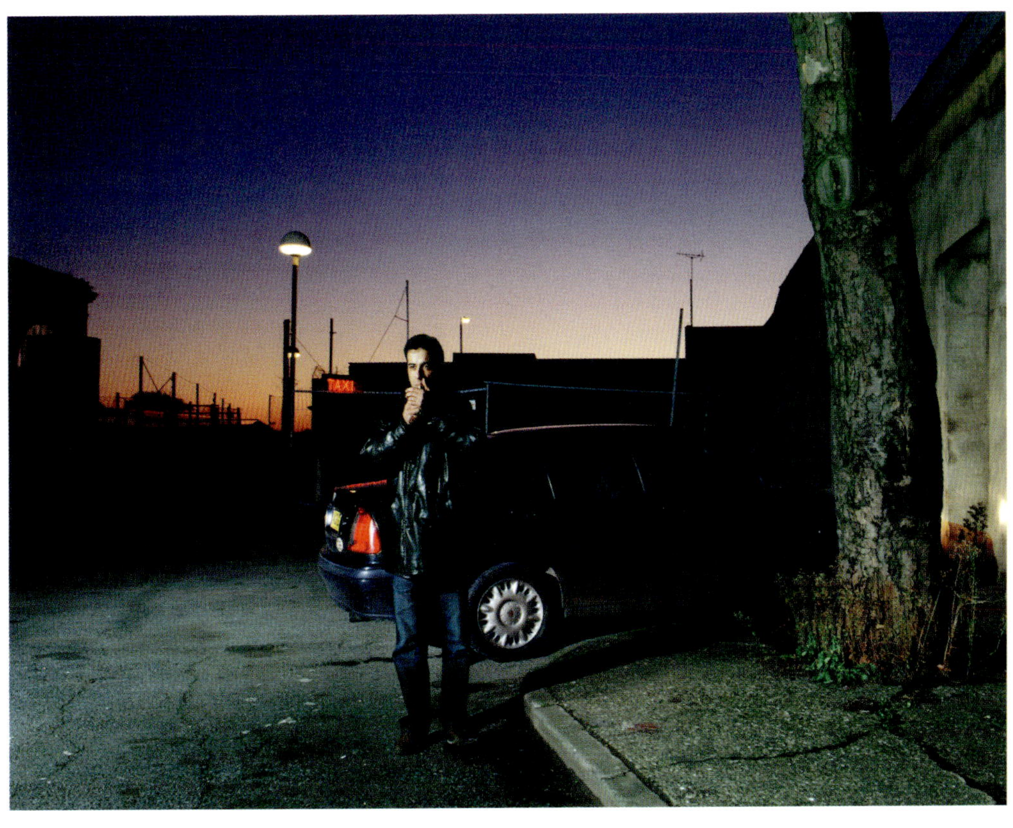

The Long Wait
Somewhere in the Night
From the series *Border*, 2005–06

MITRA TABRIZIAN (b 1956)

Two Iranian migrants are posed in scenes that reflect how the night might feel very long, as they perhaps contemplate their personal circumstances in London.

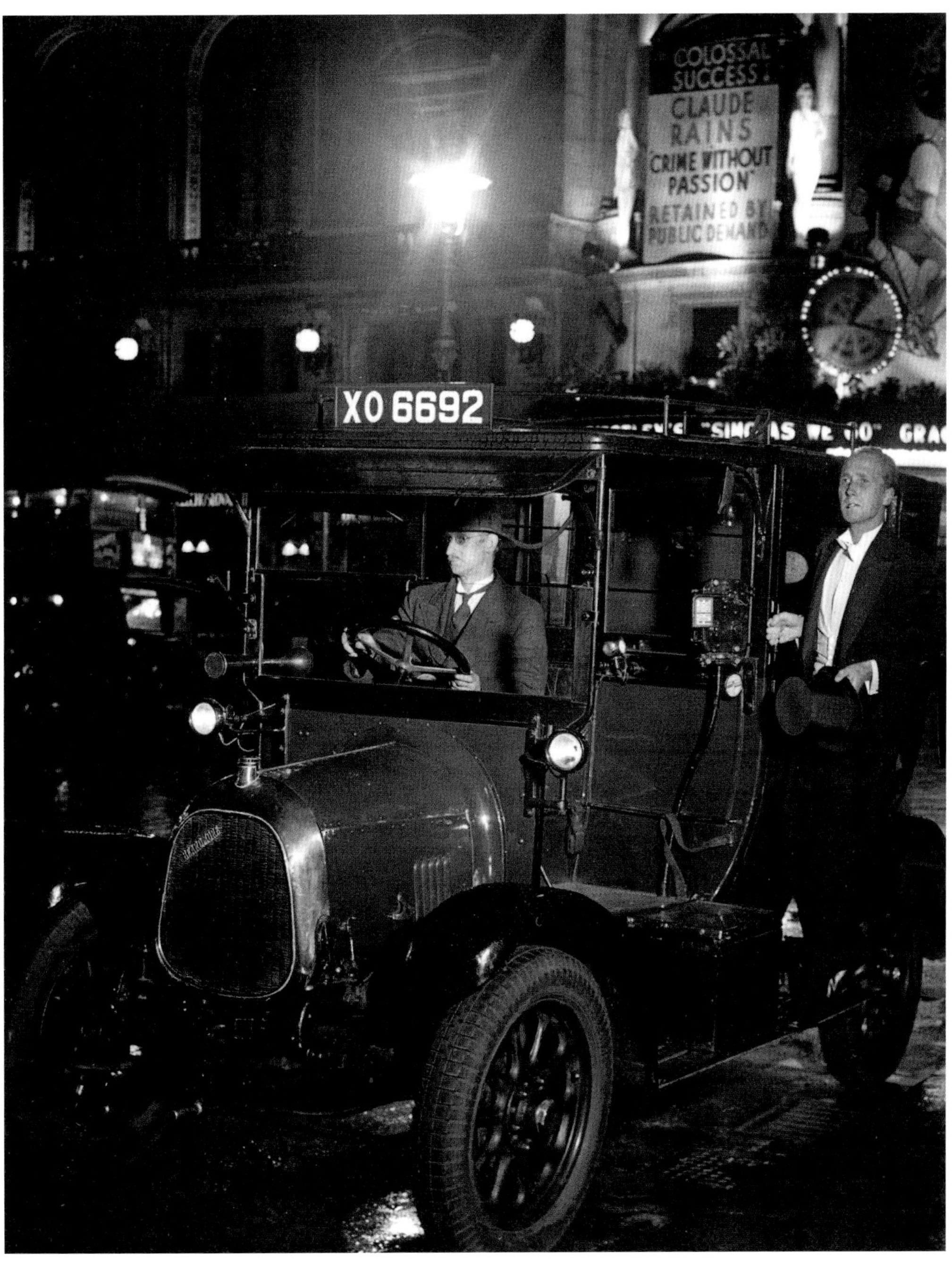

After The Theatre, Taxi in Lower Regent Street, 1934

BILL BRANDT (1904–83)

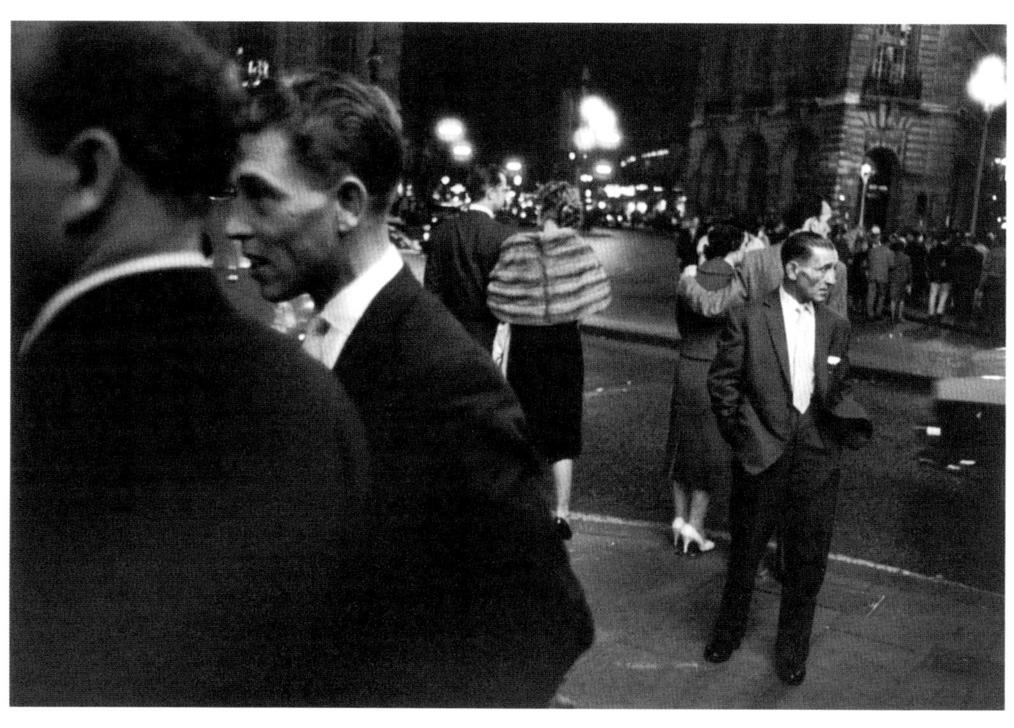

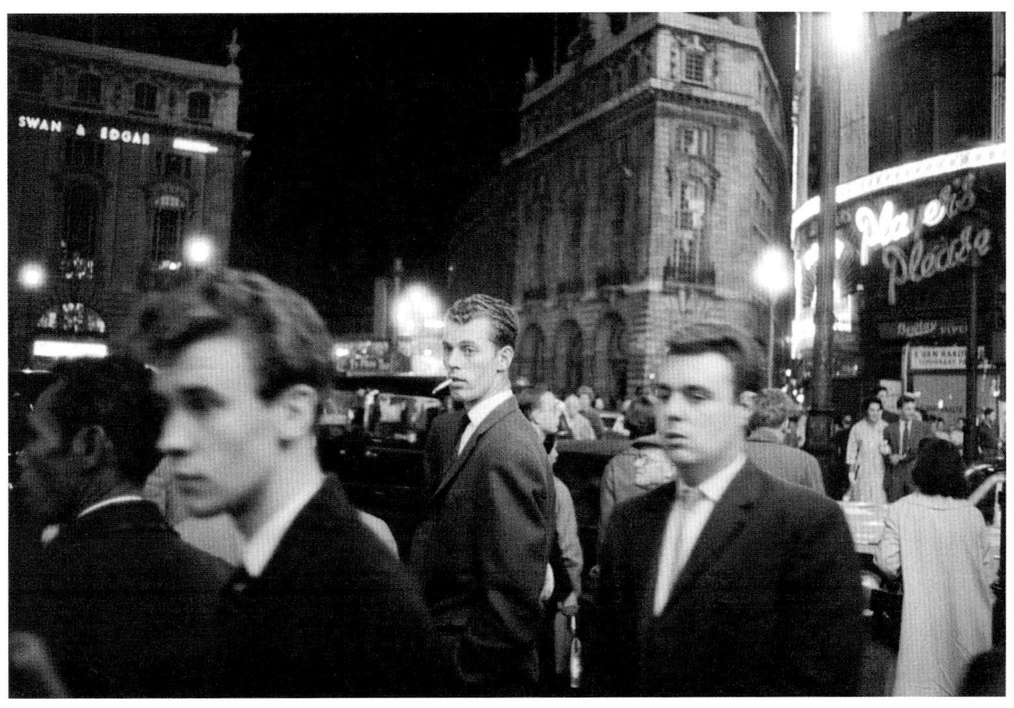

The West End at night, 1960

BOB COLLINS (1924–2002)

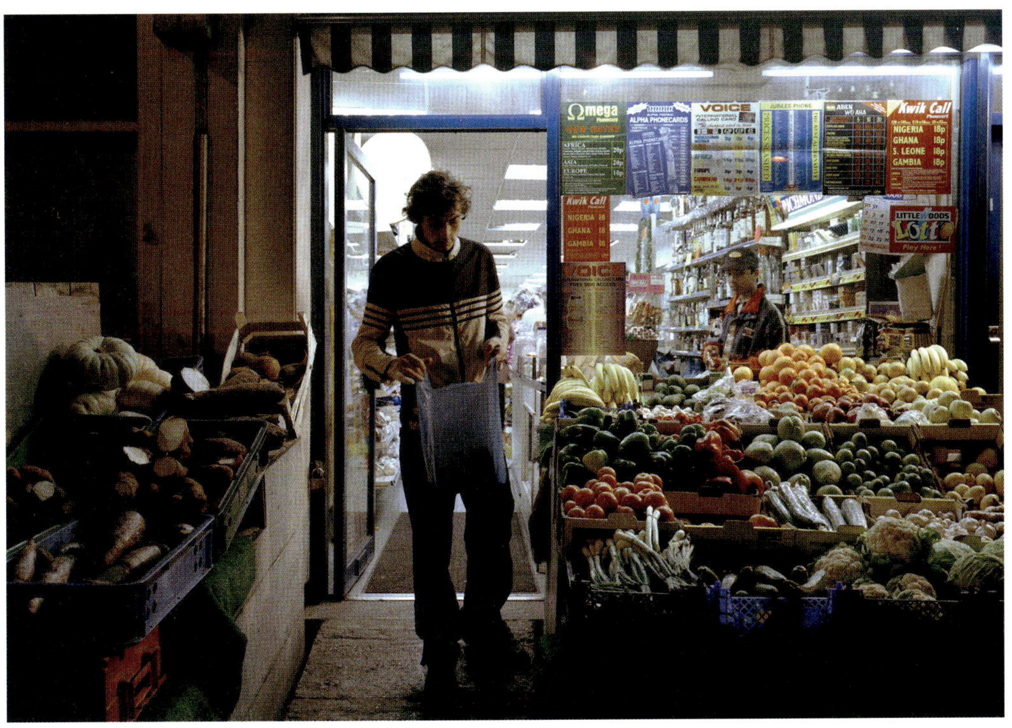

Jason, 2000

SEAMUS NICOLSON (b 1971)

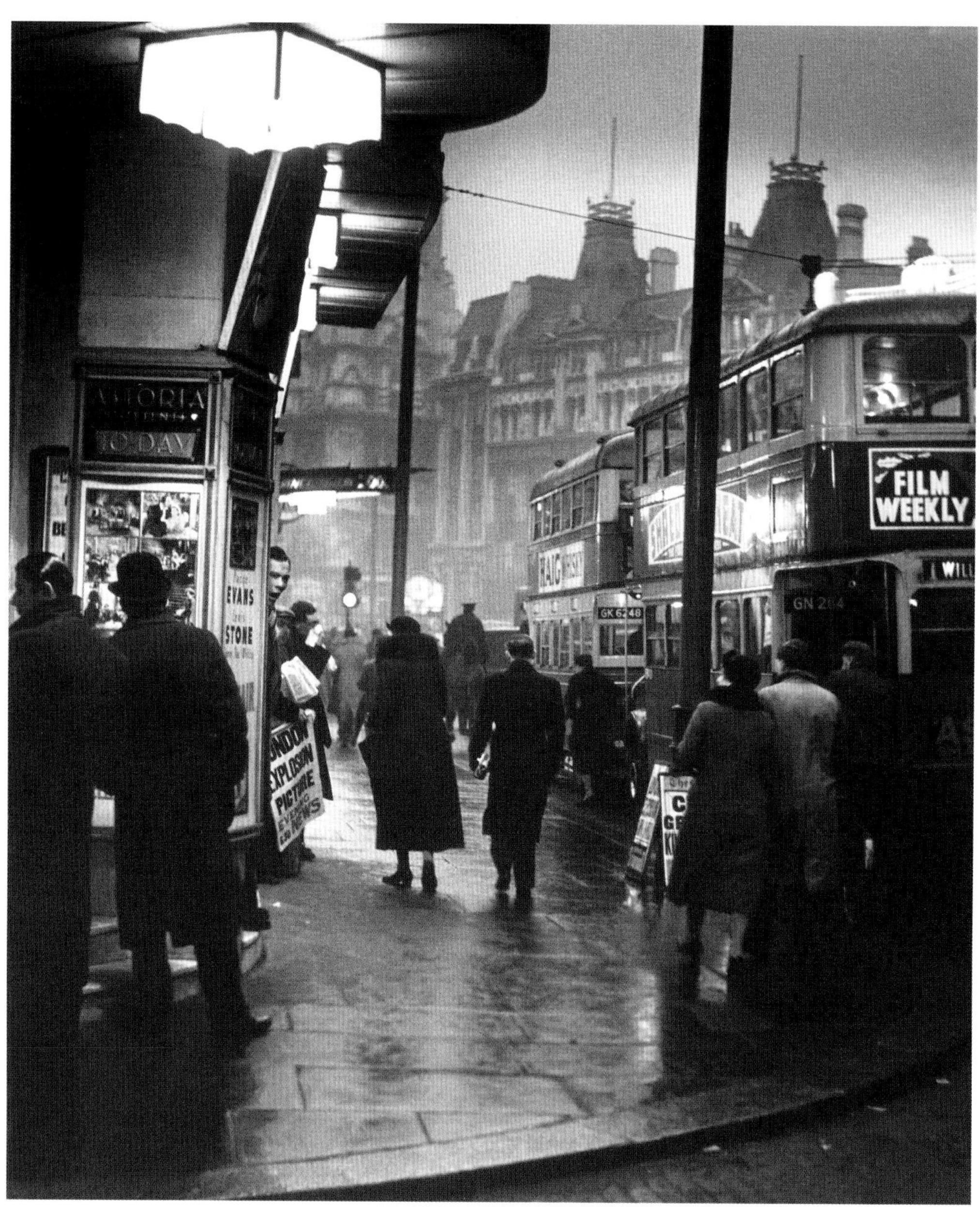
EVANS
STONE
EXPLOSION
PICTURE
HAIG
GK 6248
FILM
WEEKLY

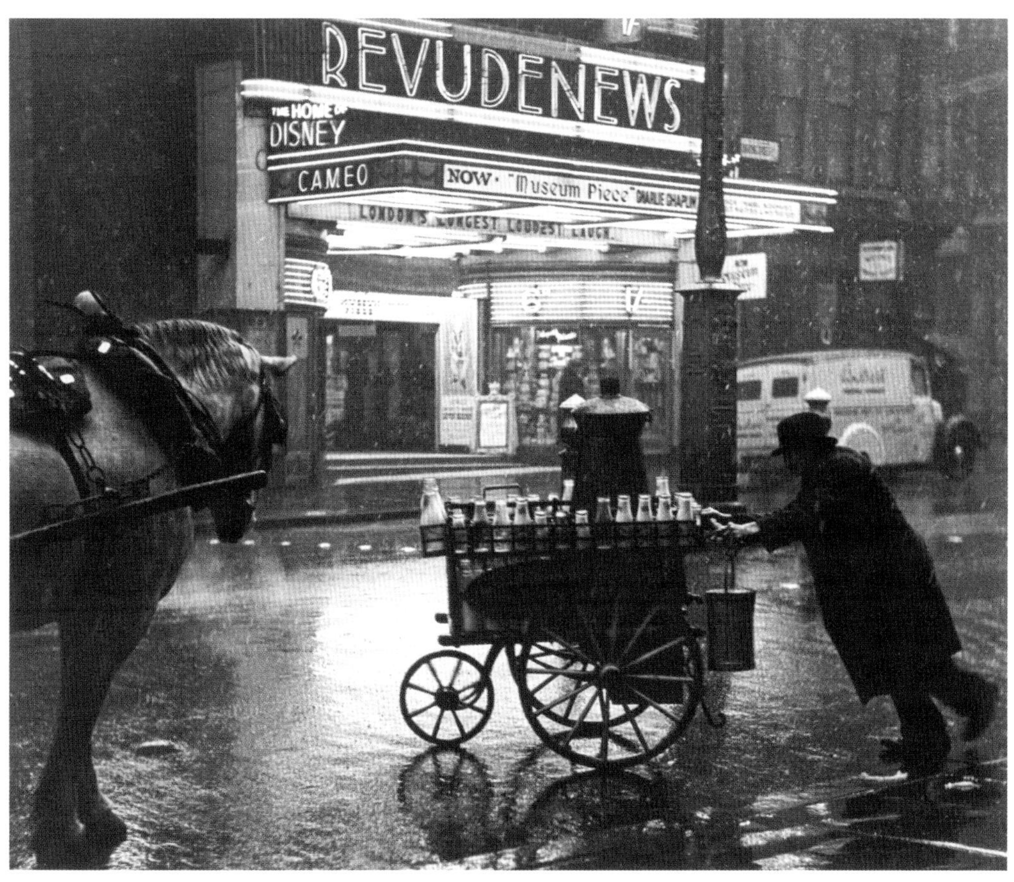

Charing Cross Road, St Giles Circus, c 1935
Milkman on the Charing Cross Road, 1935

WOLF SUSCHITZKY (1912–2016)

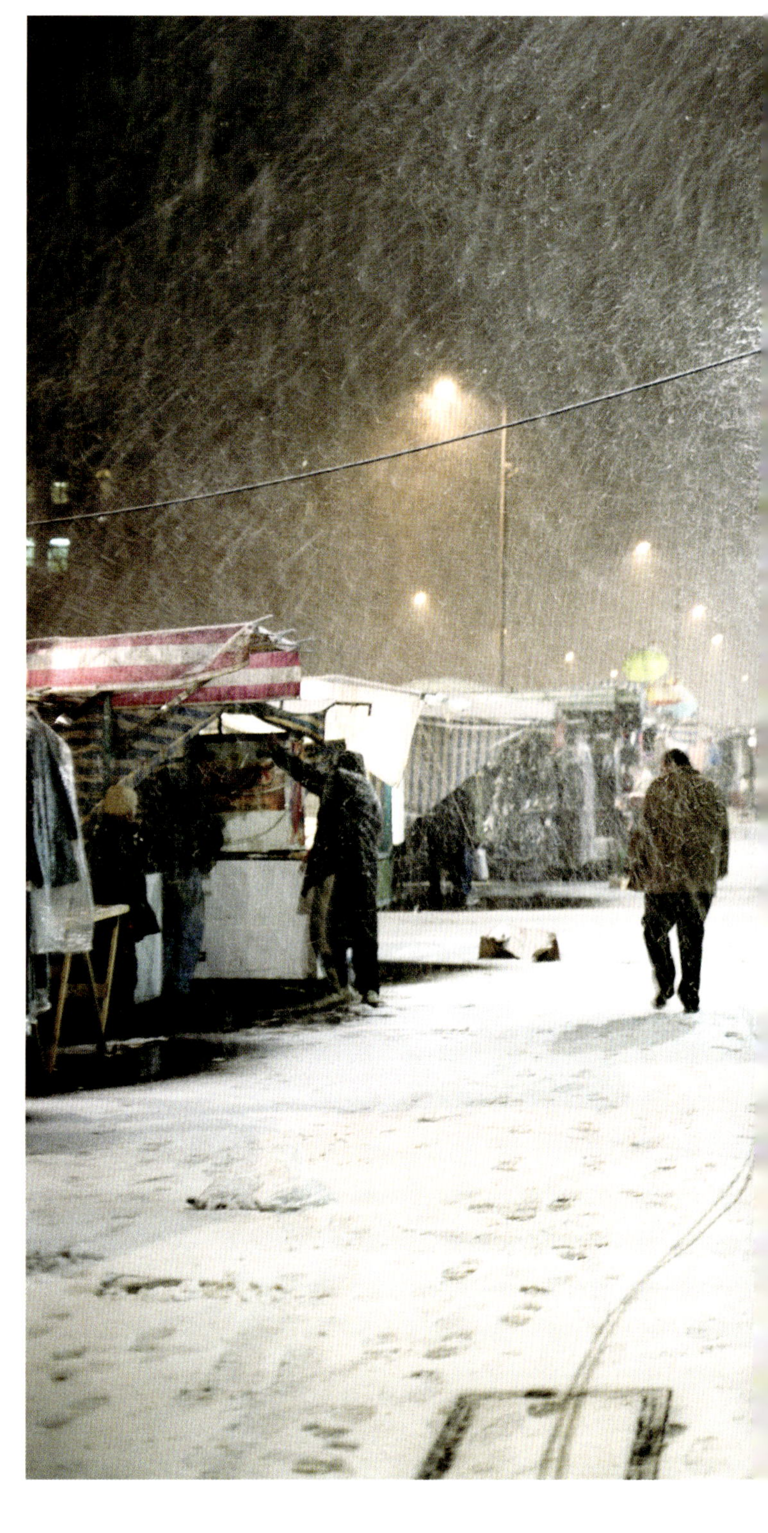

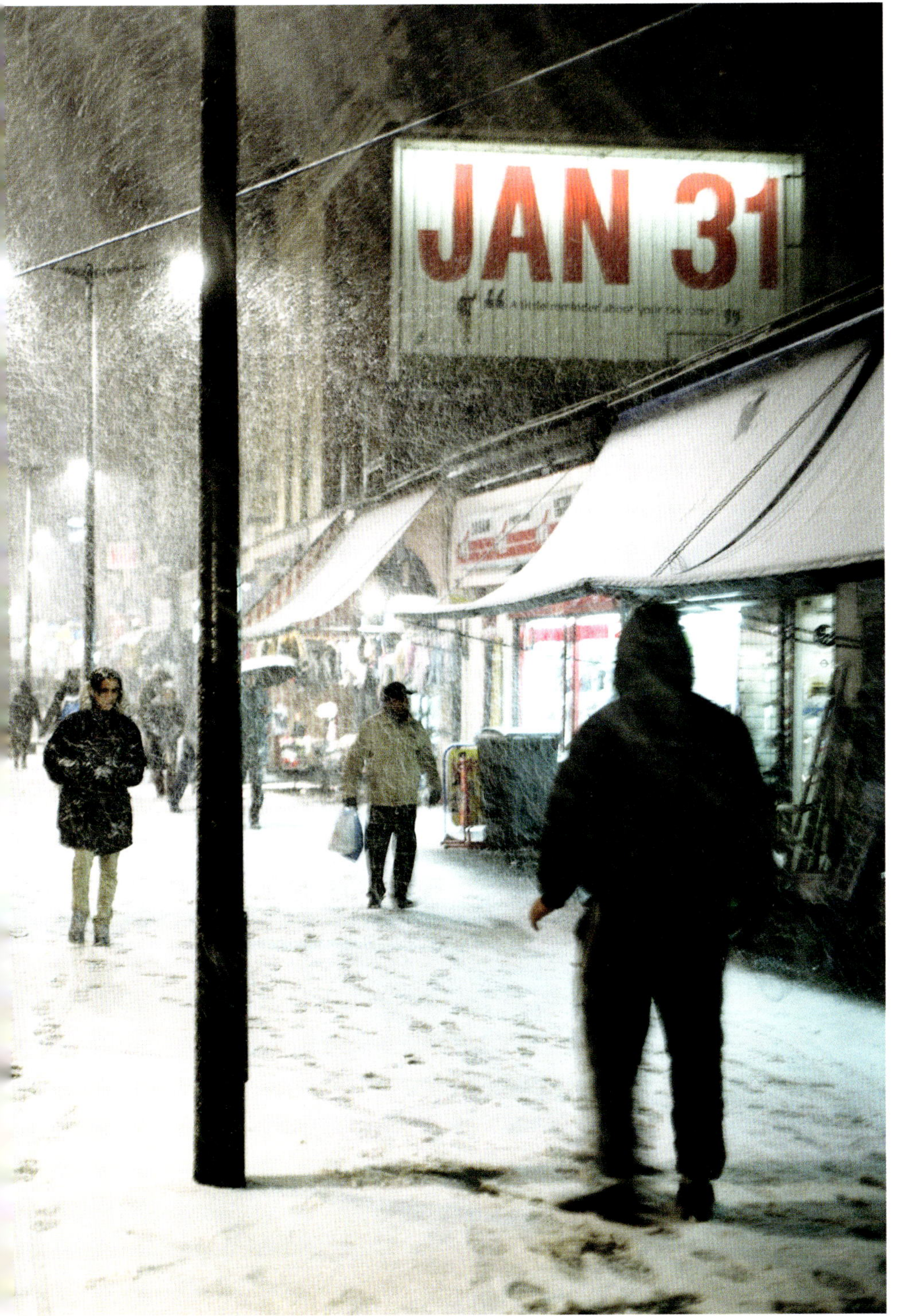
JAN 31

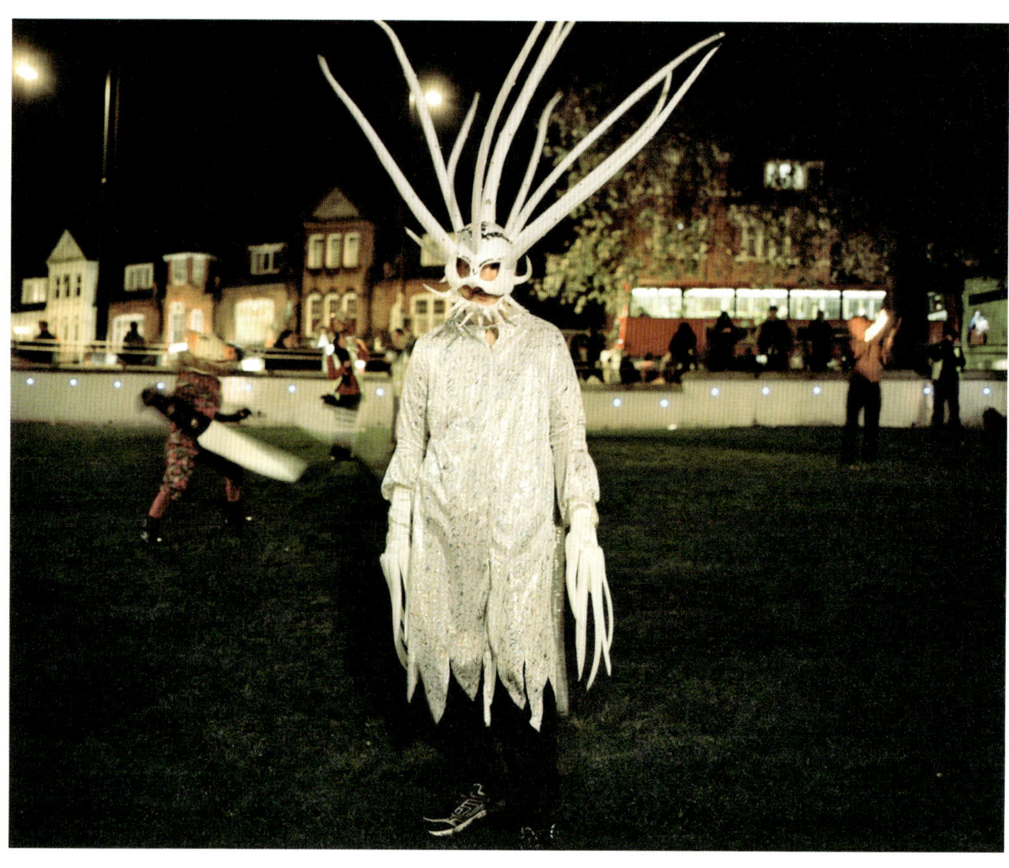

Whitechapel Market, Tower Hamlets (PREVIOUS PAGES)
Winter Carnival, Streatham Green, Lambeth (ABOVE)
from the series *London Ends*, 2008–13

PHILIPP EBELING (b 1977)

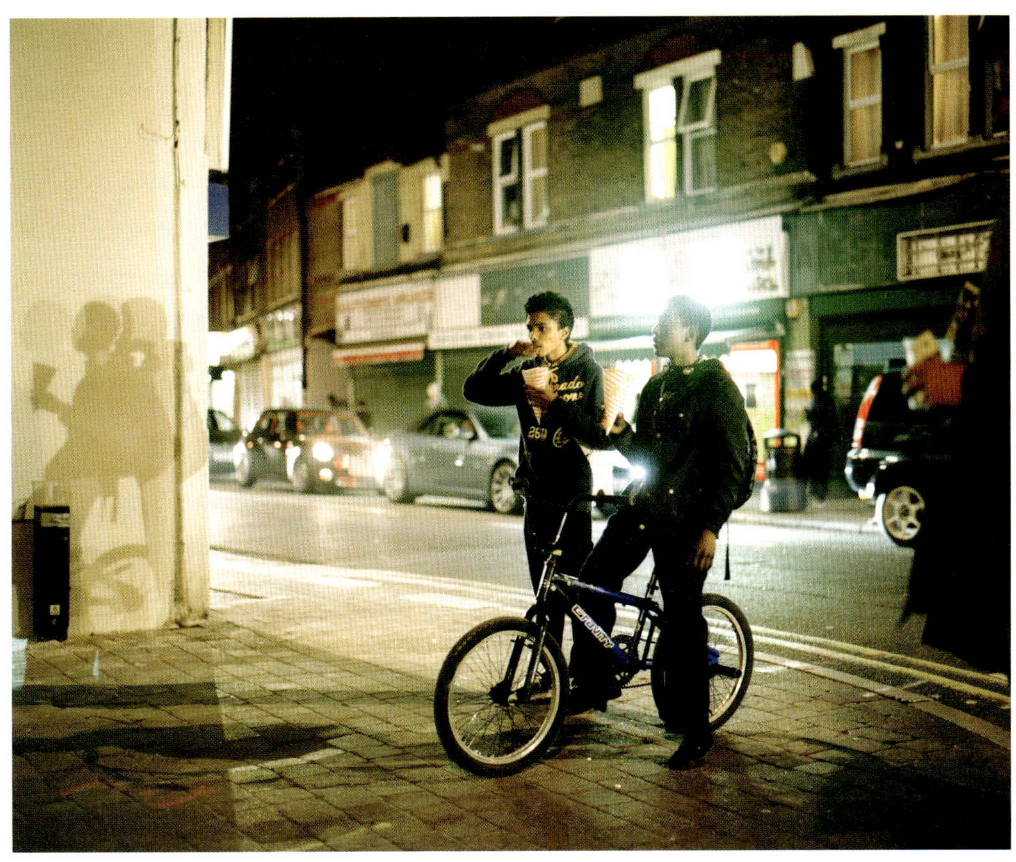

Outdoor Cinema Projection, Wood Street, Waltham Forest
from the series *London Ends*, 2008–13

PHILIPP EBELING (b 1977)

These photographs taken from Ebeling's exploration of the wider extent of the city reflect the capital's varied nightly activity through both familiar and unusual scenes.

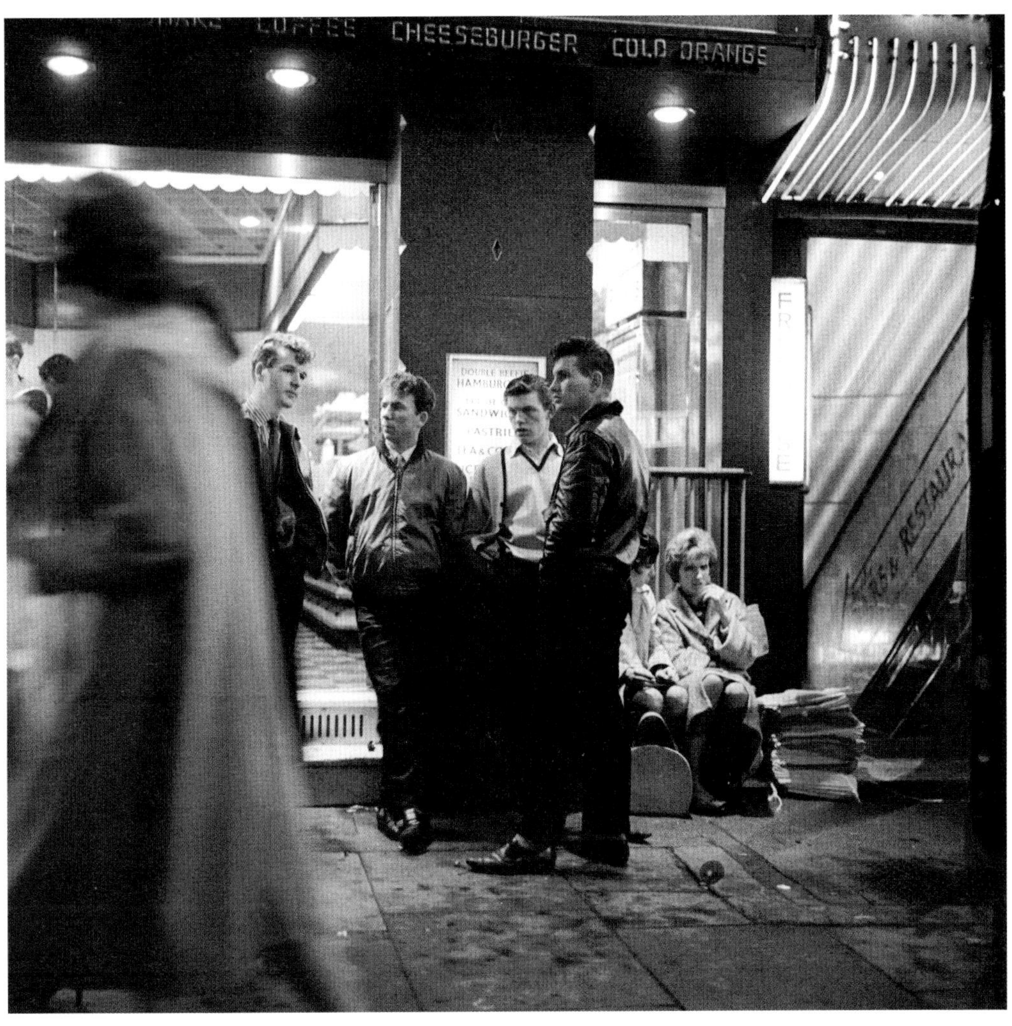

Group of Teddy Boys outside a burger bar,
West End, 1962

HENRY GRANT (1907–2004)

PAGES 168–71
The words of a paying customer, 1983
Song and Dance, 1983
Karen with punters at the Sunset Strip, 1983
From the series *London by Night*

TISH MURTHA (1956–2013)

Murtha photographed the Soho sex trade, befriending several individuals as she recorded through word and image their relationships with the district at night.

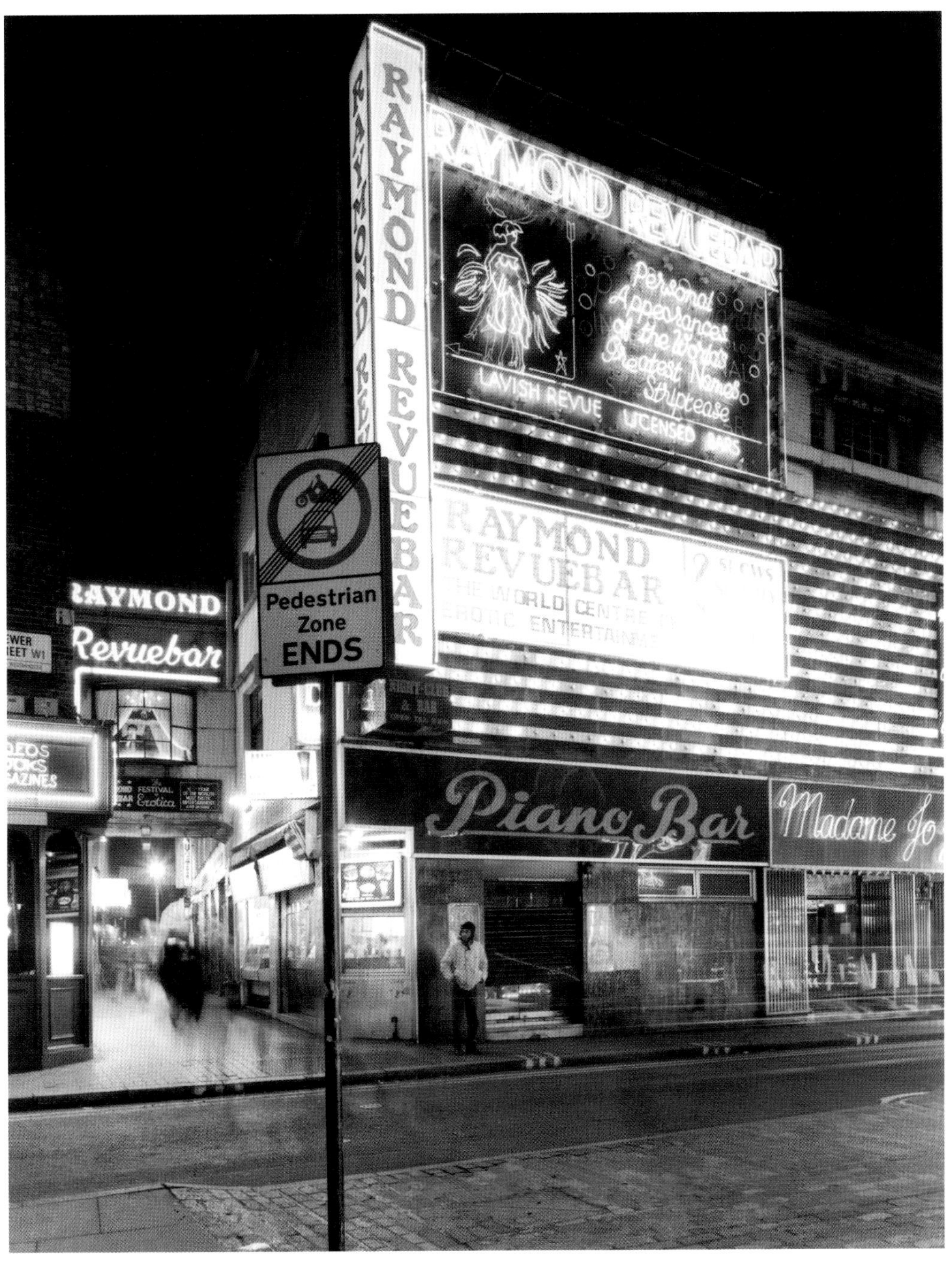

Brewer Street, W1, 1993

ALAN DELANEY (b 1958)

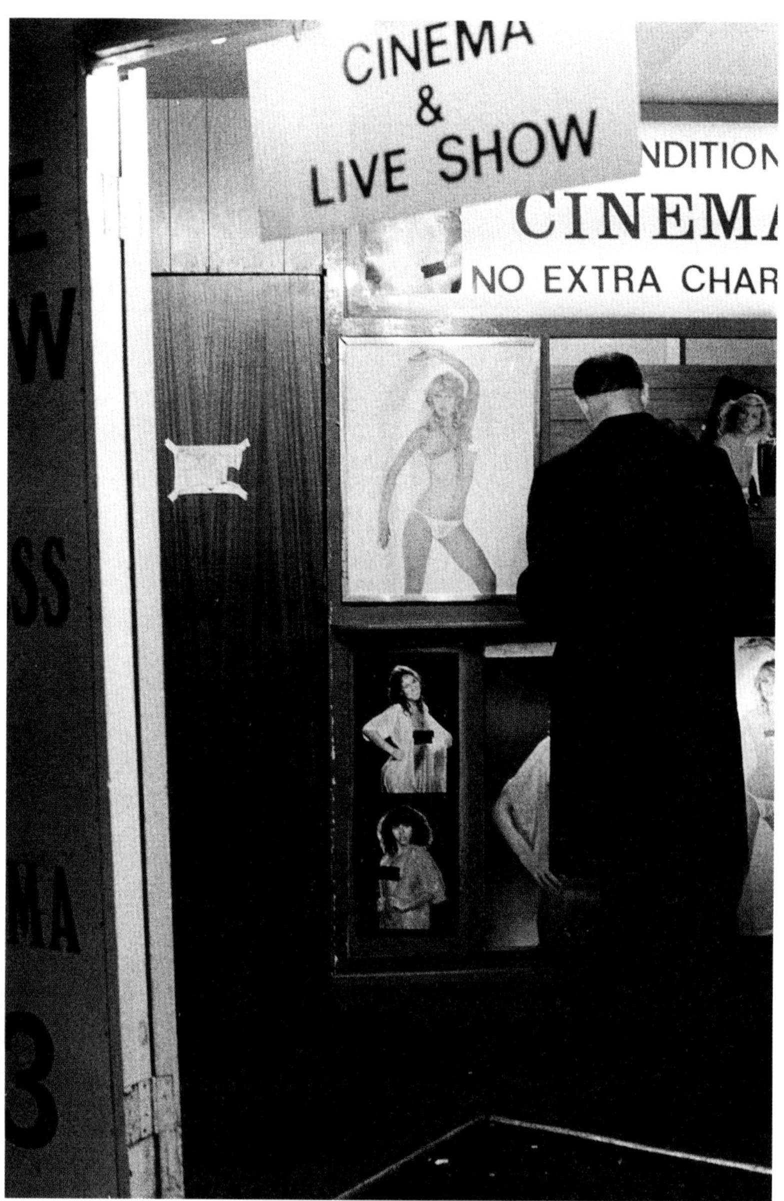

'My girlfriend wanted a 4 week break or something and I was in the West End anyway and I had £20 in my pocket and discovered myself walking up the stairs to one of those "models".'

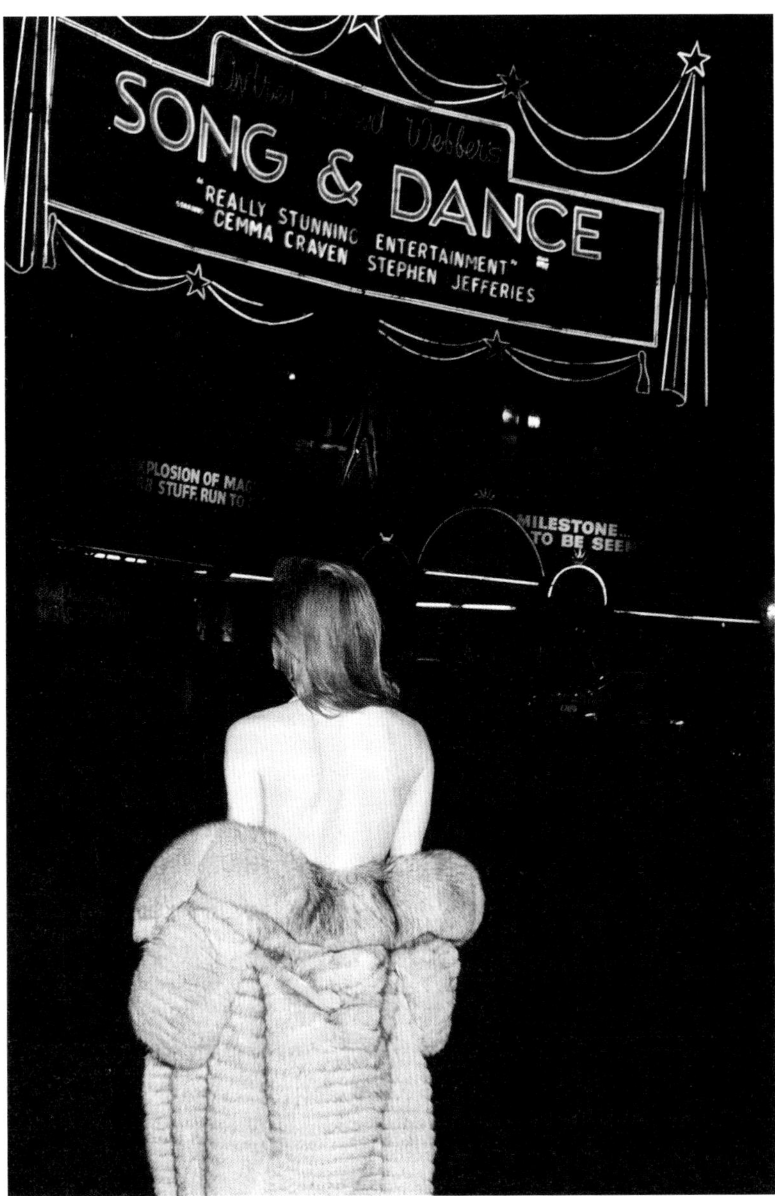

'I went out with Linda one night when Soho was quiet. She shouted out "You want to make love darling" and exposed her breasts on the street as usual but didn't get much attention.'

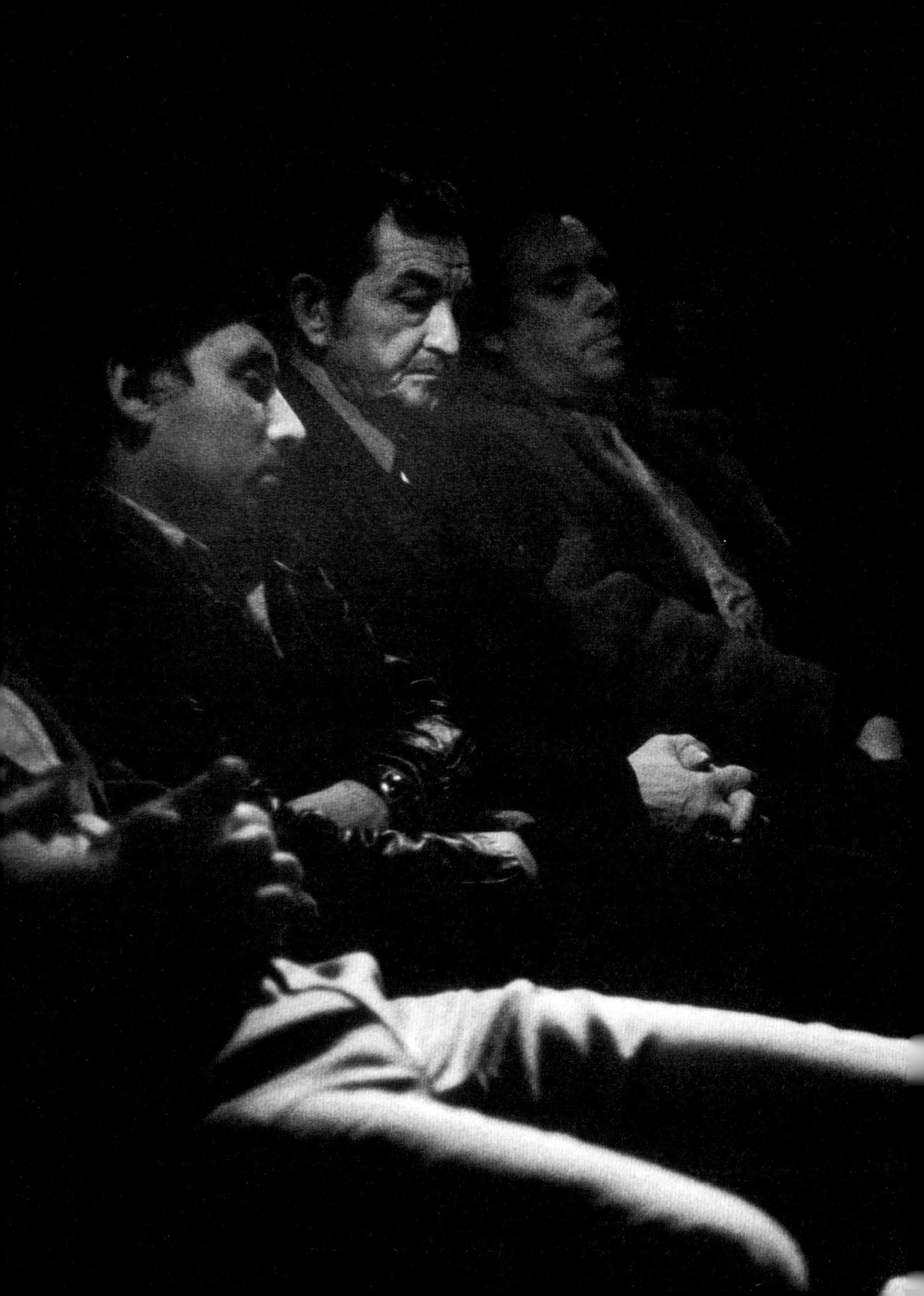

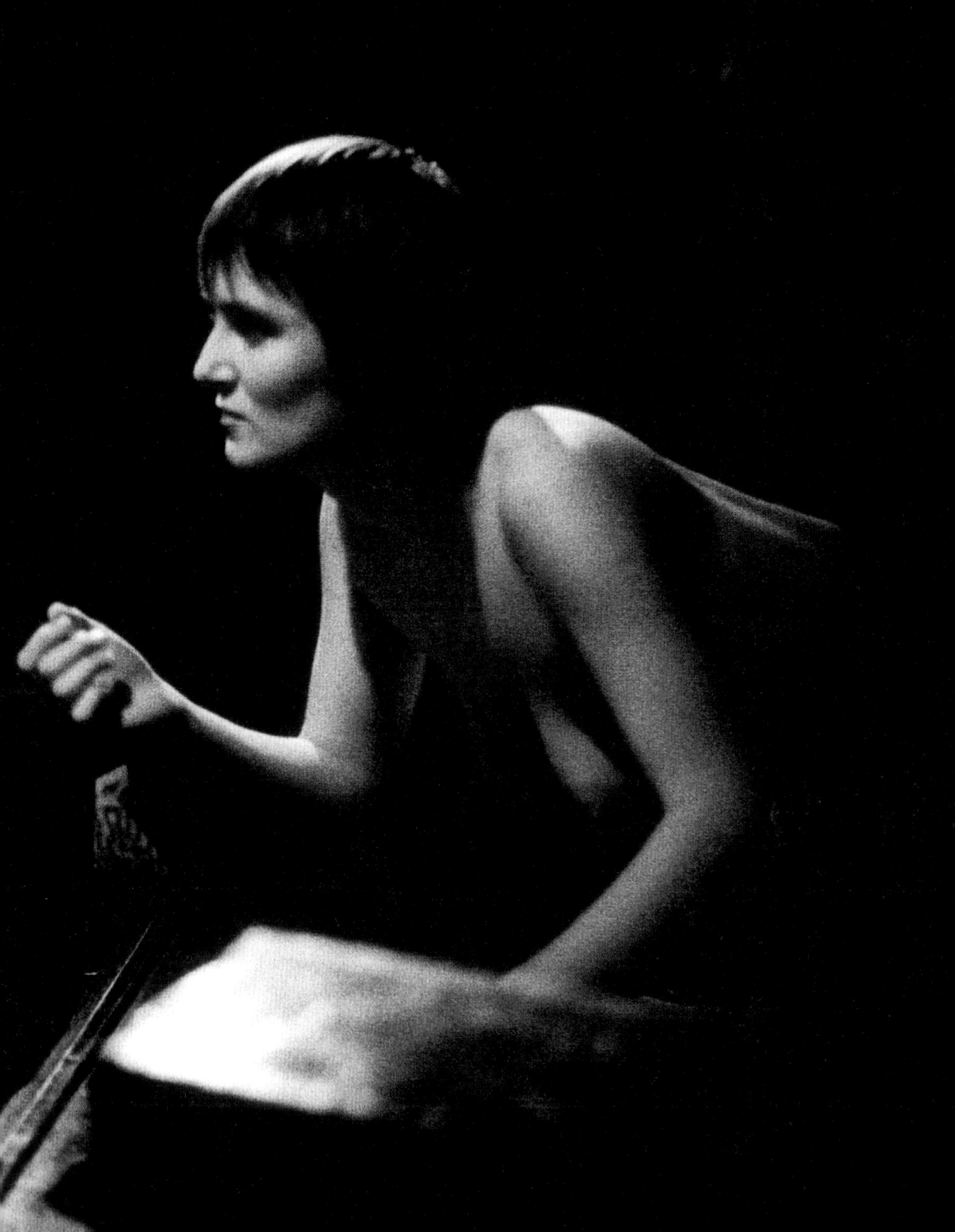

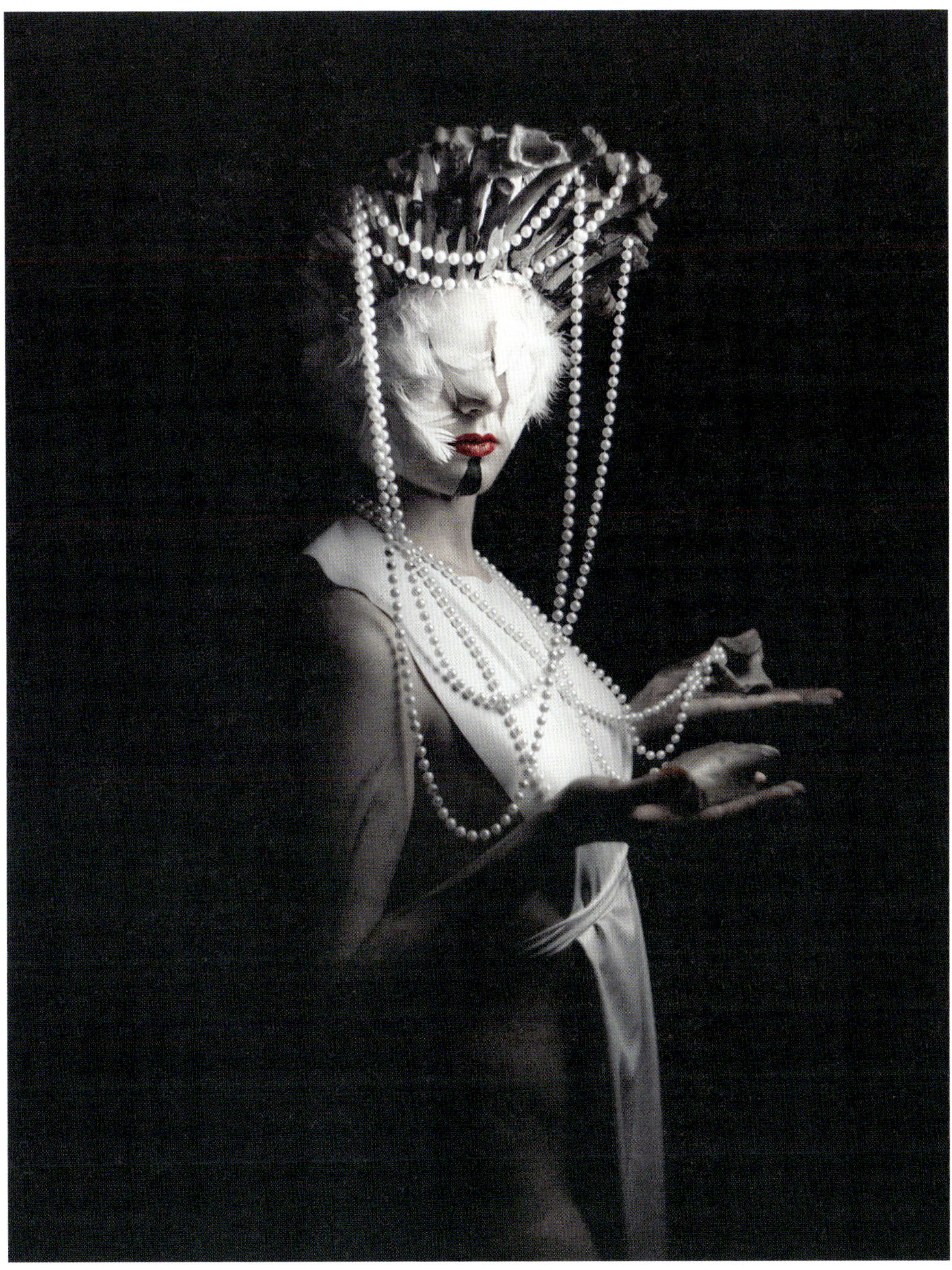

Cynth Icorn at C O V E N, 2016

DAMIEN FROST (b 1975)

Photographed on the street and at clubs in the middle of the night, Frost's captivating 'Night Flowers' shine brightly and illustrate London's vibrant, alternative nightlife.

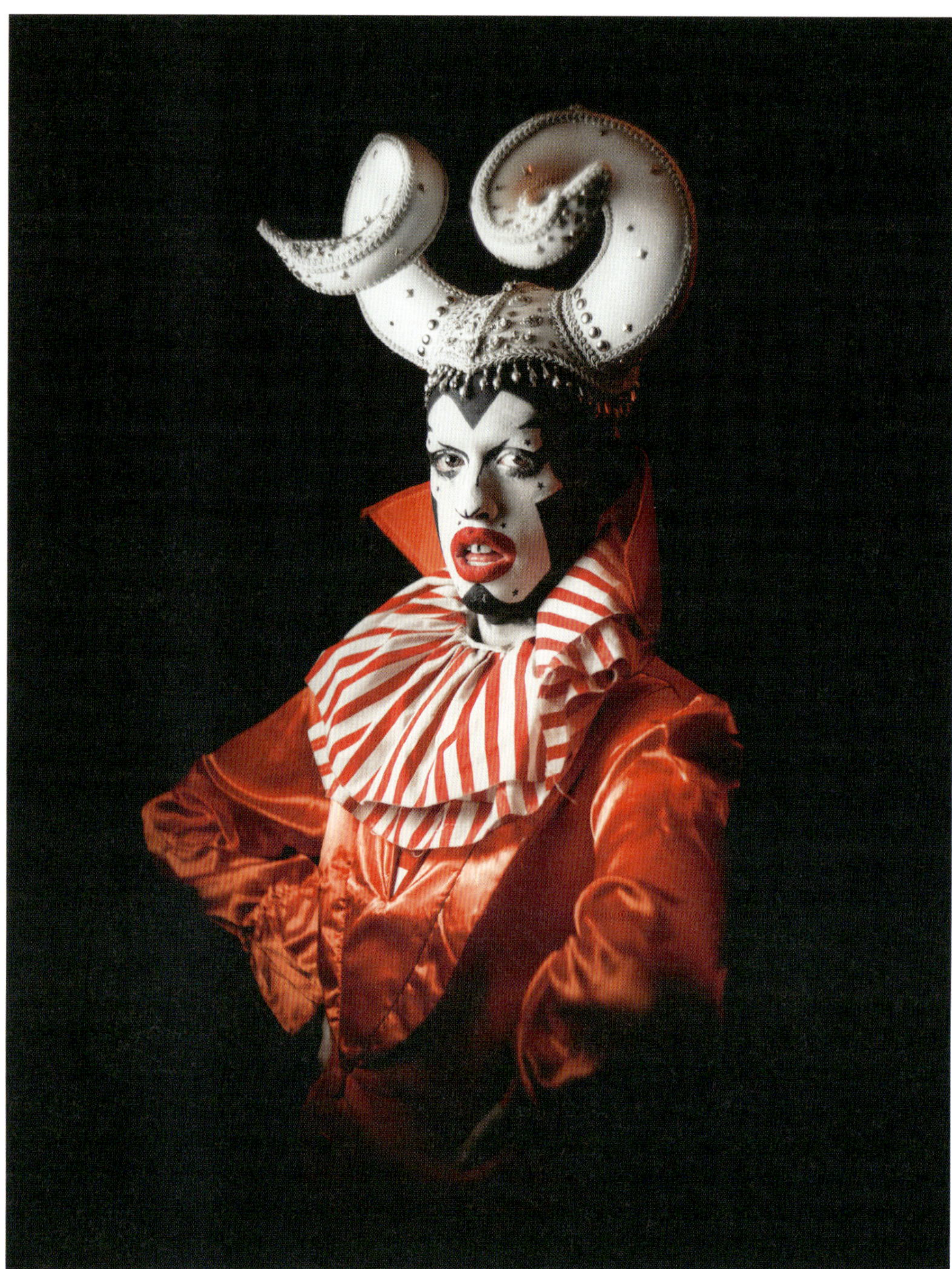

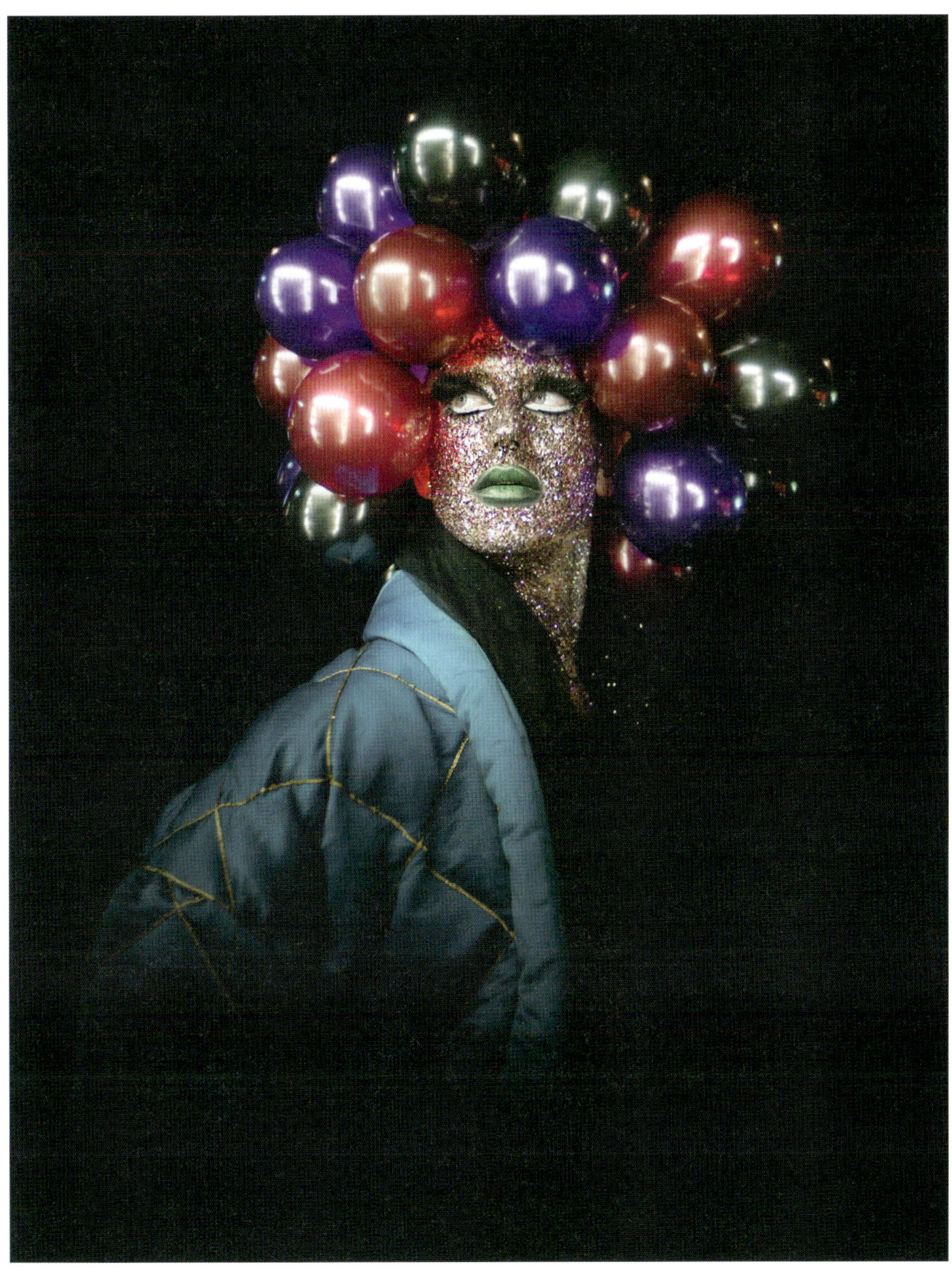

Sussi at Sink the Pink, 2016
Bourgeoisie on Old Compton St, 2014

DAMIEN FROST (b 1975)

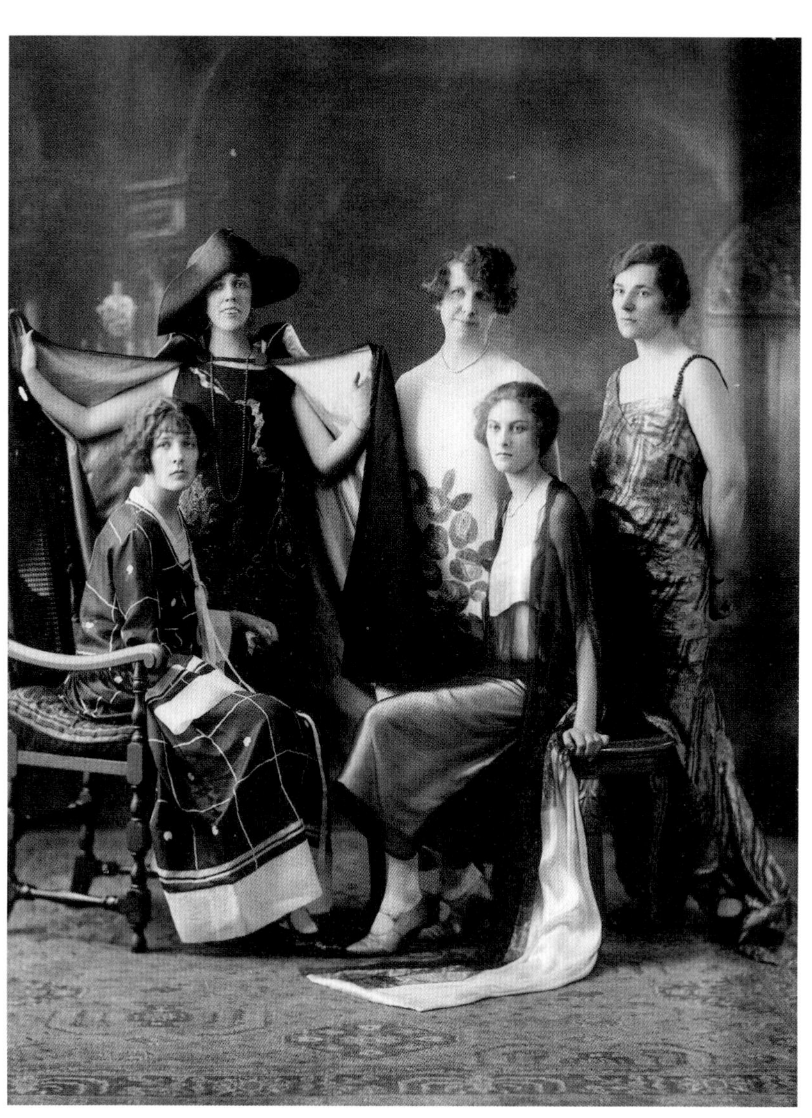

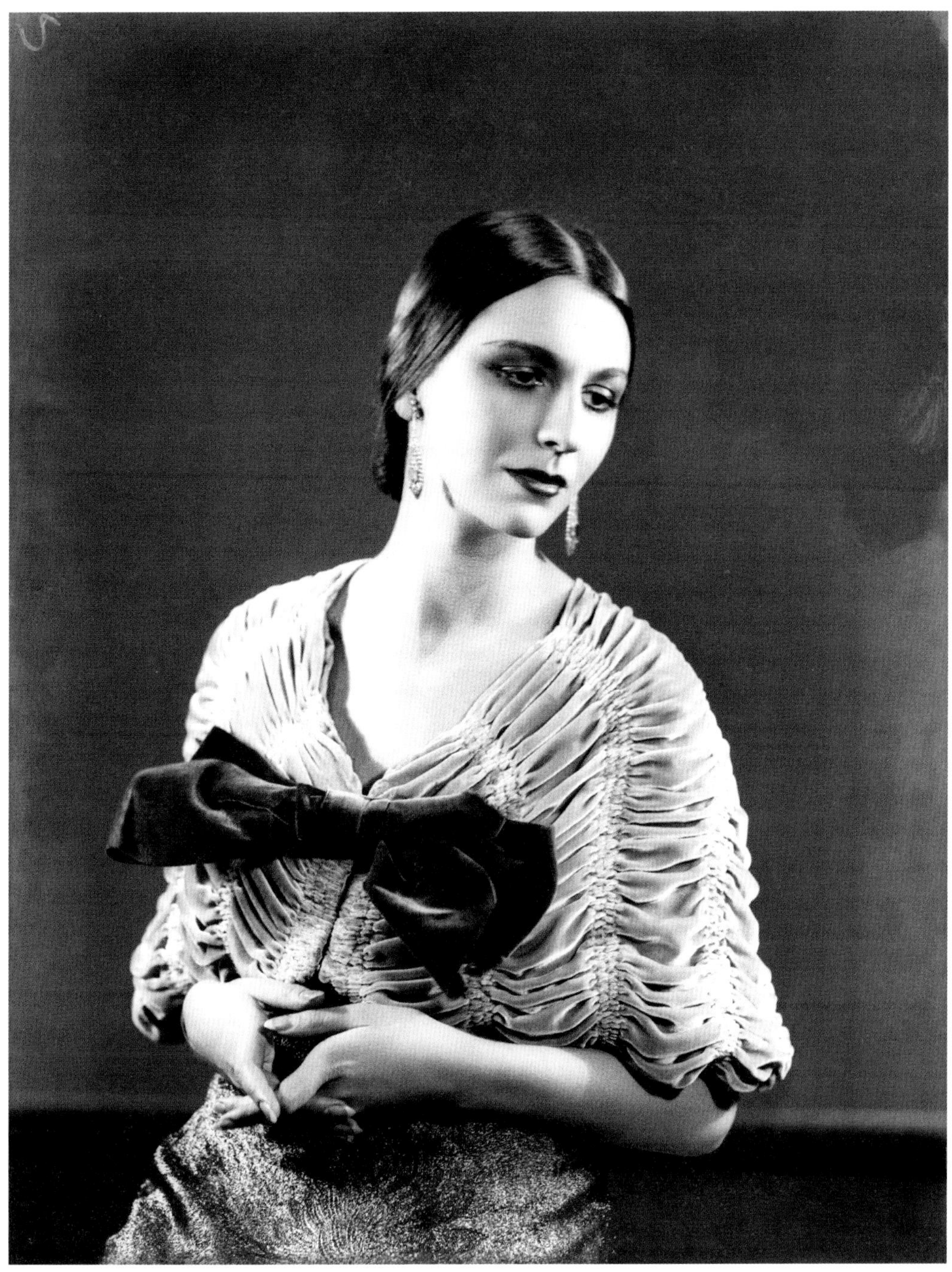

Commercial fashion photography, 1924 & 1935

ANONYMOUS (Bassano Studios)

Eveningwear modelled in the studio for advertisement photography to feature in leading magazines or department store catalogues.

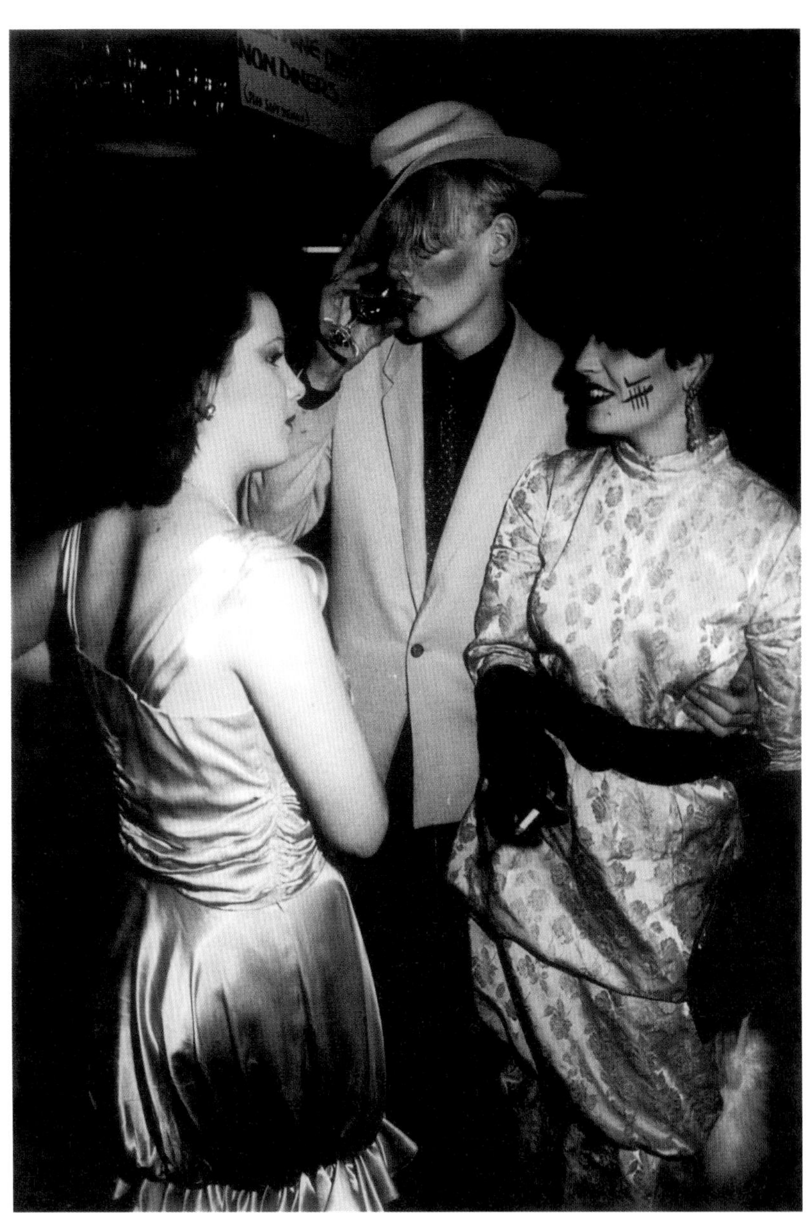

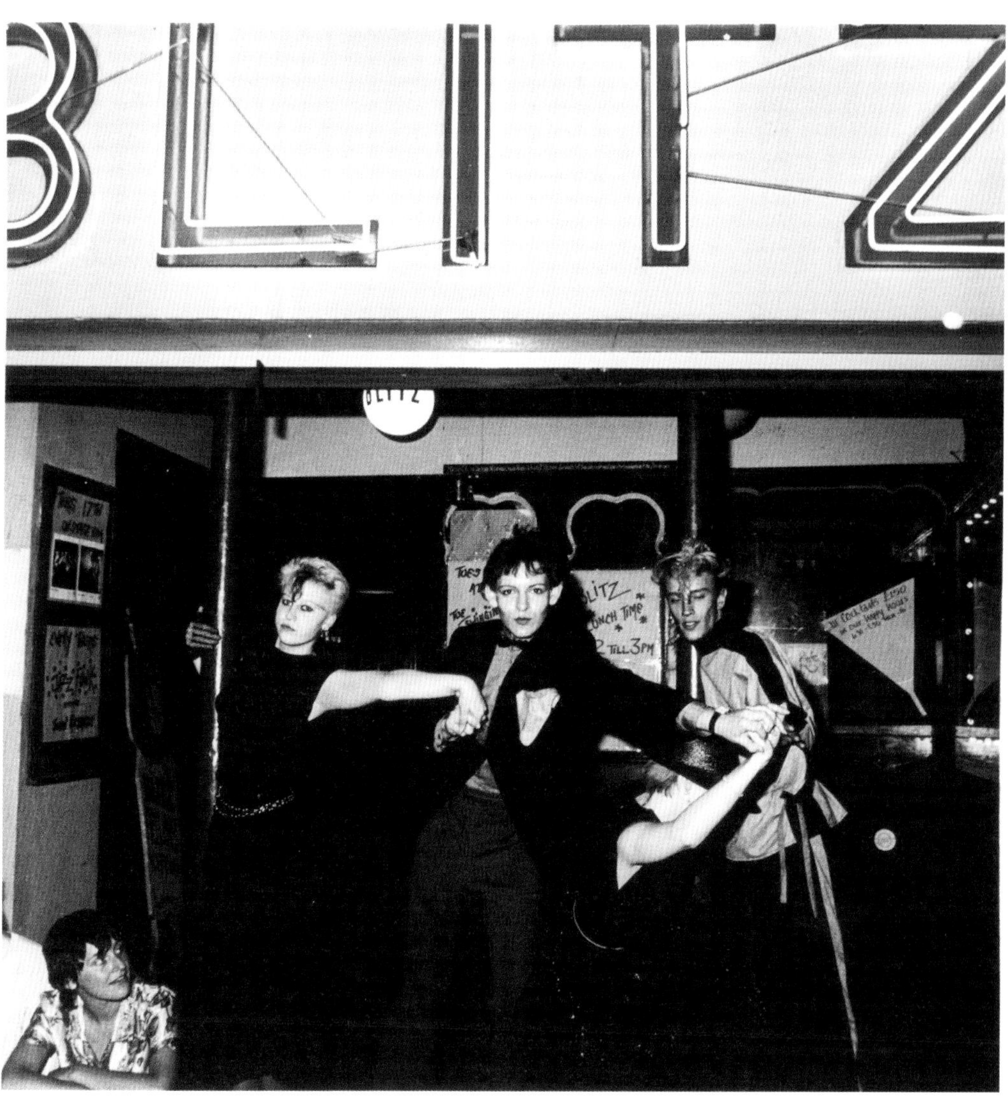

The Blitz club, 1981

DICK SCOTT-STEWART (1948–2002)

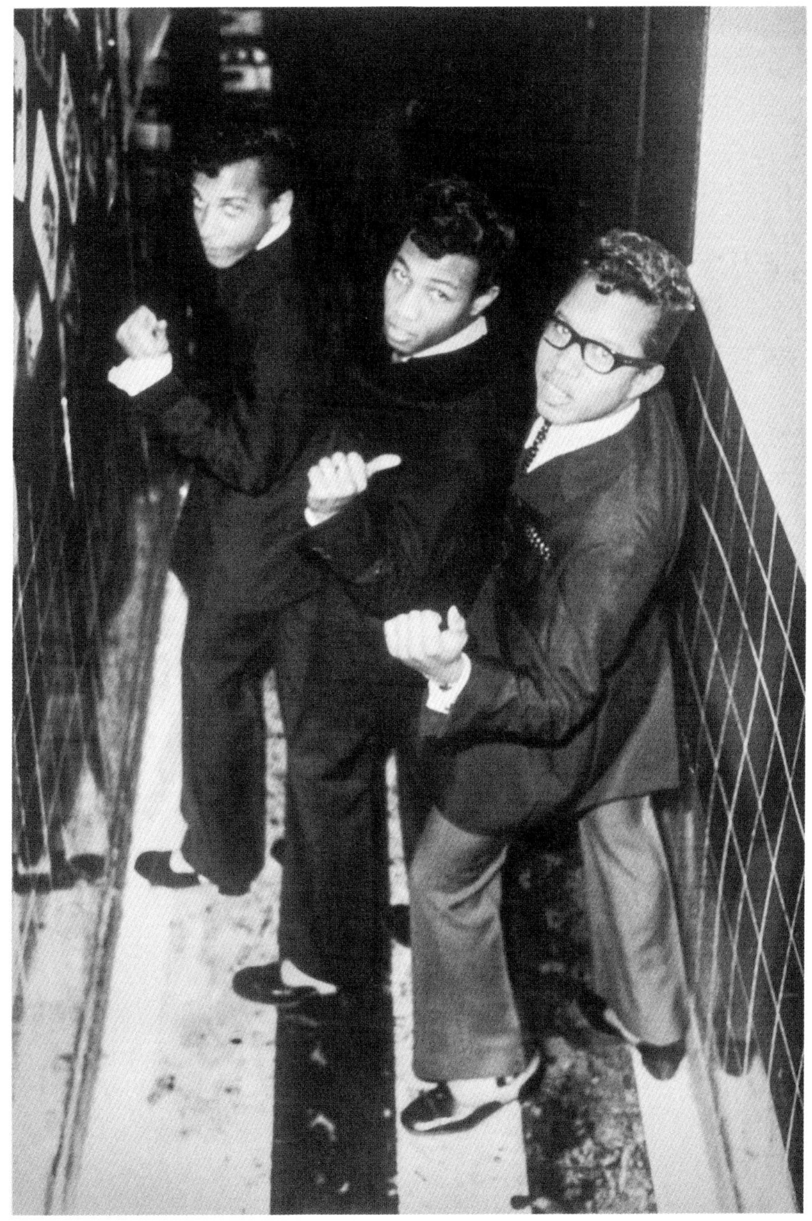

Pedro and his 'posse', regulars at the Cue Club,
Praed Street, Paddington, 1966

CHARLIE PHILLIPS (b 1944)

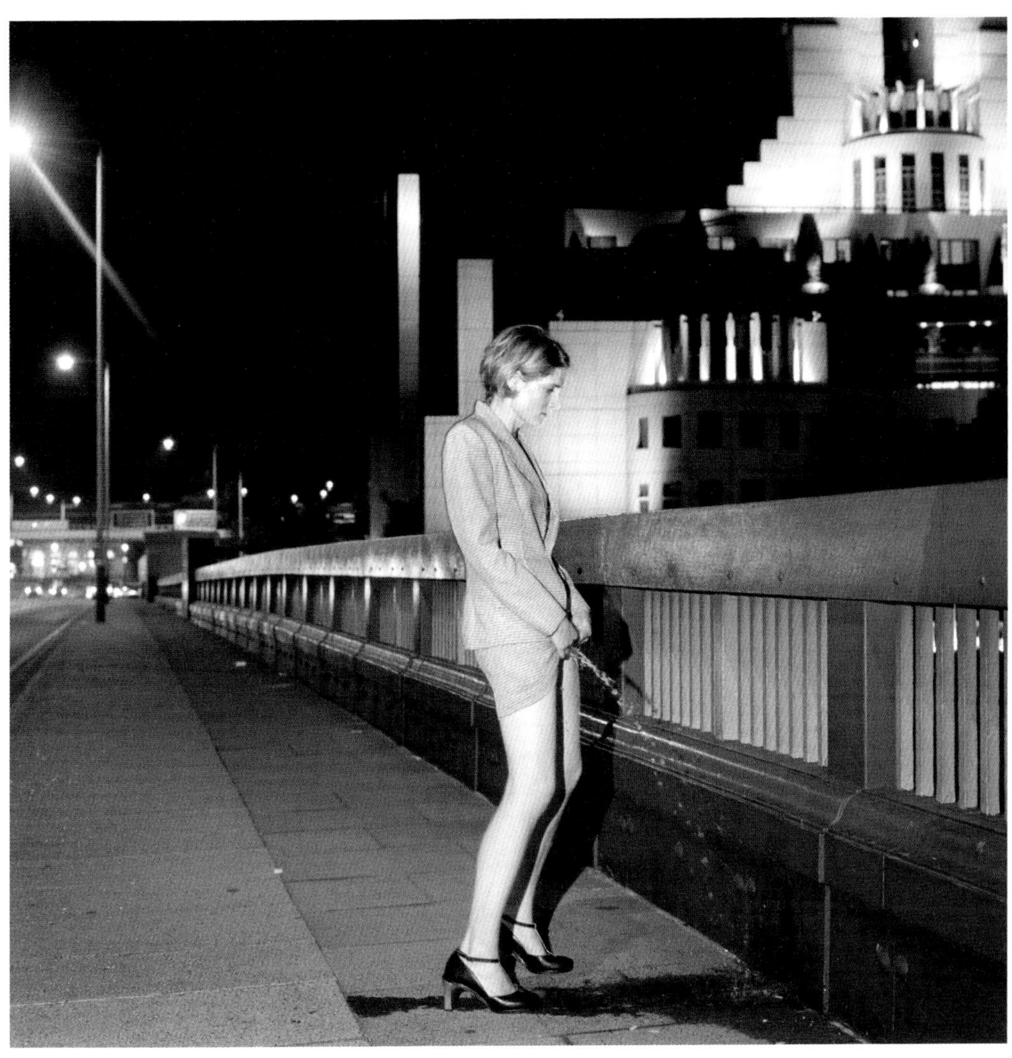

Vauxhall Bridge from the series *Pissing Women*, 1995

SOPHY RICKETT (b 1970)

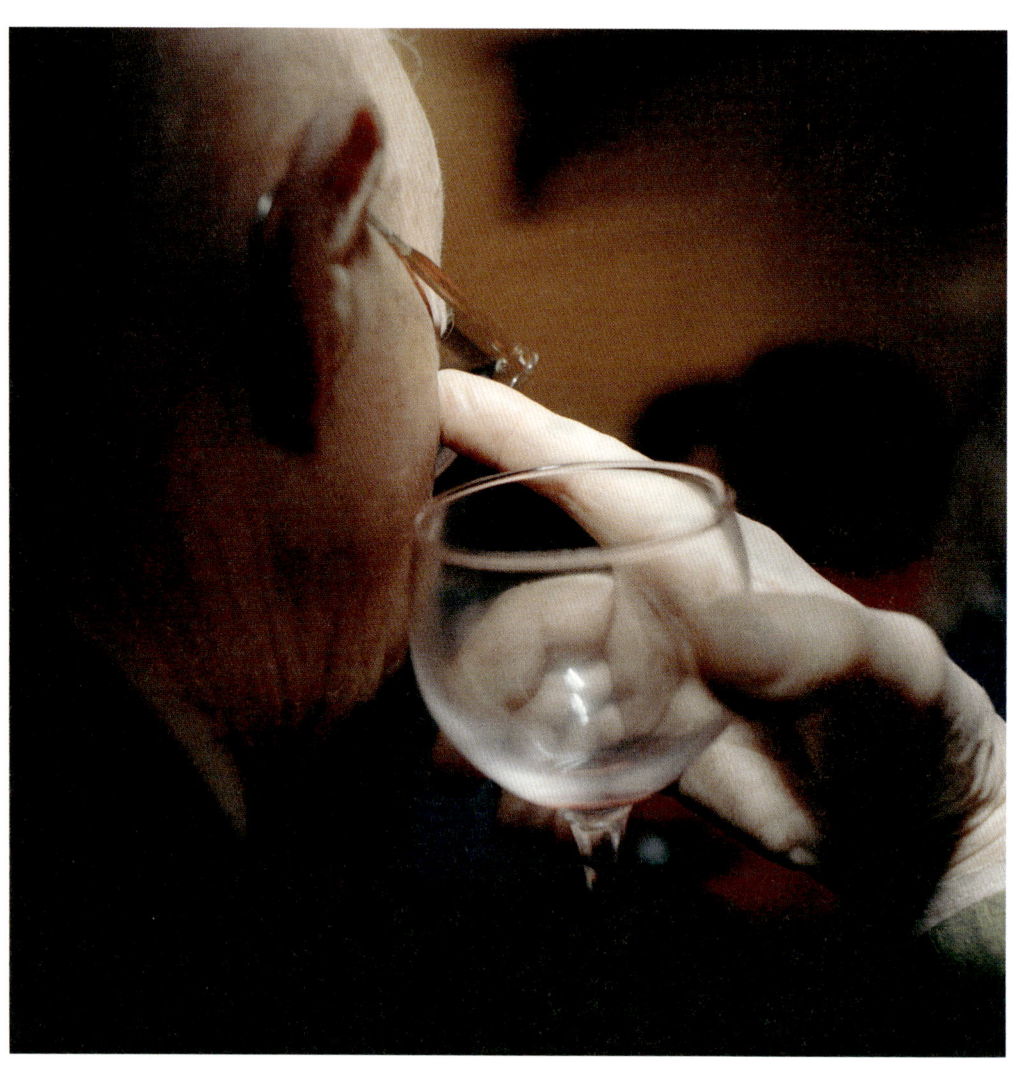

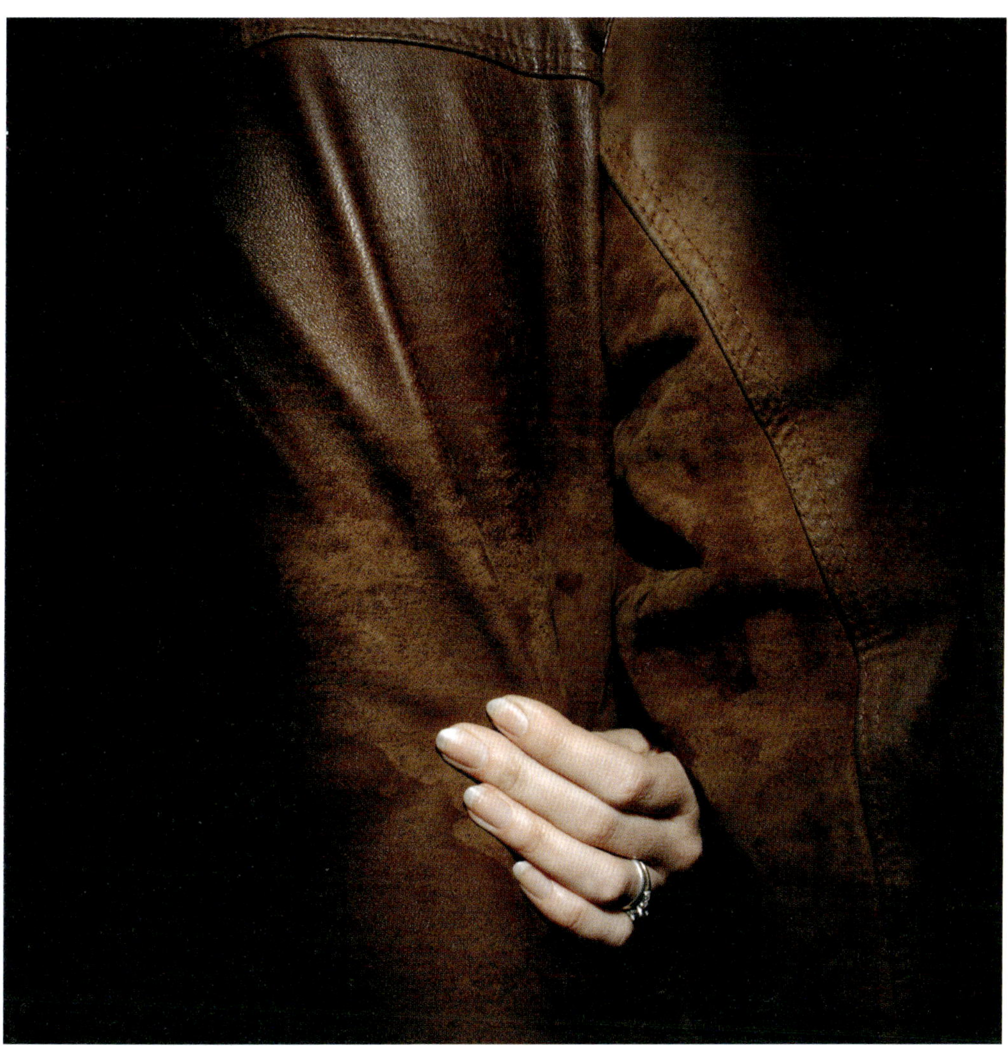

From the series *The Velvet Arena*, 1994

DAVID MOORE (b 1961)

Fragments of clothing and telling gestures disclose insight into the characters and behaviour at society occasions Moore observed.

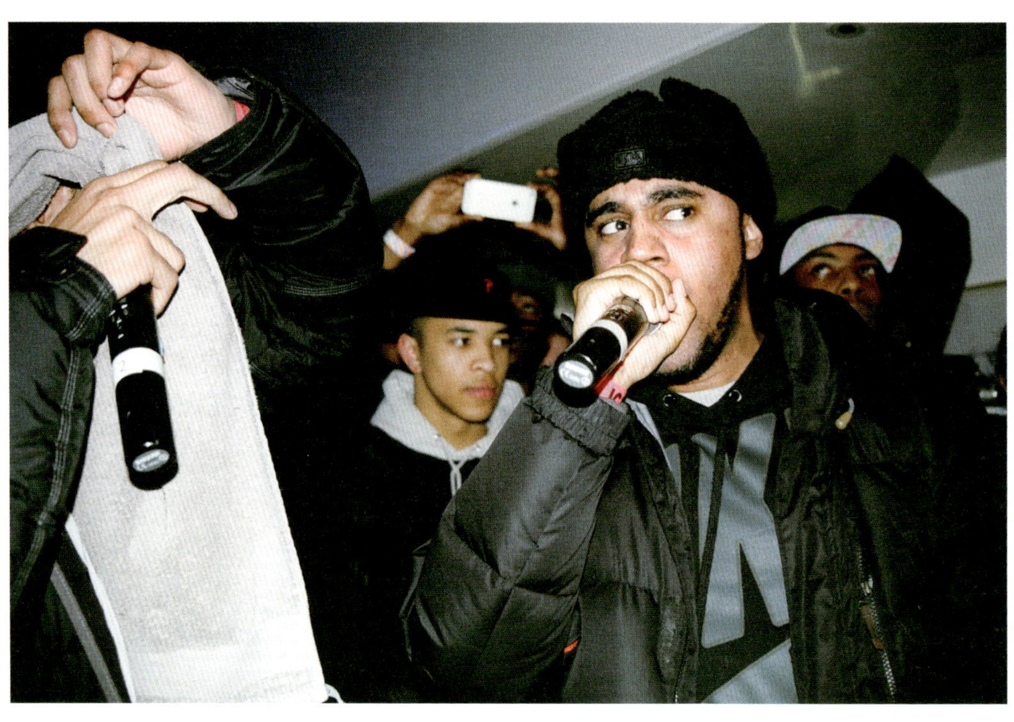

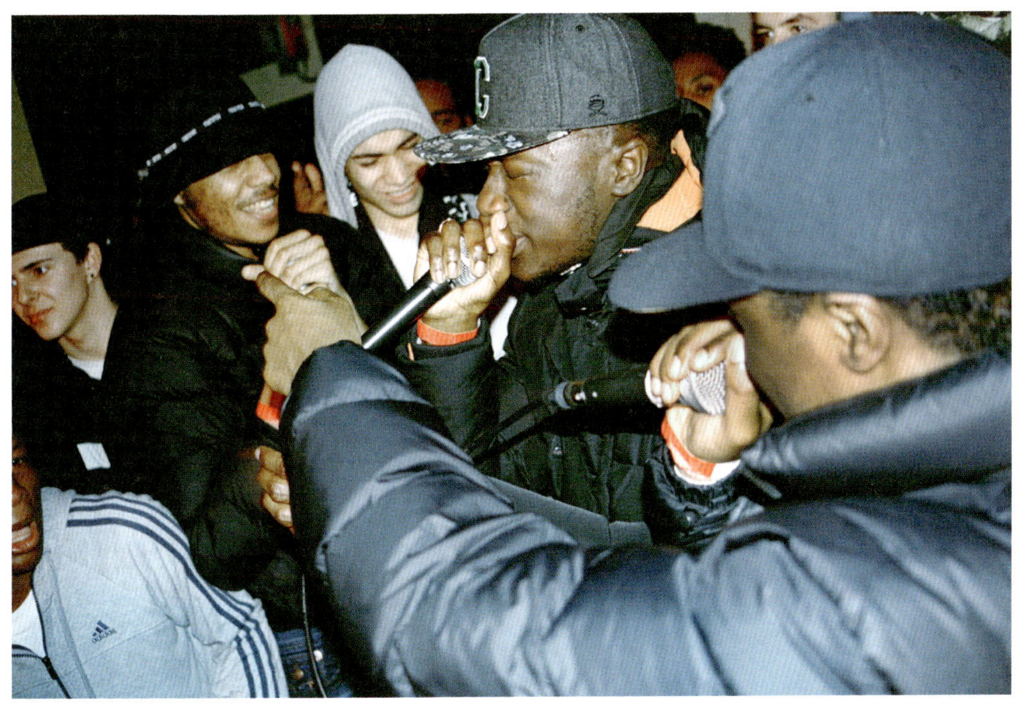

Jammz at Boiler Room, 2015
A J Tracey, ETS, Saint and PK at Ace Hotel, 2015
Novelist and Spooky at The Alibi, 2014 (FOLLOWING PAGES)

VICKY GROUT (b 1996)

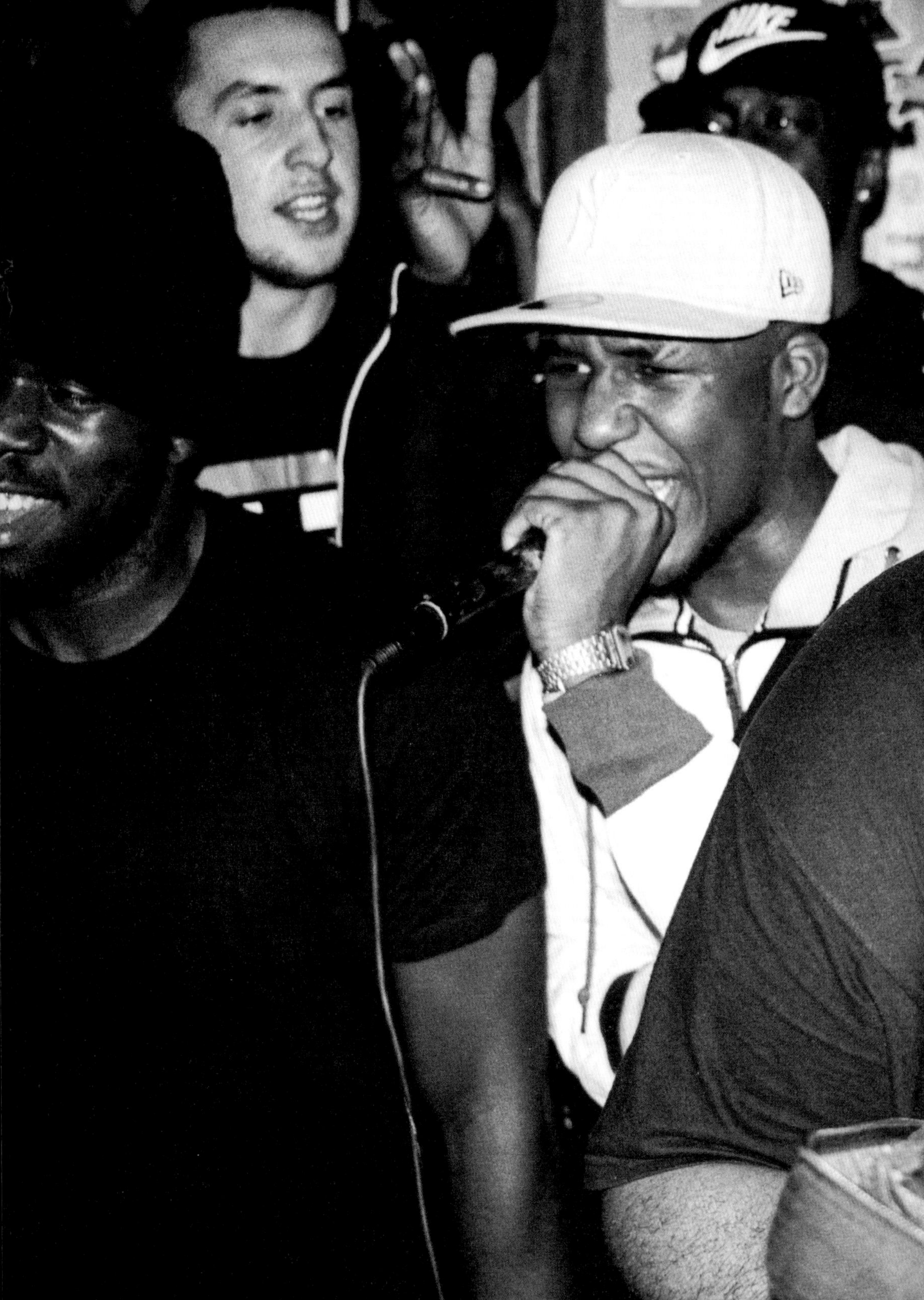
NIKE

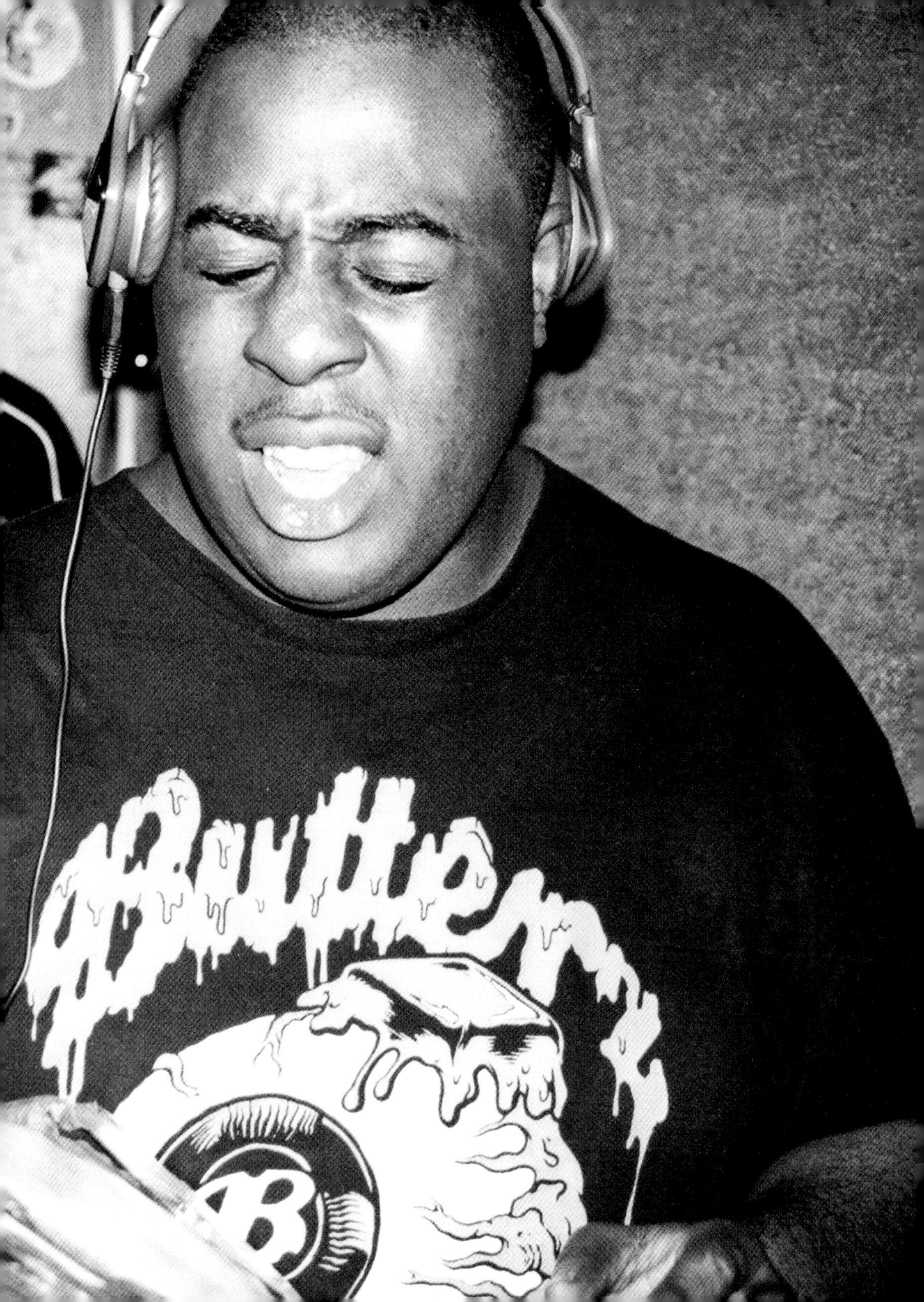
Butter

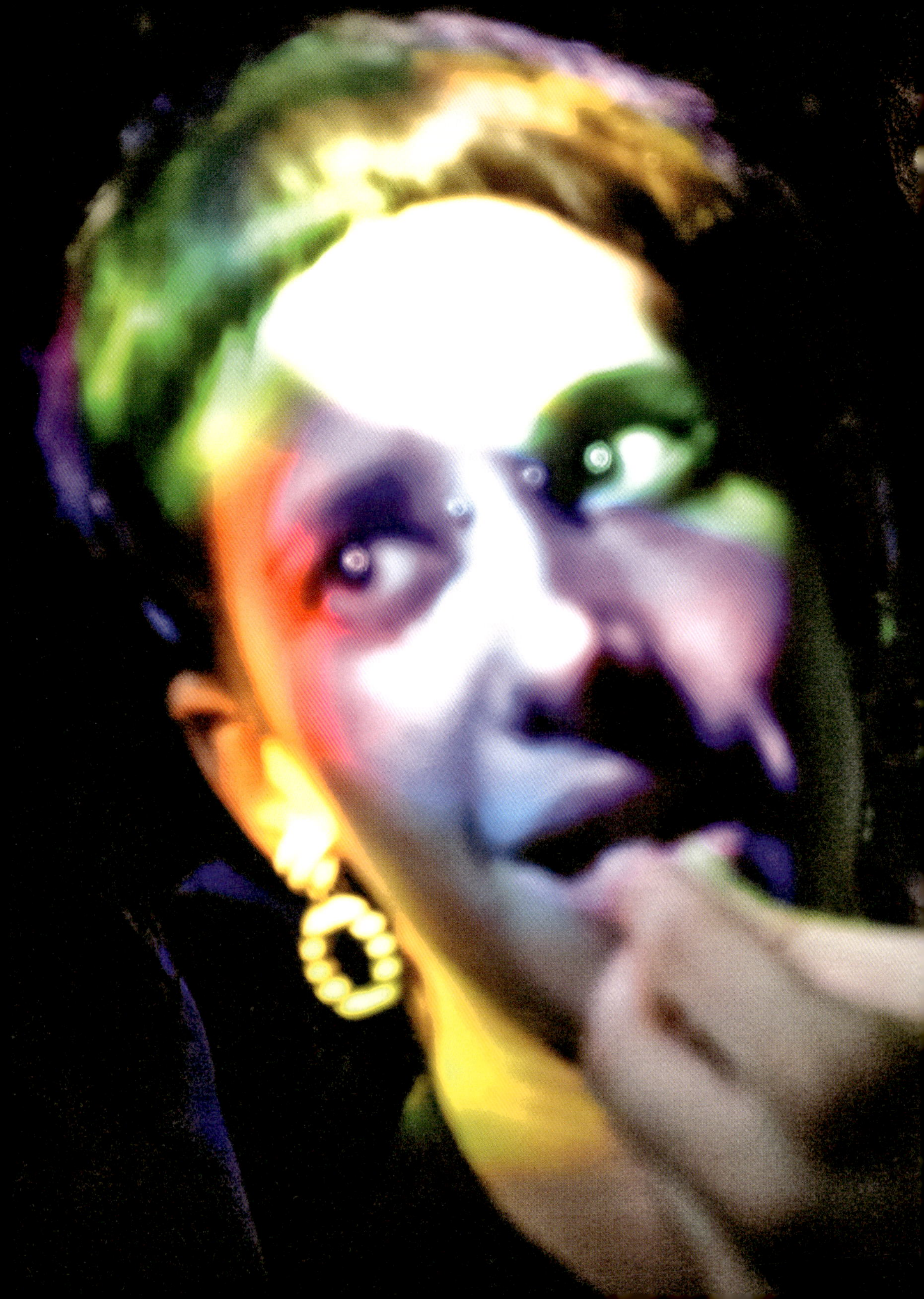

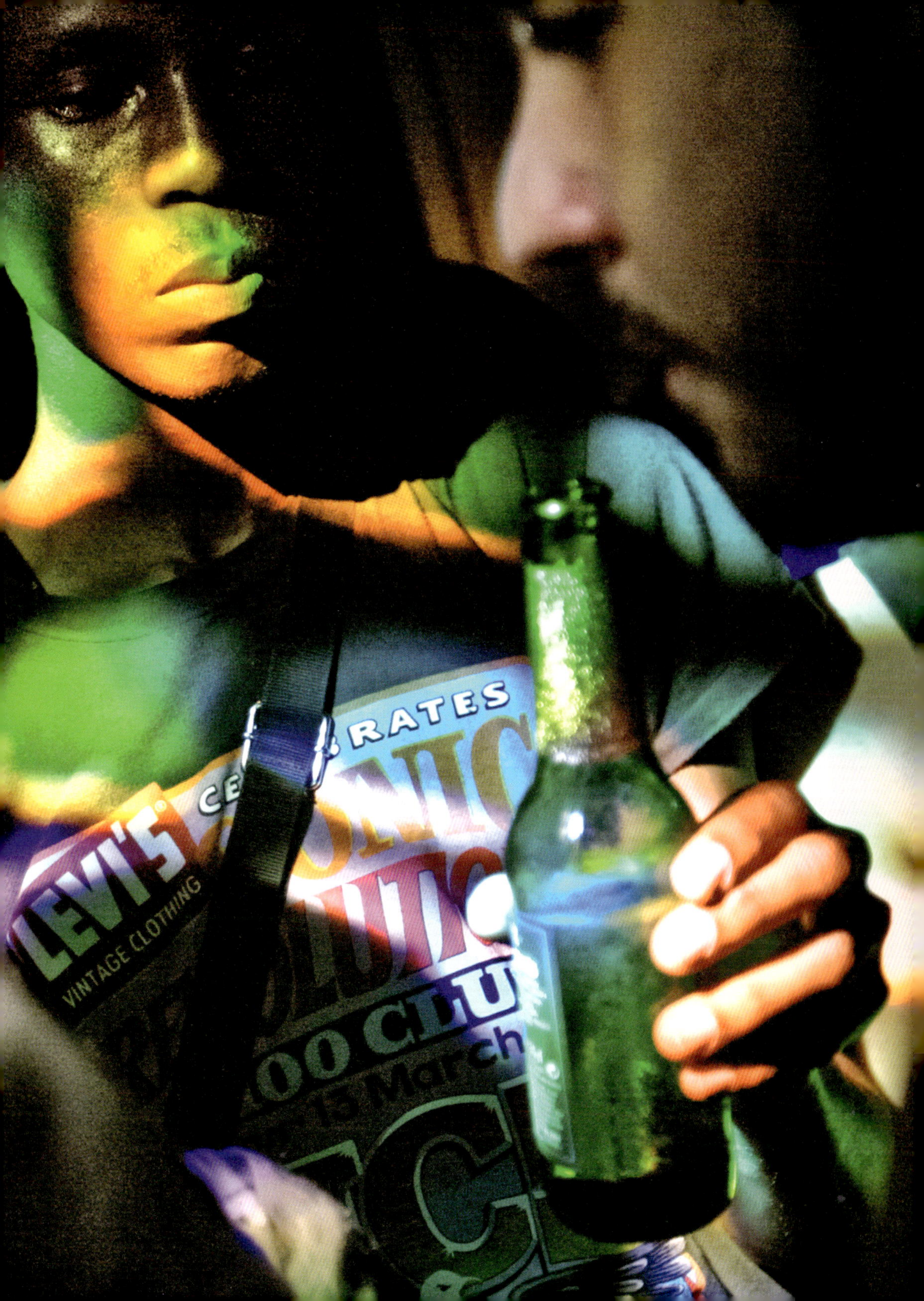

LEVI'S
VINTAGE CLOTHING
15 March

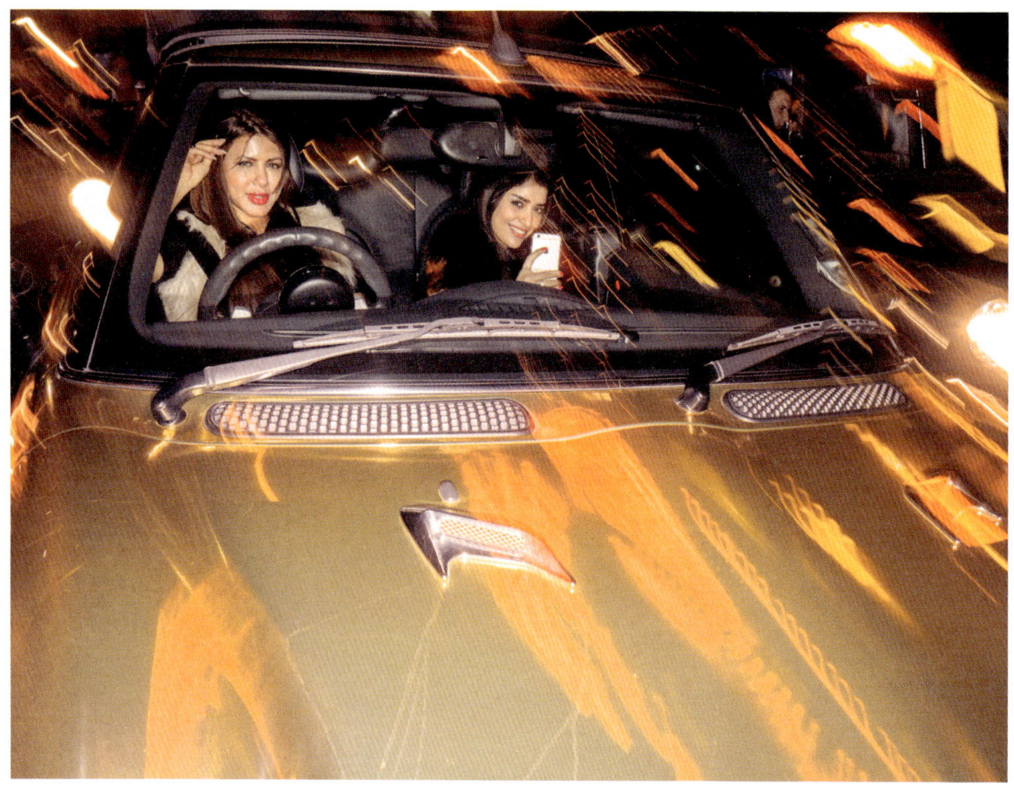

From the series *Shoreditch Wild Life*, 2014 (PREVIOUS PAGES)
From the series *Harrodsburg*, 2013–16 (ABOVE)

DOUGIE WALLACE (b 1974)

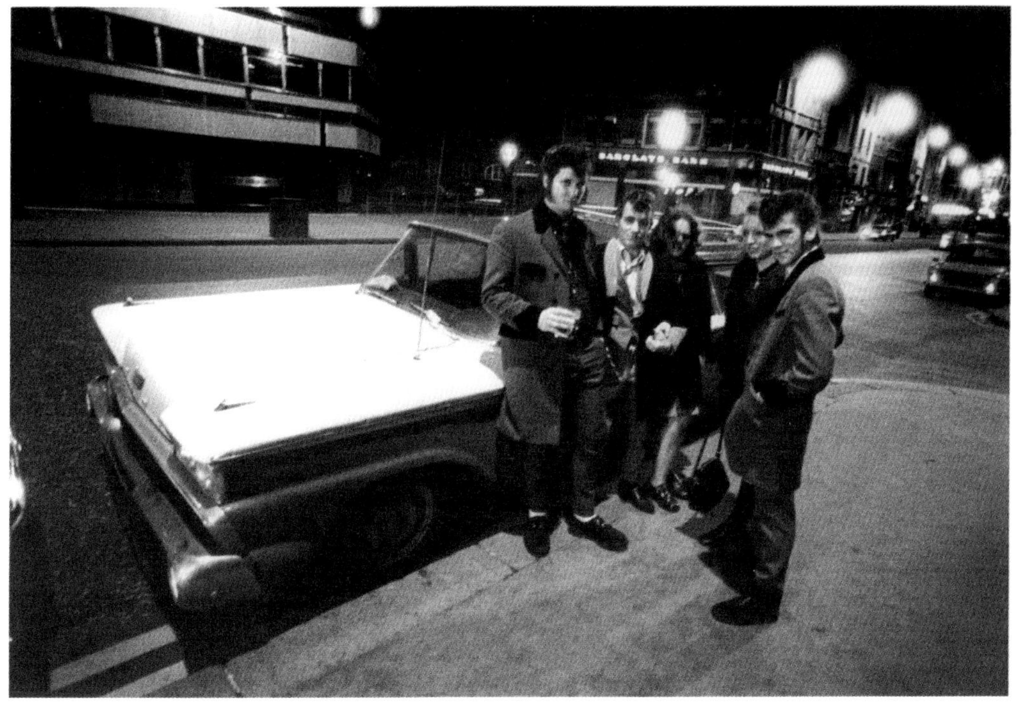

'Teds' Outside The Black Raven Pub, Bishopsgate, c 1972

ROGER PERRY (1944–91)

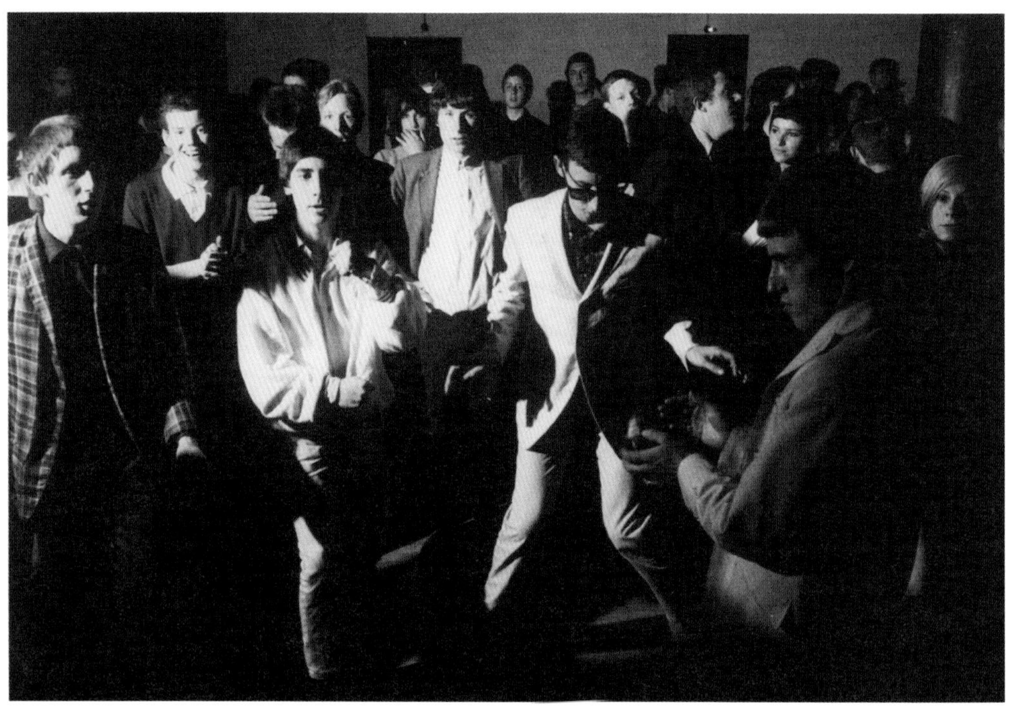

The Who (The High Numbers) dancing
at The Scene, Soho, 1964
Mods on the street, Borehamwood, 1969

TERRY SPENCER (1918–2009)

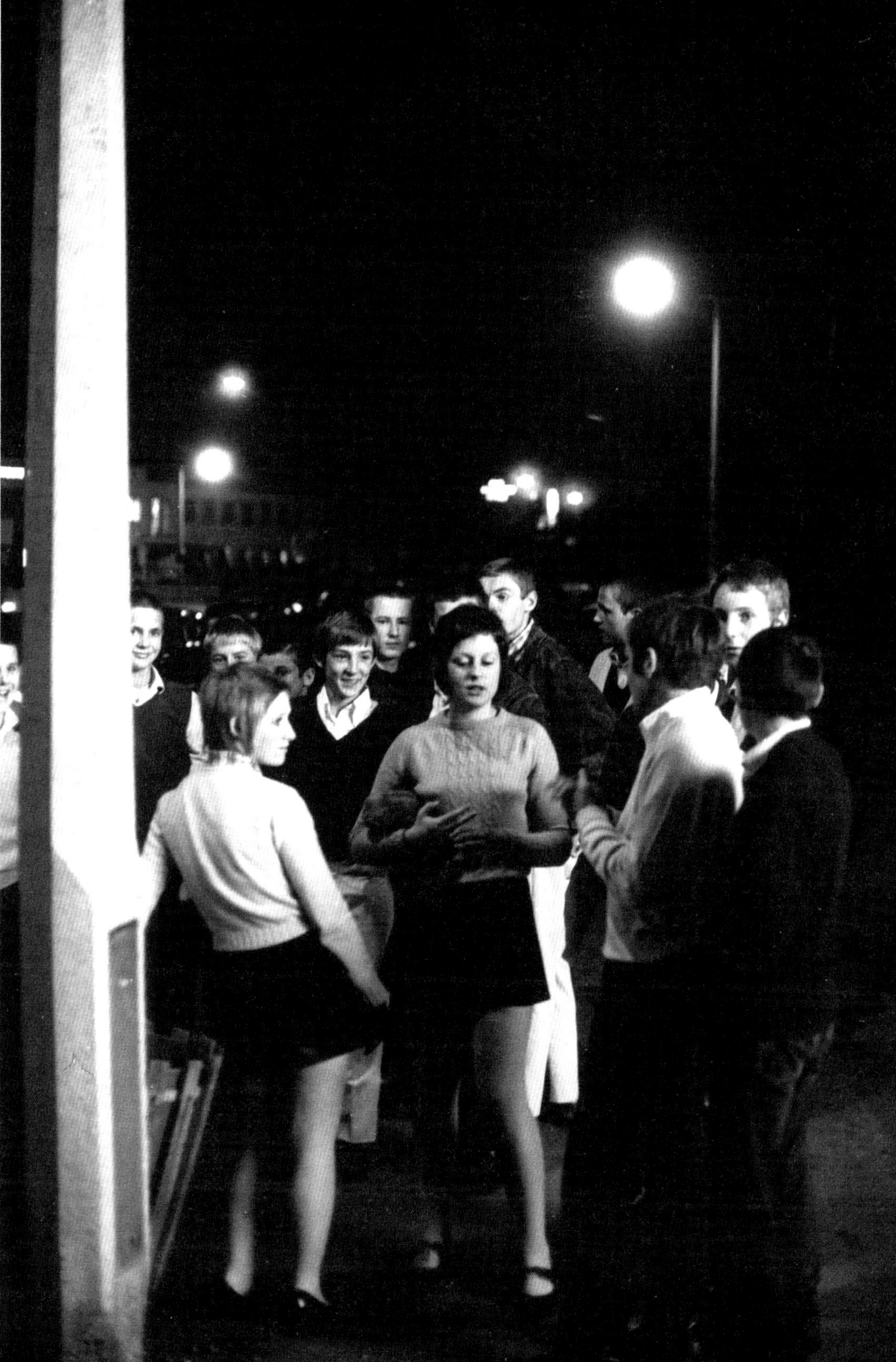

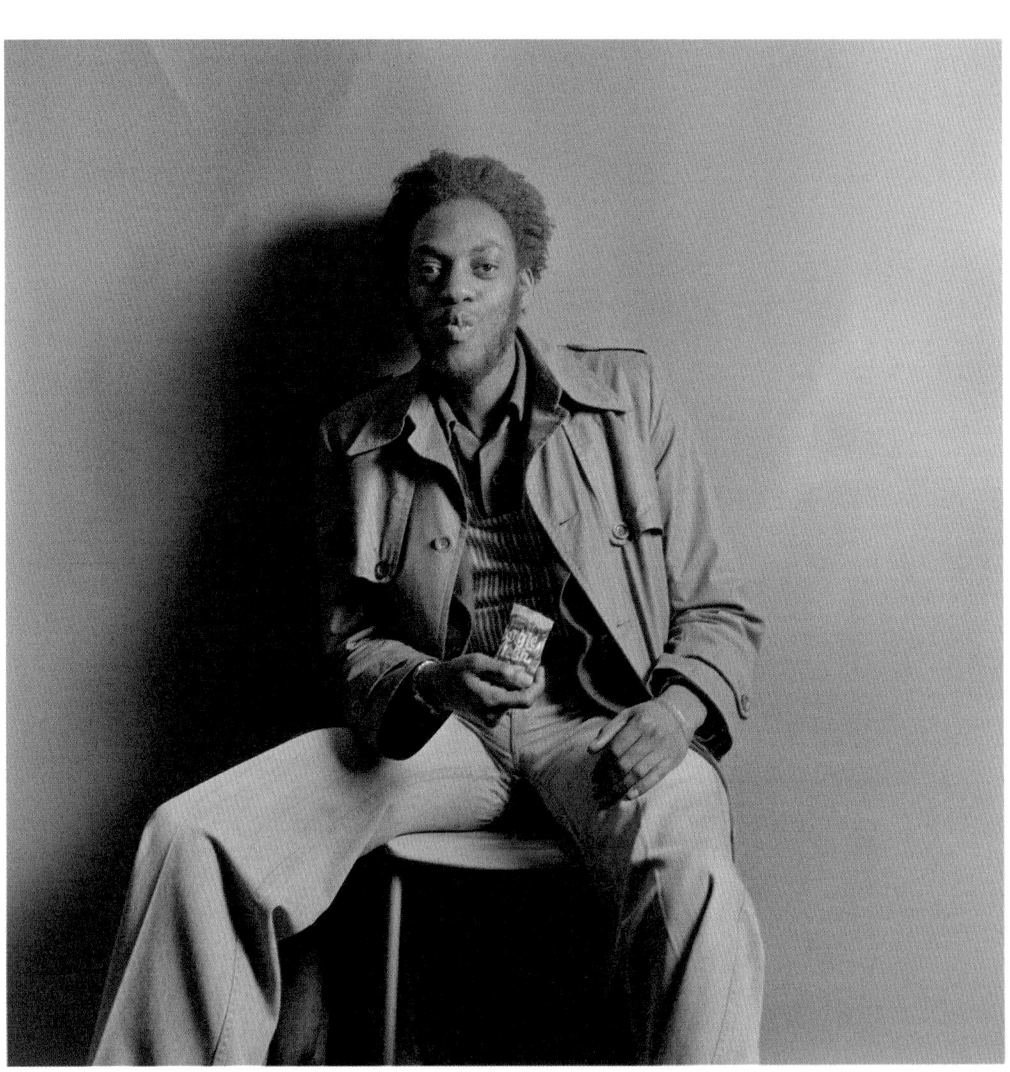

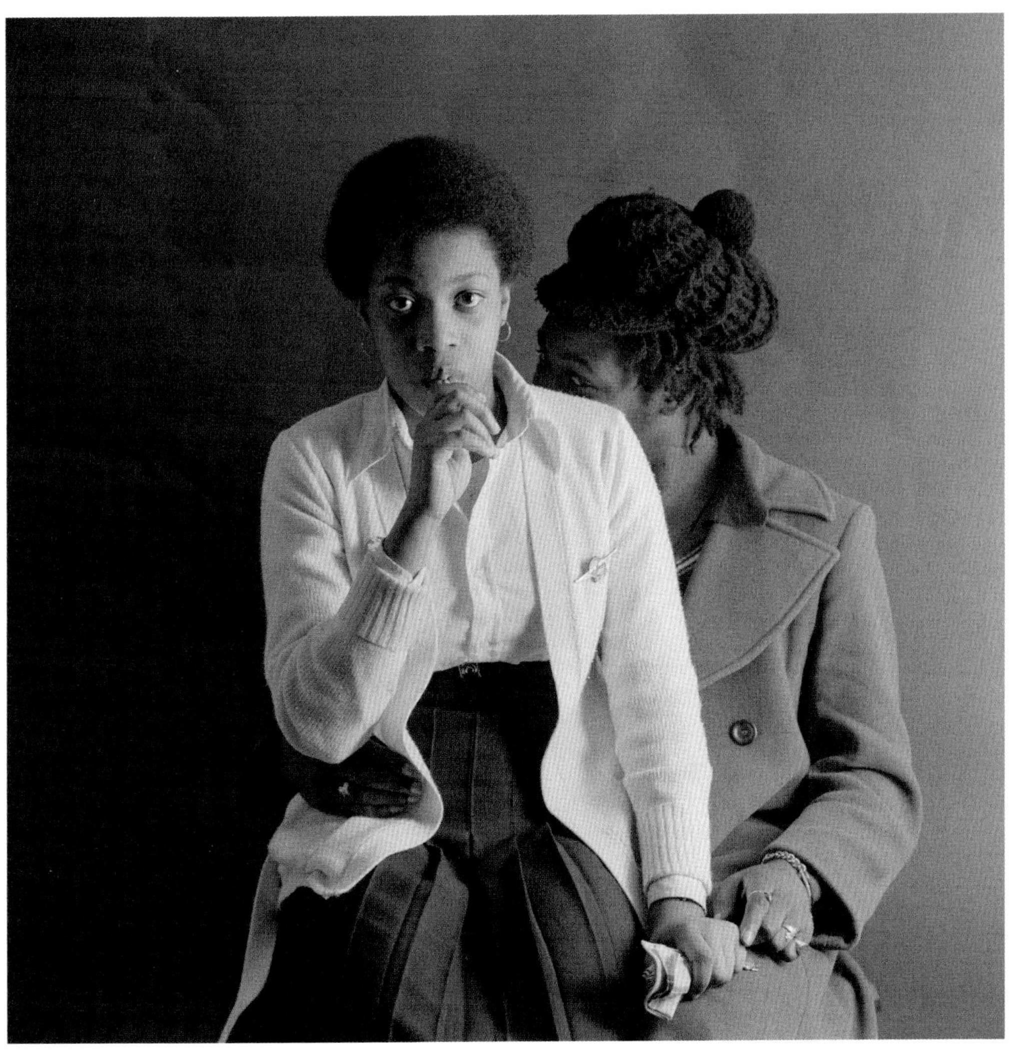

From the series *Lovers' Rock*, 1977

JOHN GOTO (b 1949)

Young people, comfortable with the camera, photographed before their evening of music and dance at Lewisham Youth Centre, where Goto taught evening classes in photography.

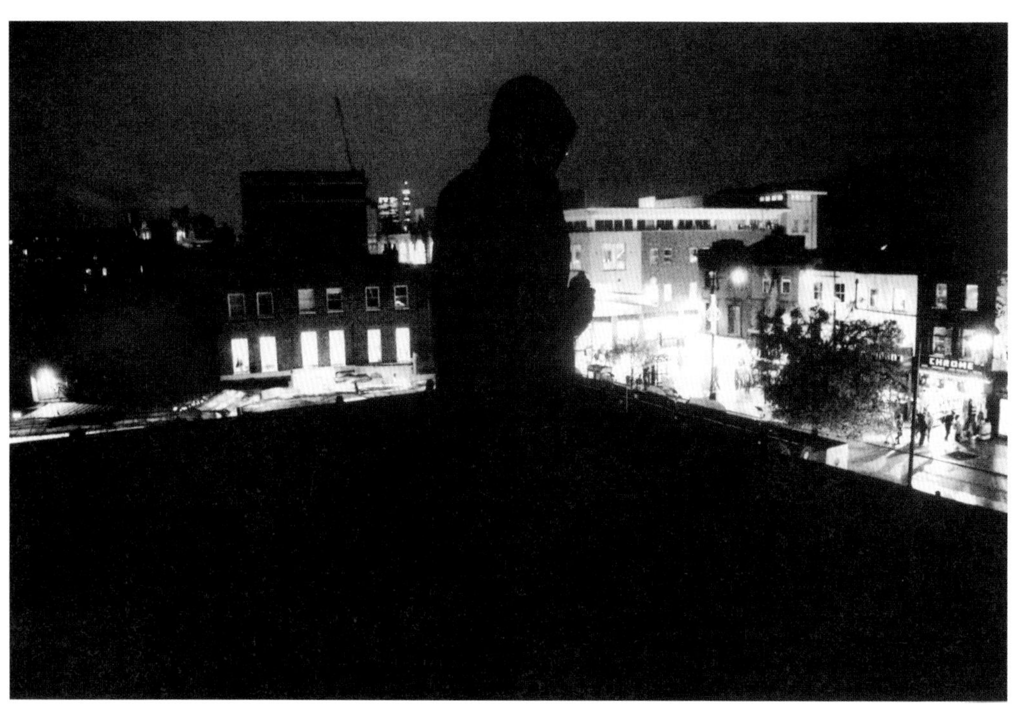
CHROME

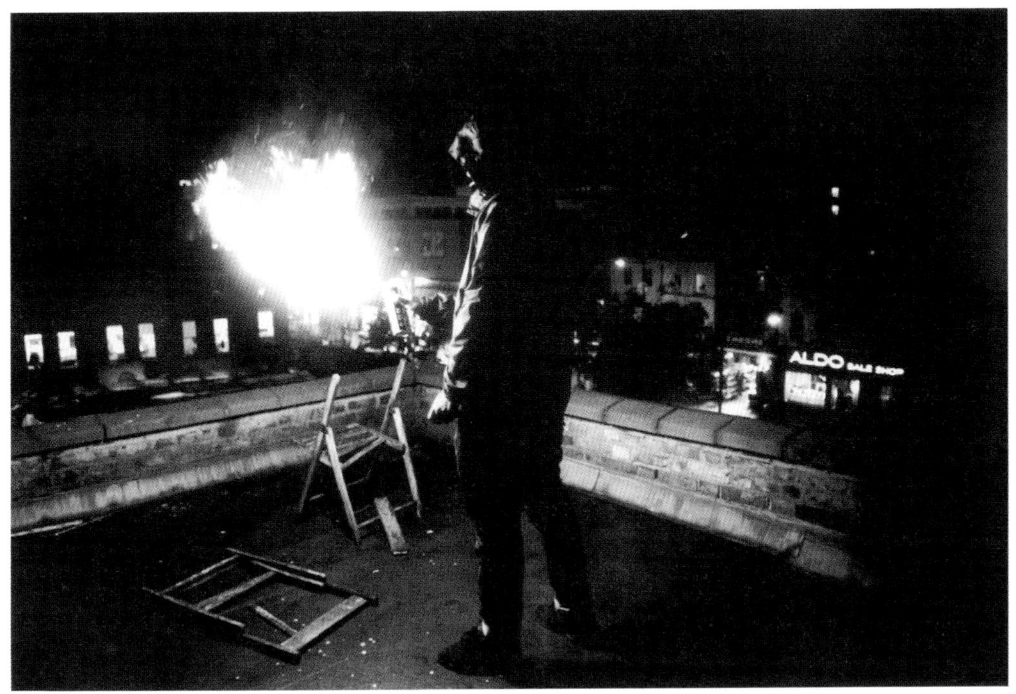

From the series *Vandals and the City*, 2015–16

MARC VALLÉE (b 1968)

Fabric nightclub, Farringdon, 5am, 2017

SARAH GINN (b 1980)

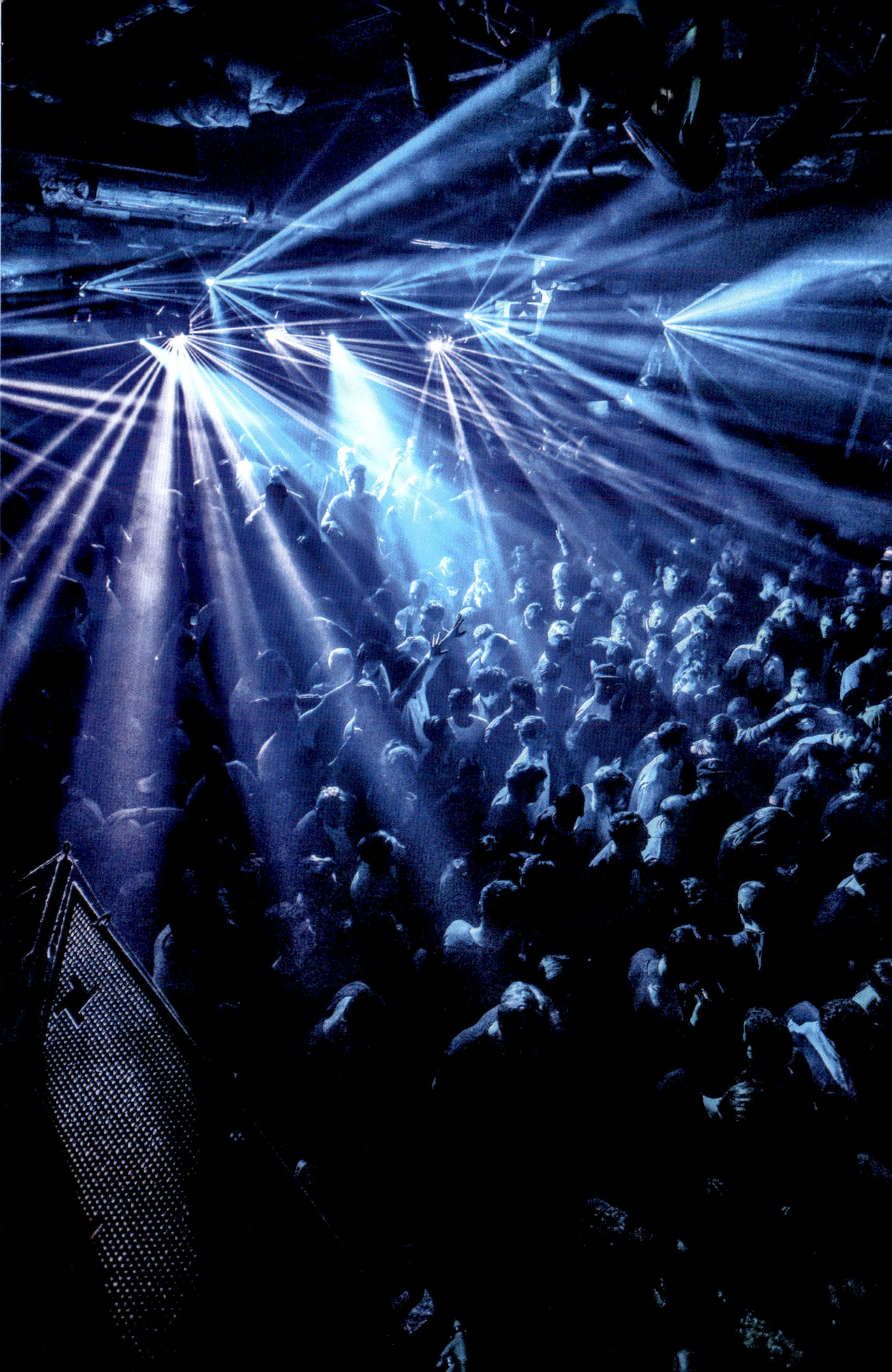

ENDNOTES

1 John Thomson, Adolphe Smith, *Street Life in London*, London: Sampson Low, Marston, Searle & Rivington, 1877, p 92

2 Photograph titled *Westminster by Night* by Walter Edmunds, 1895, acknowledged in Roy Flukinger, Larry Schaaf and Standish Meacham, *Paul Martin Victorian Photographer*, London: Gordon Fraser, 1978, p 55

3 Roy Flukinger, Larry Schaaf and Standish Meacham, *Paul Martin Victorian Photographer*, London: Gordon Fraser, 1978, p 56

4 Thomas Burke, *Nights in Town*, London: George Allen & Unwin Ltd., 4th edition, 1919, pp 20–1

5 Susan Sontag, *On Photography*, Penguin Books, 1979, p 55

6 Matthew Beaumont, *Nightwalking: A Nocturnal History of London*, London: Verso, 2015, p 355

7 Sontag, p 85

8 Roy Flukinger, Larry Schaaf and Standish Meacham, *Paul Martin Victorian Photographer*, London: Gordon Fraser, 1978, p 54

9 Matthew Beaumont, *The Night Museum*, London: Museum of London, 2016, p 13

10 Helmut Gernsheim, Alison Gernsheim, *The History of Photography*, Oxford: Oxford University Press, 1955, p 342

11 Francoise Heilbrun, 'Camerawork Defence and Illustration of Pictorialist Photography' in *Camerawork: Steiglitz, Steichen and their contemporaries*, London: Photofile, Thames and Hudson Ltd., 1991, p 3

12 H.V. Morton, *The Nights of London*, London: Methuen & Co. Ltd., 3rd edition, 1930, pp 1–2

13 John Morrison, Harold Burdekin, *London Night*, London: Collins, 1934, p 4

14 Zelda Cheatle, 'Introduction' David George, *Hackney By Night*, London: Hoxton Mini Press, 2015, pp 2–3

15 Antony Cairns, *LDN*, London: Roman Road Publishing, 2014, pp 29–34

16 Morton, p 21

17 Francis Hodgson, 'Darkened Cities', 2011, www.thierrycohen.com/pages/texts/text.html (accessed December 2017)

18 Paul Delany, *Bill Brandt: A Life*, London: Jonathan Cape, p 166

19 Bill Brandt photographs reproduced alongside drawings by Henry Moore, London: *Lilliput*, Vol. 11 No. 6, Issue No. 66, December 1942

20 Delaney, p 171

21 Rupert Martin, *London by Night*, exhibition poster, The Photographers Gallery, 1983

22 Lewis Bush, *Metropole*, www.lewisbush.com/category/metropole (accessed December 2017)

23 Bill Kouwenhoven, 'Into The Night', in *British Journal of Photography*, Vol. 159 No. 7800, p 32

24 Lucy R. Lippard, 'Hands On', *Alexis Hunter: Radical Feminism in the 1970s*, Norwich: Norwich Gallery, NSAD 2006

25 Celia Fremlin, 'Walking in London at Night', London: *New Society* magazine, 19 April 1979, p 132

26 Colin Wiggins, *Tom Hunter: Living in Hell and Other Stories*, London: Yale University Press, The National Gallery, 2005, p 60–1

27 Zelda Cheatle, 'Introduction', David George, *Hackney By Night*, London: Hoxton Mini Press, 2015, p 1

28 Rut Blees Luxemburg, Alexander García Düttmann, *Liebeslied, My Suicides*, London: Black Dog Publishing, 2000

29 Sadiq Khan, Mayor of London, *From Good Night to Great Night: A Vision for London as a 24-hour City*, London: Greater London Authority, July 2017, p 6, www.london.gov.uk/24hourvision (accessed December 2017)

30 Nick Turpin, 'Photographer's Note', *On the Night Bus*, London: Hoxton Mini Press, 2016, p 6

31 Hamid Naficy, 'The Embodied Protest' from Mitra Tabrizian, *Another Country*, Germany: Hatje Cantz, 2012, p 17

32 Chris Shaw, *Life As a Night Porter*, Santa Fe, USA: Twin Palms Publishing, 2006

33 Martin, 1983

34 Tish Murtha, *Creative Camera* magazine, No. 239, November 1984, p 1588

35 Philipp Ebeling, *London Ends*, London: Fishbar, 2016, p 92

36 Damien Frost, *Night Flowers*, London: Merrell Publishing, 2016

37 Paul Gilroy, 'There is Love in the Heart of the City', from John Goto, *Lovers' Rock*, London: Autograph, ABP, p 18

38 Tim Hilton, 'Spirits in the Material World', exhibition review *Independent on Sunday*, 1994, davidmoore.uk.com/projects/the-velvet-arena (accessed Dec 2017)

39 Khan, 2017

SELECT BIBLIOGRAPHY

Nancy W. Barr, *Detroit After Dark*, US: Detroit Institute of Arts, Yale University Press, 2016

Katy Barron, *Unseen, London Paris New York, Photographs by Wolf Suschitzky, Dorothy Bohm, Neil Libbert*, London: Ben Uri Gallery & Museum, 2016

Matthew Beaumont, *Nightwalking, A Nocturnal History of London*, London: Verso, 2015

Hilaire Belloc, Alvin Langdon Coburn, *London*, London: Duckworth and Co., 1909

Rut Blees Luxemburg, *Liebeslied My Suicides*, London: Black Dog Publishing, 2000

Rut Blees Luxemburg, Michael Bracewell, *London: A Modern Project*, London: Black Dog Publishing Ltd., 1997

Bill Brandt, James Bone, *A Night in London*, London: Country Life, 1938

Bill Brandt, *A Camera in London*, London: Focal Press, 1948

Bill Brandt, *Shadow of Light*, London: Gordon Fraser Gallery, 1977

Thomas Burke, *Nights in Town*, London: George Allen & Unwin Ltd, 1915

Lewis Bush, *Metropole*, London: 2015

Antony Cairns, *LDN*, London: Roman Road Publishing, 2014

David Campany, *Art & Photography*, London: Phaidon, 2003

Alan Delaney, Robert Cowan, *London After Dark*, London: Phaidon Press, 1993

Paul Delany, *Bill Brandt: A Life*, London: Jonathan Cape, 2004

Philipp Ebeling, *London Ends*, Fishbar Books, 2016

William Eckersley, *Dark City*, London: Stucco Press, 2011

W. D. Emanuel, *The All-in-One Camera-Book*, London and New York: Focal Press, 51st edition, 1962

Roy Flukinger, Larry Schaaf, Standish Meacham, *Paul Martin, Victorian Photographer*, London: Gordon Fraser, 1978

Damien Frost, *Night Flowers*, London: Merrell Publishing, 2016

Anna Fox, *Workstations*, London: Camerawork, 1988

David George, *Hackney By Night*, London: Hoxton Mini Press, 2015

John Goto, *Lovers' Rock*, London: Autograph ABP, 2013

Bert Hardy, *My Life*, London: Gordon Fraser, 1985

E. O. Hoppe, *A Camera on Unknown London*, London: J.M. Dent and Sons, 1937

Alexis Hunter, Lucy R. Lippard, John Roberts, Lynda Morris, *Alexis Hunter: Radical Feminism in the 1970s*, Norwich: Norwich Gallery, NSAD, 2006

Tom Hunter, *The Way Home*, Germany: Hatje Cantz, 2012

John Morrison, Harold Burdekin, *London Night*, London: Collins, 1934

H. V. Morton, *The Nights of London*, London: Methuen & Co. Ltd., 3rd edition, 1930

Michael Pritchard FRPS, *A History of Photography in 50 Cameras*, London: Bloomsbury Visual Arts, 2014

Sukhdev Sandhu, *Night Haunts*, London: Artangel; Verso, 2007

Mike Seaborne, *Photographers' London 1839–1994*, London: Museum of London, 1994

Chris Shaw, *Life as a Night Porter*, Santa Fe, USA: Twin Palms Publishing, 2006

Adolphe Smith, John Thomson, *Street Life in London*, London: Sampson Low, Marston, Searle & Rivington, 1877–1878

Susan Sontag, *On Photography*, London: Penguin, 1979

Homi K. Bhabha, David Green, Hamid Naficy, Mitra Tabrizian: *Another Country*, Germany: Hatje Cantz, 2012

Nick Turpin, *On the Night Bus*, London: Hoxton Mini Press, 2016

Marc Vallée, *Vandals and the City*, London: Marc Vallée, 2016

Dougie Wallace, *Harrodsburg*, Stockport: Dewi Lewis, 2017

IMAGE CREDITS

Images reproduced on pp 20, 26, 27, 28, 29, 31, 32, 33, 34, 36, 38, 39, 51, 90, 91, 118, 119, 176, 177: all © Museum of London. Several images acknowledged below are also held in the Museum of London's photographs collection. pp 8, 97: © Rut Blees Luxemburg; pp 14-15, 135, 154, 155 and cover image: © Estate of Bob Collins; p 18-19: © Victoria and Albert Museum, London; p 35: From an original postcard © Judges of Hastings www.judgesampson.com; p 37: © Estate of Felix H. Man/TATE; p 41: © Estate of Hannes Kilian/TATE; pp 42, 165: Henry Grant Collection/Museum of London; p 43: © John Hinde Studios; pp 44-45: © Jim Friedman; pp 46, 47, 48-49: © Will Eckersley; pp 52, 53: © Niall McDiarmid; pp 55, 57, 107: © David George; pp 58, 59, 167: © Alan Delaney; pp 60-61: © 2011 Suki Chan; pp 62, 63: © Antony Cairns; pp 64-65: © Thierry Cohen represented by the Danziger Gallery, New York; pp 67, 69: © Chloe Dewe Mathews; pp 70-71: © ESA/NASA; pp 74-75, 82-83, 85: © Lewis Bush; p 76: © Andrea Luka Zimmerman; p 87: © Herbert Mason/Daily Mail/Solo Syndication; p 89, 113, 137, 139, 153: © Bill Brandt Archive; pp 92-93, 94-95: © Tim Bowditch & Nick Rochowski; pp 99, 100, 101: © Brian Griffin; p 103: © Estate of Colin O'Brien/Spitalfields Life Books; pp 104, 105: © Peter Marlow/Magnum Photos; p 109: © Chris Moyse; p 111, 117, 141, 146-147: © Bert Hardy/Hulton Archive/Getty Images; p 112: © The Estate of Alexis Hunter, Courtesy of Richard Saltoun Gallery; p 115: © Tom Hunter; pp 122-123: © Bruce Davidson/Magnum Photos; p 124: © Anna Fox. Courtesy of James Hyman Gallery, London; pp 130, 131: © Chris Shaw/TATE; pp 132, 133: © Emma Charles; p 134: John Murray/Hulton Archive/Getty Images; pp 142, 143, 144-145: © Nick Turpin; pp 148, 149: © Barry Lewis; pp 150, 151: © Mitra Tabrizian; p 157: © Seamus Nicolson; pp 158, 159: © Estate of Wolf Suschitzky; pp 160-161, 162, 163: © Philipp Ebeling; pp 168, 169, 170-171: Images by Tish Murtha © Ella Murtha; pp 173, 174, 175: © Damien Frost; pp 178, 179: © Dick Scott-Stewart Archive; p 181: © Charlie Phillips/www.nickyakehurst.com; p 183: © Sophy Rickett; pp 184, 185: © David Moore; pp 186, 187, 188-189: © Vicky Grout; pp 190-191, 192: © Dougie Wallace; p 193: © The Estate of Roger Perry; pp 194, 195: © Cara Spencer; pp 196, 197: © John Goto; pp 198, 199: © Marc Vallée; p 201: © Sarah Ginn

ACKNOWLEDGEMENTS

Many people have contributed to the making of this publication. I would especially like to thank each of the contributing photographers who have been so generous in supporting this book and the London Nights exhibition. Without their time, patience and above all brilliant creativity this book would not be possible. I would also like to thank the copyright holders who have enabled these images to be reproduced. Special thanks also to Inua Ellams for the mesmerising words that so beautifully complement the photographs. I'm also grateful to Bronwen Colquhoun for her time in reviewing draft text and to Liz Marvin for copy-editing. At the Museum of London sincere thanks go to all colleagues, but particularly Thomas Ardill, Nikki Braunton, John Chase, Glyn Davies, Louise Doughty, Nicola Fyfe, Francis Marshall, Lois Neville, Helen Parkin, Oliver Perry, Richard Stroud, Sean O'Sullivan, Victoria Tremble, Sean Waterman, Rosalie Wiesner and Alex Werner. A great thank you to Martin Usborne, Ann Waldvogel, Ruth Brooks and everyone at Hoxton Mini Press and Friederike Huber for the wonderful design. Lastly, enormous thanks to my ever-supportive family.